Praise for *Journeys Toward Ge...*

'By means of a series of interviews with key activists and writers in the story of the struggle for justice for women in Islam in recent decades, Ziba Mir-Hosseini – pioneering activist and erudite scholar herself – offers us an insightful and illuminating meditation on the history of this struggle in our time, in its fierce hopes and commitments as well as its most vexing and recalcitrant problems. Essential reading on the subject, her book will surely become a classic.'

Leila Ahmed, Victor S. Thomas Research Professor of Divinity, Harvard University

'Long one of our age's most gifted scholars on Islam, gender and equality, Ziba Mir-Hosseini has written a new book that takes readers through a conversational journey about gender equality with six leading Muslim intellectuals. Both deeply personal and scholarly, the journey's narratives offer state-of-the-field commentaries on not just gender equality but Shari'a law and Muslim ethics in our late-modern age. The result is one of the most important and enjoyable books on Islam and gender that I have ever read.'

Robert W. Hefner, Professor of Anthropology and Global Affairs, Boston University

'Among today's most innovative and influential Islamic thinkers, Ziba Mir-Hosseini has worked for decades to promote gender equality in Muslim family law. The fascinating and engaging dialogues in this volume, carried out with a diverse array of interlocutors who are important thinkers in their own right, reflect her twin commitments to conceptual precision and real-world transformation. These interviews could only have been carried out by someone with her intellectual range and collaborative spirit. This volume is essential reading for anyone interested in contemporary Muslim thought.'

Kecia Ali, Professor of Religion, Boston University

'At once personal and scholarly, diverse yet focused on particular issues, presenting both spiritual and intellectual journeys, this work represents an original way of broaching the ever-elusive subject of gender in Islam.'

Omaima Abou-Bakr, Professor of English and Comparative Literature, Cairo University

Journeys Toward Gender Equality in Islam

Ziba Mir-Hosseini

ONEWORLD
ACADEMIC

Oneworld Academic

An imprint of Oneworld Publications

Published by Oneworld Academic in 2022

ISBN 978-0-86154-327-4
eISBN 978-0-86154-328-1

Typeset by Hewer Text UK Ltd, Edinburgh
Printed and bound in Great Britain by Clays Ltd, Elcograf S.p.A.

Oneworld Publications
10 Bloomsbury Street
London WC1B 3SR
England

Stay up to date with the latest books,
special offers, and exclusive content from
Oneworld with our newsletter

Sign up on our website
oneworld-publications.com

Contents

Acknowledgements

This book has been in the making since 2009, when I began the conversations without which it would not exist. I am deeply grateful to Abdullahi An-Na'im, amina wadud, Asma Lamrabet, Khaled Abou El Fadl, Mohsen Kadivar and Sedigheh Vasmaghi for their willingness to become my interlocutors, in our shared quest for gender equality and justice from within Islamic tradition. Thank you all for your generosity with your time, patience, and trust, and for speaking so honestly and reflectively about your own journeys to knowledge of Islam and its sources. If I have in any way misrepresented your stories and views, please forgive me.

I have the great good fortune to be part of a community of activists and scholars working toward the same ends. My colleagues in Musawah are unfailingly supportive, kind and generous. I owe special thanks to Zainah Anwar, Jana Rumminger, Mulki Al-Sharmani and Sarah Marsso for invaluable comments on the parts of the manuscript that they have read, and to Lena Larsen, Lynn Welchman and Marwa Sharafeldin for their comradeship and support. Homa Hoodfar has long insisted that I write a book such as this, to help make reformist approaches in Islam accessible to a wider audience of non-specialists. Thank you, Homa jan, for your faith in me and for your friendship and encouragement all these years.

My special gratitude goes to Sarah Hobson for her friendship and her encouraging comments on an early draft, and to Muhammad Khalid Masud, who mentored me for many years, sharing his vast insight and knowledge. He is one of the best teachers I have ever had.

In the first decade of the new century I spent four semesters as Hauser Visiting Professor Global Law at New York University; it was during this time, and the year I spent as Fellow of the Wissenschaftskolleg zu Berlin (2004–5), that I developed the notion of this book. During two more recent semesters at NYU I had two outstanding research assistants – Maliheh Zare in 2017 and Shirin Shahidi in 2019 – who helped with the transcription and translation of the two conversations conducted in Persian. Shirin also checked all the transcriptions against the recordings, and edited each of them diligently for which I am truly grateful.

An invitation to give the 2020 British Society of Middle Eastern Studies Annual Lecture came as I was putting the final manuscript together, and I am extremely grateful for the opportunity this gave me to share the main ideas in the book – and to receive some helpful comments from the organizers and our virtual audience. Thank you to John Chalcraft, Nicola Pratt and Zahra Tizro for making this possible.

Above all, I could not have finished this book without Richard Tapper's help; thank you, Richard jan, for patiently reading various drafts, for your wonderful edits that improved the book in ways that were beyond me, and above all for your love and support.

Note on Transliteration and Translation

I have used a simplified version of the transliteration system adopted by the *International Journal of Middle Eastern Studies*, using a full range of English vowels, but excluding all diacritical marks; I do employ symbols for the letters *ayn* (') and *hamza* ('). Non-English terms are italicized. However, where appropriate, I have used familiar English forms of Arabic and Persian terms and names, for example halal, haram, fatwa, hijab – though I have preferred *Shari'a* to Shariah. All these words have entries in the Concise Oxford English Dictionary. As is conventional in English – see Brown, 2009 – I have used the word Hadith as both a singular and a collective plural.

Islamic sciences – like other branches of knowledge – are replete with specialist jargon and technical terms that are filtered through everyday life in Muslim contexts. Some of these terms have multiple and indeterminate meanings that are made clear by context and usage. One key word is *hukm*, which can mean: Qur'anic injunction, divine law, judgement, determination, decision, order, command, sentence, decree; in the plural (*ahkam*), it denotes religious rulings, principles, precepts. Another such term is *shar'*; as a noun, it can mean religion, religious law, divine law, canon; in adjectival form (*shar'i*), it can mean religious, legitimate, legal, lawful, permissible, licit, authorized, admissible, jural, de jure. These key terms, along with some others, are kept in their original form (italicized) and translated at first use, leaving the context to illuminate their meanings. All English translations of the Qur'an are from *The Qur'an, A New Translation* by M.A.S. Abdul Haleem, unless stated otherwise.

The conversations in the final two chapters were conducted in Persian and inevitably involved *ta'arof* – a mixture of tact and politeness that is inherent to the language. In the translations, I have reduced the *ta'arof* but tried to keep the spirit of these exchanges; and in transliterating technical terms I have kept to the Persian pronunciation whenever they are part of everyday language.

Introduction

The only way that we can come to knowledge is through dialogue
Paul Ricoeur

In the early 1980s, when I first started attending the Tehran branches of the post-revolutionary family courts, presided over by Islamic judges, women who came to court were astonished to learn that their husbands could now not only take another wife but also divorce them, all without securing their consent. Some were incredulous, and would ask more than one judge, 'Can he really divorce me, if I don't agree? Is this justice? Is this what Islam says?' They used every occasion – sometimes thumping the judge's desk – to remind the judge of his role as custodian of the Shari'a, and of the injustice of a system that could not protect them. The judges had no answer.

My research in these family courts was the beginning of my search to make sense of the gap between the ideals of Islam and legal practices in countries such as post-revolutionary Iran, where the government and the judiciary claim to be implementing 'Shari'a'. My quest has changed course over the years, but since the early 1990s two questions have been at the centre of my work: If justice is an intrinsic value in Islam, why have women been treated as second-class citizens in Islamic legal tradition? Now that equality has been established as an essential principle in contemporary conceptions of justice, is it possible to argue for equality between men and women from within the Islamic tradition?

This book examines these questions in conversations with six Muslim reformists (three men and three women) conducted between 2009 and 2020.[1] All six are public intellectuals; I have interacted with some in academic workshops and conferences, and collaborated in research with others. I chose them

---

1 Some of these conversations are ongoing as I write this in June 2021.

because they have all shaped my own thinking in some way, they have all transcended the limitations of classical jurists, and because I wanted to develop a way to argue for gender equality through Islamic law with them.

My initial aim in the project was to make these thinkers' writings accessible to a wider audience, and in particular to women's rights activists. As the project progressed, I found that what I was doing was tracking how these reformist thinkers came to know Islam and its textual sources in the ways they do; and how their experiences became a source of theological and juristic discoveries. At the same time, I realized that I was bringing their journeys to knowledge of Islam into conversation with my own.

So let me begin with an account of my own trajectory and how I came to develop this methodology of conversation and collaboration as a way of exploring and producing knowledge to challenge patriarchy in Muslim legal tradition. It all started with my experiences in post-revolutionary Iran.[2]

THE SEARCH: OUT OF THIS DEAD END

In July 1979, six months into the revolution that brought political Islam into power in Iran, the renowned Iranian poet Ahmad Shamloo wrote a poem, "*Dar in Bombast*" (In This Dead End), that proved to be prophetic of what was to come.

In This Dead End

They smell your mouth.
Lest you have said, 'I love you.'
They smell your heart.
These are strange times, my dear . . .
And they flog love
at the roadblock.
We had better hide love in the closet . . .
In this crooked dead end and twisting chill,
they feed the fire
with the kindling of song and poetry.

---

2 The following account draws on my earlier writings, especially Mir-Hosseini, 1999, 2010a and 2013a.

Do not risk a thought.
These are strange times, my dear . . .
He who knocks on the door at midnight
has come to kill the light.
We had better hide light in the closet . . .
Those there are butchers
stationed at the crossroads
with bloody clubs and cleavers.
These are strange times, my dear . . .
And they excise smiles from lips
and songs from mouths.
We had better hide joy in the closet . . .
Canaries barbecued
on a fire of lilies and jasmine,
these are strange times, dear . . .
Satan drunk with victory
sits at our funeral feast.
We had better hide God in the closet.[3]

در این بن‌بست

دهانت را می‌بویند
مبادا که گفته باشی دوستت می‌دارم
دلت را می‌بویند
روزگار غریبی‌ست، نازنین
و عشق را
کنار تیرکِ راهبند
تازیانه می‌زنند
عشق را در پستوی خانه نهان باید کرد
آتش را
به سوخت‌بارِ سرود و شعر
فروزان می‌دارند
به اندیشیدن خطر مکن
روزگار غریبی‌ست، نازنین
آن که بر در می‌کوبد شباهنگام

---

3 Shamloo, 1979. The translation is a modified version of the anonymous one on YouTube; see Bibliography.

به گشتنِ چراغ آمده است
نور را در پستوی خانه نهان باید کرد
آنک قصابانند
بر گذرگاه‌ها مستقر
با گنده و ساتوری خون‌آلود
روزگار غریبی‌ست، نازنین
و تبسم را بر لب‌ها جراحی می‌کنند
و ترانه را بر دهان
شوق را در پستوی خانه نهان باید کرد
کبابِ قناری
بر آتش سوسن و یاس
روزگار غریبی‌ست، نازنین
ابلیس پیروزمست
سورِ عزای ما را بر سفره نشسته است
خدا را در پستوی خانه نهان باید کرد

Shamloo's poem spoke to me then as it does now, and as it has done to many Iranians of my background and generation. In the aftermath of the revolution, the clerical leaders who took over politics banished love, beauty, joy and pleasure from public space, and anyone expressing them risked punishment. The new authorities justified this policy in the name of Islam: it was God's law, the Shari'a. This was a new encounter with Shari'a, the core of the faith into which I was born, and a vision of it that I had not experienced before and now – like the women litigants who came to court – found unjust and frightening.

At the time of the revolution – which I supported – I was in my late twenties, finishing my studies in England. In 1980 I returned home, newly married and with a doctorate in hand. I had looked forward to becoming a university teacher and living happily with my husband. But neither expectation was to be fulfilled; I found myself in Shamloo's 'dead end'. Under the new regime's 'Islamization' policy the universities were closed down, and when they reopened three years later there was no place for people like me. Not only was I not qualified to teach 'Islamic anthropology', I was not a 'good Muslim': the file on me contained a report that I had never 'fully observed the rule of hijab'.[4] My marriage also broke down, and the 'Shari'a' marriage contract I had signed left me at my husband's mercy; he would neither agree to a divorce nor give me permission to leave the country. My only option was

---

4 For the interview that led to my rejection, see Mir-Hosseini, 2010a.

to negotiate my release in a court presided over by a religious judge. I began to educate myself in Islamic family law; I read widely, and I also attended some of the new family courts, intrigued to discover how the new regime was implementing 'Shari'a' in practice. I learned the new law well enough to secure my own divorce.

In 1984 I returned to the UK, and to academic life in Cambridge. I started a new research project on a topic of which I now had some knowledge and personal experience. Between 1985 and 1989, I did fieldwork in family courts in Iran and Morocco. I wanted to know, as an anthropologist, what it means to be married and divorced under a law whose advocates claim it to be sacred. Investigating the details of marital disputes that came to court, I focused on the strategies of the litigants, and how judges came to their decisions. I went beyond the letter of the law, to examine the complexity of human relations, how individuals understand and relate to the 'sacred' in the law. This research led to my first book, *Marriage on Trial* (1993). In retrospect, I see that I was seeking to understand how Shamloo's 'dead end' came about in Iran, and how to get out of it.

During those months of sitting in courts and listening to litigants, observing and conversing with judges, I learned that by the time a marital dispute reached court, whatever was sacred and ethical in the law had evaporated. Neither the judges nor the disputing couple were concerned with the sacred. What was left of the Shari'a was a strong patriarchal ethos that privileged men and placed women under male authority: it was an ideology to legitimize unequal and unjust power relations in marriage and society and to curtail women's voices and choices. In fact some clerical judges in Tehran told me that the courts were not the right place to learn about the Shari'a; I should go to seminaries and read books of *fiqh*, Islamic jurisprudence.

In the early 1990s, I began to study these Islamic juristic texts, seeking to understand how their ideas of male and female nature and men's and women's roles in society were constructed. In several further visits to Iran, I worked with a young cleric who facilitated my entry into the seminaries in Qom – the centre of religious learning. He also helped me to establish a dialogue with the male clerics in charge of a woman's magazine financed by the seminaries. In the course of these conversations with clerics, I realized the importance of engaging with the Islamic legal tradition, and the need to develop a language and framework to argue for justice and equality from within the tradition. The clerics and I often talked across each other. As an anthropologist I understood law in its social context, as shaped by social, cultural and political forces; they were reluctant to acknowledge this, insisting upon upholding a set of ideal laws. They aimed to get the textual and legal arguments right, and then social practices could be changed; for them, for every problem there was a legal solution in the Shari'a, which they were attempting to find. Where I put the emphasis on changing norms and practices around notions of gender and social justice, they stressed textual sources as containing the ideals to shape reality. Yet I saw how these contemporary custodians of the Shari'a – the ulema – modified and reconstructed classical *fiqh* rulings that did not benefit women. I was also spending a lot of time with women visiting the shrine in Qom, and became enraged at how badly the shrine custodians treated them; and I saw how the strict codes of gender segregation and hijab worked to marginalize women and undermine their experiences.

Recordings of these conversations formed the basis of my next book, *Islam and Gender*.[5] The format followed a pattern established in anthropology since the 1970s (with the recognition that knowledge/culture is constructed in the process of conversation). By then I was aware of the links between ideas, identity and politics, and I began to observe – and reveal – my own motives and changes in perspective in the course of my research. I began with an account of the development of my thinking up to that point, and described how the material in the book had been collected, as well as my efforts to understand the background and ways of knowing of my interlocutors.

While writing *Islam and Gender*, I also started working with Kim Longinotto, an experienced independent British filmmaker. We co-directed an observational documentary (inspired by *Marriage on Trial*), in which the presence and concerns of the film crew were evident throughout. *Divorce Iranian Style* was shot in 1997, premiered in 1998, and during the ensuing years broadcast on TV in several countries, winning prizes in numerous festivals. I have written an account of this, which was my first experience in filmmaking, and how it involved me in a long series of negotiations, not only with the Iranian authorities for permission and access, and with British television film producers, but also with myself: I had to deal with personal ethical and professional dilemmas as well as with theoretical and methodological issues of representation.[6]

---

5 See Mir-Hosseini, 1999, pp. xi–xx. As described there, my research in Iran had also included extensive fieldwork among women in many other contexts, exploring their religious language and their understandings of religious texts; but all my fieldnotes were confiscated in Tehran airport as I left for England in November 1995.

6 Mir-Hosseini, 2002.

All these experiences gave a new edge to my research, which became more focused on rulings on marriage, divorce, custody, hijab and *zina* (sex outside marriage). I sought to unveil the theological and rational arguments as well as the social and legal theories that underpin juristic notions of gender, specifically the constructs on which the whole edifice of gender inequality in Muslim legal tradition has been built. My aim was to undermine this edifice, to show that there is nothing 'sacred' about it, and that consequently it is open to change.

In 2001, Zainah Anwar, founder of the Malaysian NGO, Sisters in Islam, invited me to write a paper on the 'construction of gender in Islamic legal tradition and strategies for reform' for a conference in Kuala Lumpur.[7] At the time, my research was focused on the idea of 'Islamic feminism', and writing this paper moved me further over the line toward activism. Subsequent trips to conferences and meetings in Malaysia and Indonesia opened a new world to me, where I felt at ease. There was none of the tension between religious and secular feminists that I was used to in the forums in Europe and North America where I had been presenting my work. I now spoke and wrote, not just as an academic merely concerned to analyse and explain, but also as an activist in search of solutions. This I found liberating.

It was, moreover, a welcome change from my experiences with secular-minded women's groups and NGOs in other Muslim-majority countries. For them, feminism was only possible within a secular framework; they had a visceral mistrust of religion, which was not the source of inspiration and liberation but an obstacle and a hurdle that should be ignored for the time being and would eventually be overcome. They saw my approach and my work, attempting to address women's issues from within a religious framework, as futile and counter-productive. At the same time, almost all the ulema I encountered voiced suspicions about my approach and my engagement with international human rights and feminism, both of which they saw as alien and Western-inspired.

Meanwhile, three other new experiences were having a profound impact on my thinking and my approach to research. First, in 2000, I was invited to teach at New York University School of Law for a semester in 2002. I accepted, for what was to be the first of six visits.[8] With my students – and among my law school colleagues – I experienced a new culture: the tradition of learning

---

7 Mir-Hosseini, 2003b.
8 As Hauser Global Law Visiting Professor in 2002, 2004, 2006, 2008, 2017 and 2019.

of American academic lawyers. I was struck by the similarities between this tradition and that of the Qom seminaries. Both were founded on the conviction of the law's ability to be neutral and to deliver justice. Lawyers – like the ulema – dislike uncertainties and seek legal remedies for social issues, while my own training as an anthropologist taught me to observe and to seek to understand the social context, the contingencies of social practice and the causes of legal disagreements.[9]

It was during my visits to NYU that I came to know Carol Gilligan, the pioneering feminist psychologist whose work I knew and respected. I would attend the seminar course that she taught with constitutional lawyer David Richards on the roots of ethical resistance, exploring questions such as: Why do people resist injustice? Why does resistance succeed or fail? I loved these seminars and found Gilligan's talks, the readings and discussions so enriching.[10] Apart from Gilligan's own books, I came to be very much influenced in my teaching and writing by *Women's Ways of Knowing*, a book by some of her admirers, which gave me insight into the cognitive processes involved when women acquire knowledge and relate to authority.[11]

Another important influence stemmed from my involvement in the project "New Directions in Islamic Thought and Practice", initiated by the Oslo Coalition on Freedom of Religion or Belief.[12] The project was conceived in 2002 when I was invited to Oslo by Lena Larsen to teach in a short course on divorce in Islamic law. Dismayed by the excessive focus of the media and academia on 'Islamic fundamentalism', a group of us recognized that we as academics have a responsibility to provide a forum for Muslim reformist thinkers to meet and exchange ideas. With support from the Oslo Coalition, and in consultation with an international committee of experts, the project developed into a series of closed workshops and public fora in collaboration with universities in different Muslim countries. The first workshop was held in Jogjakarta in 2004, followed by others in Sarajevo (2005), Istanbul (2007), Marrakesh (2008) and Cairo (2009 and 2010). The project has so far produced three books.[13] The workshops were occasions for honest debate and exchange

---

9 See Mertz, 2000.

10 See, for example, Gilligan, 1982, 2011, 2018.

11 Belenky et al., 1986.

12 The project is part of the Norwegian Centre for Human Rights; I am still part of the working group, though not as actively as before; see https://www.jus.uio.no/smr/english/about/programmes/oslocoalition/islam/

13 Vogt et al., 2008; Mir-Hosseini et al., 2013; Masud et al., 2021.

of ideas about reform and strategies for bringing these ideas to the public. As an active member of the working group, I was involved in organizing the meetings, where I not only met with key Muslim thinkers but gained insights into their diverse ways of thinking and approaching the textual tradition.

Thirdly, a fellowship at the Wissenschaftskolleg zu Berlin (Wiko) in 2004–5 provided me with the space and intellectual environment that I needed at the time. Among the fellows that year was the prominent Iranian philosopher and reformer Abdulkarim Soroush, whose work I had followed since the early 1990s and which continues to influence me. In the course of my research in Qom and my conversations with the clerics, I was also listening to recordings of Soroush's lectures and reading his interviews and writings. He had opened my eyes to new ways of thinking about Islam and its textual tradition. In the following years I had met Soroush several times in London and elsewhere; now in Berlin I learned much more of his approach and had a chance to develop our discussions. I found his approach to Islam coherent and inspiring – though I still could not agree with his gender perspective, as I had written in *Islam and Gender*.[14]

One of the most interesting fellows at Wiko was the feminist philosopher Nancy Fraser, whose work I very much admired. I joined the reading group that she and other feminist scholars formed that year. I came to appreciate feminism as a knowledge project, and started to ask new questions, to understand its relevance to my own research and context; that there are different ways of knowing; that there is no such a thing as value-free, 'objective' knowledge, so there can be neither definite nor final answers to what we know about Islam; 'the more value-neutral a conceptual framework appears, the more likely it is to achieve the hegemonic interests of dominant groups.'[15] I was increasingly convinced that, until patriarchal interpretations of the Shari'a are challenged from within the tradition, there can be no meaningful and sustainable change in family laws in Muslim contexts. I saw one problem to be the antagonism between 'secularist' and 'Islamic' approaches to the issue of women's rights; this divide, partly a legacy of colonial policies, blocked any fruitful debate and prevented women's groups from forging a viable strategy for Muslim family law reform. It was essential, I believed, to bring feminist methodology and knowledge into conversation with Islamic legal tradition, starting with gender as a category of analysis.

14 See Mir-Hosseini, 1999, pp. 217–246.
15 Harding, 2004, p. 6.

These varied experiences and discussions have strongly shaped my 'formation' in the years since, and influenced my input into the new movement that came to be called Musawah.

THE MAKING OF MUSAWAH

Zainah Anwar of Sisters in Islam, who shared my views, organized a workshop in Istanbul in March 2007, bringing together a diverse group of activists and scholars from a range of countries to discuss Islamic Family Law Reform. A planning committee was formed, charged with setting out the vision, principles and conceptual framework of Musawah (Arabic for equality), a new movement for the reform of Muslim family laws and practices.

We aimed to link academics and activists and to bring fresh perspectives on Islamic teachings. We began by commissioning a number of concept papers by reformist thinkers such as amina wadud,[16] Khaled Abou El Fadl and Muhammad Khalid Masud. We used these papers, published as the book *Wanted: Equality and Justice in the Muslim Family*,[17] to show how the wealth of resources within Islamic legal tradition, and the Qur'anic verses on justice, compassion and equality, can support the promotion of human rights and a process of reform toward more egalitarian family relations. In the course of two other workshops in Cairo and London, we developed a *Framework for Action*, in which we integrated Islamic teachings, universal human rights principles, national constitutional guarantees of equality and the lived realities of women and men, as the basis of our claim for equality. We presented both *Wanted* and the *Framework for Action* at the launch of Musawah in Kuala Lumpur in February 2009.

The *Framework for Action* grounds our claim to equality and arguments for reform simultaneously in Islamic and human rights frameworks. Taking a critical feminist perspective, we work from within the tradition of Islamic legal thought and invoke two of its main distinctions. The first, which underlies the emergence of the various schools of Islamic law and within them a multiplicity of positions and opinions, is between Shari'a and *fiqh*. Shari'a ('the way') in Muslim belief is God's will, as revealed to the Prophet Muhammad. *Fiqh*

---

16 Wadud no longer capitalizes her name; I have honoured her choice, apart from when quoting an older citation, and at the beginning of sentences.
17 Anwar, 2009.

('understanding') is Islamic jurisprudence, the process and the methodology for discerning and extracting legal rulings (*ahkam*) from the sacred sources of Islam: the Qur'an and the Sunna (the practice of the Prophet, as contained in Hadith, Traditions). Like any other system of jurisprudence, *fiqh* is human, temporal and local.

The second distinction is between the two main categories of legal rulings: *'ibadat* (ritual/devotional acts) and *mu'amalat* (social/contractual acts). Rulings in the first category, *'ibadat*, regulate relations between God and the believer: here jurists contend there is limited scope for rationalisation, explanation and change, since such rulings pertain to the spiritual realm and divine mysteries. This is not the case with *mu'amalat*, which regulate relations among humans and remain open to rational considerations and social forces, and to which most rulings concerning women and gender relations belong.

These distinctions have given us the language and the conceptual tools to argue for gender equality from within Muslim legal tradition. Contemporary Muslim family laws, we argue, are neither divine nor immutable; they are the product of *fiqh*, as developed by classical jurists in vastly different historical, social and economic contexts. They belong to the realm of *mu'amalat*, an area of *fiqh* rulings that is open to reinterpretation in line with the demands of time and place. These rulings, we argue, must now conform with contemporary notions of justice, to which gender equality became inherent during the course of the twentieth century. Women's concerns and voices were silenced by the time the *fiqh* schools emerged, early in the history of Islam; today we are reinserting them into the processes of the production of religious knowledge and law-making.[18]

It was against this background that I began this book project in September 2009. By then my search for a way out of the 'dead end' that Shamloo so eloquently depicted had merged with my work for Musawah and the wider struggle for the democratization of knowledge in Islam. Two events earlier that year gave me cause for optimism: the first was the launch of Musawah in February and the second was the rise of the Green Movement in Iran in the aftermath of the disputed June presidential elections, in which women and youth were at the forefront. I saw both events as promising early signs of collective challenges, from within, to patriarchal and despotic versions of Islam.

---

18 These paragraphs appear in several of Musawah's publications, drawn from my own writings; I had a role in formulating Musawah's approach, but it was and is an essentially collective work.

CONVERSATIONS: ORGANIZATION OF THE BOOK

There are seven chapters, framed by this introduction and a conclusion; Chapter One sets the scene for the six that follow, which are devoted to my conversations with leading Islamic reform thinkers.

The first section of Chapter One contextualizes the competing gender discourses and perspectives in contemporary Islamic tradition. I examine the challenge that the idea of gender equality has presented to established understandings of the Shari'a, and how, by the end of the twentieth century, this challenge had given birth to 'Islamic feminism'. The second section introduces three reformist texts that engaged with gender issues in Muslim tradition in ways that have inspired myself and all my interlocutors. These texts appeared at three key moments in the development of Muslim discourses on gender rights – the codification of family laws, the zenith of political Islam, and the rise of Islamic feminism. Their authors – Tahir Haddad, Fazlur Rahman and Nasr Hamid Abu Zayd – are no longer with us, but their approaches to Islam's textual sources became the building blocks of ideas of gender equality from within the Islamic legal framework.

Chapter Two presents my conversations, beginning in September 2009, with Abdullahi An-Na'im, the well-known Sudanese academic teaching in the United States at Emory University, whose pioneering work on Islam and human rights has inspired me and many other women. Following his mentor Mahmoud Mohamad Taha, the late Sudanese religious thinker and leader, in the 1990s An-Na'im proposed a methodology for a comprehensive reformation from within Islamic tradition. In 2007, as the idea of Musawah was taking shape, Zainah Anwar invited An-Na'im to contribute a concept paper on Islam and human rights from a reformist perspective. To our surprise, he responded to the effect that 'I am done with this type of approach.' Puzzled, I now asked whether he had departed from his earlier project of reformation from within Islam. If so, why and in what ways? He responded:

It is not a departure at all, in fact it is going deeper within the same approach that has two tracks. One is about the internal transformation of Muslim understandings of Shari'a and the practices of the Shari'a. The second track is the external conditions that enable this internal transformation and conversation to take place. In other words, I have [first] to address the political, legal, constitutional, and human rights dimensions not as an end itself but as a means to the end. I need the external conditions to protect the space that I need in order to be as radical as I care to be in the internal conversation among Muslims about Islam.

As our conversation progressed our differences in approach and strategy became apparent. They concern two issues. One is An-Na'im's use of Shari'a and *fiqh* interchangeably in his work. For him it is 'intellectual dishonesty' to distinguish them, as well as a futile strategy for opening space for debate. The other issue is engagement with traditional ulema and religious centres of learning, which he also sees as futile. By contrast, I see the distinction between Shari'a and *fiqh* as essential for challenging patriarchy from within, and engagement with the ulema to be a key strategy for achieving the internal transformation of Muslim understandings of Shari'a.

My next conversations are with two feminist scholars of the Qur'an – amina wadud and Asma Lamrabet. I know both of them well and have worked with them closely; we share the same vision. These conversations unfolded between 2010 and 2014, during the progress of Musawah's first research project (I was convenor) to re-examine *qiwama* and *wilaya*, two juristic concepts rooted in the Qur'an, which Muslim jurists have interpreted and constructed to justify male authority over women.[19] Both have chapters in one of the resultant books: *Men in Charge? Rethinking Male Authority in Muslim Legal Tradition* (2015).

In Chapter Three I talked with amina wadud, an African-American who converted to Islam in 1972. Her first book, *Qur'an and Woman: Rereading the Sacred Text from a Woman's Perspective*, first published in 1992, translated into many languages, has become a seminal text for Muslim feminists. I asked her to talk about her conversion and her evolving journey from adherence to a Salafi version of Islam to breaking a taboo in 2005 when she led a mixed Friday Prayer in New York. I also wanted to know why, despite having been a founding member of Sisters in Islam in 1988, she refused for a long time to identify as feminist.

In the 1990s I struggled with the two discourses led by Muslim women who argued that feminism and Islam are irreconcilable. The best way I can describe this time is that feminism was not wide enough to embrace

---

19 https://www.musawah.org/knowledge-building/qiwamah-wilayah

Islam, and Islam was not universal enough to embrace feminism. It was a living reality for many people including myself, who weren't willing to give up one for the other. I just had to take them both. The launch of Musawah in 2009 was really transformative for me. It was there that I began to see the political, social, cultural impact of this gender-inclusive analysis of Islam. And I said, well there it is. That's what Islamic feminism is and I was more comfortable with it.

Wadud also explained how she came to develop a gender-inclusive approach to the Qur'an, the impact of the 2005 controversy, and how her vision of feminism and Islam was formed.

Chapter Four introduces Asma Lamrabet, who started from the opposite position. A Moroccan medical doctor, around 1990 she felt betrayed and disillusioned by secularism and began to study her own faith and to write about it. I came to know her through her much-discussed book *Women in the Qur'an: An Emancipatory Reading*. Published in French in 2007, it appeared while I was doing research on recent family law reforms in Iran and Morocco, and Lamrabet and I met during one of my field trips in Rabat. We became friends, and I was also able to connect her with Fatima Mernissi – strangely, they lived in the same city but had never met. In 2011, Lamrabet became director of the women's studies centre in the Rabita Mohammedia, which made her a public figure. It was then that she became involved in Musawah's research project. She resigned her directorship in March 2018 during the women's campaign for equal rights in inheritance laws. Her opinion that the Qur'an teaches equality between men and women in inheritance was widely reported in the press, but it ended her strained relationship with the ulema.

I asked Lamrabet about her journey, how she became an 'Islamic Feminist', i.e. the move from secularism to Islam in her search for justice and equality for women, and why she decided to join Rabita and then leave. She described the abyss between her approach and that of the ulema in the Rabita:

Ninety per cent of the Qur'an refers to the human being, laying the path for proper actions or behaviour. It gives a great deal of importance to other concepts that are interconnected with the human, such as reason ('aql) ... When you have a holistic vision of the text and fully grasp its textual and contextual meanings, it is impossible to conclude that there is discrimination ... The ulema study and memorize the Qur'an, but their knowledge of the text is superficial . . . They have locked the Qur'an in the closet and are relying on the exegesis. You are being diverted from using your 'aql or reason, against engaging with justice, and we are simply guided to perform the ulema's orders, something that the political authorities approve. This is my problem inside this institution, my limits are political limits; I am gradually hitting a wall; because I ask, why is there no justice? Why is there discrimination? Why are they not using their reason, 'aql? Why, Why?

The next three conversations were with scholars who have critically engaged with *usul al-fiqh*, legal methodology, and have proposed strategies for substantive reform. All three are well versed in traditional religious sciences and modern education, and in different ways, have redefined the conventional relationship between Shari'a, *fiqh* and state law.

The subject of Chapter Five is Khaled Abou El Fadl, a distinguished and prolific Egyptian scholar of Islam, Professor of Law at the University of California, Los Angeles. His criticism of modern puritanical jurists is widely regarded as enlightening and vital. I first met him in 1999 during a panel discussion; we exchanged books, and we have kept in touch since. After the 9/11 attacks he became more vocal in his critique of Salafi Islam; that made him a public figure in the US press, but also the target of Muslim extremist wrath. He contributed a paper on Islam and human rights to Musawah's first book, *Wanted*.

In January 2014 Abou El Fadl invited me to his home in Los Angeles, and we talked for several hours. As he recounted his religious and legal education in Egypt and the USA, two things became clear to me: one was his mother's deep influence on his ethical understanding of Islam and his search for justice; the other was the important role played by his wife, Grace Song, who had converted to Islam before they met, in making his work known. Abou El Fadl had just submitted the manuscript of *Reasoning With God: Reclaiming Shari'a in Modern World*. He spoke passionately about the book, in which he develops different elements of his reform methodology into a coherent system. This is how he talked about it:

The Shari'a as a moral order is a historical reality that we have lived through. This is how Islam was practised and thrived throughout the ages with such rich diversity: the Islam of Indonesia, the Islam of the Philippines, the Chinese, the Uyghurs. The Wahhabis saw all this richness and diversity as . . . 'corruption on Earth'. I say, this is *not* the corruption that the Qur'an talks about at all. If the Wahhabis see this rich diversity as corruption, that is a fundamental rejection of sociology. And religion without sociology is itself a corruption because it tries to hammer human beings into statues, sorts of idols.

The last two conversations in the book are with Mohsen Kadivar and Sedigheh Vasmaghi, Iranian scholars with whom I have been collaborating since about 2010. Both are prominent members of a trend of reformist thought in post-revolutionary Iran known as 'New Religious Thinking', which demands the separation of religion from the state. Both had to leave Iran in the aftermath of the disputed presidential elections of 2009 and the emergence of the Green Movement, in which they have remained active. Their personal and intellectual lives, like mine, were transformed by the revolution, by the Islamic Republic's ideological use of the Shari'a and its penetration into the private lives of individuals.

In Chapter Six I talk with Mohsen Kadivar, a qualified Islamic jurist who also has a doctorate in Islamic philosophy and theology from Tarbiat Modares University in Iran. Since 2009 he has been Professor of Islamic Studies at Duke University. In October 2017, I asked him to talk about his life and work: how he abandoned his university studies in engineering in the 1980s and went to the Qom seminary, his time there, and how his approach radically changed two decades later.

> I can say that around 2000/2001 I went through a huge transformation in my intellectual orientation. In effect, I experienced a kind of paradigm shift . . . I first knocked on every door in classical *fiqh*, and learned whatever was there. I tried to find any opening in support of reforms. For example, take the question of Islam and democracy, which was a hot topic early in Mr Khatami's presidency [1997–2005]. I supported the concept of 'Islamic democracy' that Khatami advocated, and even tried to explicate its basis in Islam; I wrote articles on the topic. However, in the new phase of my intellectual journey, I made it clear in my writings that I no longer defend 'Islamic democracy'; what I defend is that we can have a democratic interpretation of Islam.

Kadivar has pursued his project through an engagement with *fiqh* that can open a constructive dialogue between traditional *fiqh* and modern notions such as human rights and gender equality. He has developed a reformist methodology that he calls 'Structural ijtihad' or 'ijtihad in principles and foundations' (*ijtihad dar usul va mabani*),[20] which we discussed at length. He argues that at the time of revelation, the laws endorsed in the Qur'an and Sunna were, for the time, rational, just, moral and more effective than other existing laws in their category. The most important of those four qualities is justice, which acquires a particular significance in the area of women's rights. From this he concludes that for a ruling (*hukm*) based on textual evidence to remain valid for our time, it should meet all four criteria: to be just, ethical, reasonable according to the values and standards of our time, and more effective than other existing laws.

Chapter Seven introduces Sedigheh Vasmaghi, one of the few Iranian women to have both a seminary training and a doctorate in *fiqh* from Tehran University. She is also a renowned poet and a major voice of reform. She was elected to the first Islamic City Council of Tehran, and served as its speaker between 1999 and 2003. Then she left public office and devoted herself to writing – producing two books critical of Islamic jurisprudence and its treatment of women. In the aftermath of the 2009 upheavals, to avoid prosecution, she left the country in 2011 to be visiting professor at Göttingen University, then later moved to Uppsala; but she decided to return to Iran in July 2017.

Our conversation, which took place via Skype in November that year, revolved around her book, *Rethinking Shari'a* (*Bazkhani-ye Shari'a*) which she completed before returning to Iran. There she engages further with questions raised in her earlier books. What is a Shari'a ruling (*hukm-e shar'i*)? What is its scope? Does it relate to every aspect of law? How do jurists (*fuqaha*) come to know it? What makes this book compelling is that she uses the Usuli[21] jurists' own methodology to refute the very basis of their claims. She says:

> The biggest mistake is to use religion as the source of law . . . The idea
> that the laws regulating our everyday life should be based on Shari'a

---

20 *Ijtihad* (lit. effort/exertion) is the process of exerting independent effort to deduce laws from the textual sources. It is commonly counterposed to *taqlid* (lit. imitation), conformity to past opinions.

21 The term Usuli is derived from *usul al-fiqh* and refers to those who use its methodology when inferring religious laws (*ahkam shar'i*) from the four valid sources: Qur'an, Hadith, *'aql* (reason) and *ijma'* (consensus).

was created by the jurists (*fuqaha*) over the centuries . . . I have repeatedly said in my books that *fiqh*'s era of law-making is over, and the
fuqaha must loosen their grip over the rules guiding day-to-day life
and leave that to the discretion of the lawmakers and the people.
Muslims are going through a difficult time; women and religious
minorities living in Muslim contexts are not treated as full humans.
We must untangle the knot by which the *fuqaha* tied Islam to law so
that Muslims can live in peace and prosper, so that women can achieve
their rights.

In the Conclusion I bring the different strands of these narratives together
with those of Muslim feminist activists in Musawah, to reflect on the possibilities of constructing egalitarian gender rights in Islam. I also reflect on the
impact of these new forms of scholarship and activism, how they have persua-
sively challenged the pre-modern understandings of Shari'a and are forging
the way for an understanding of Islam that has room for gender equality as it
is understood in our time.

Each of the transcript chapters begins with a more detailed introduction
to my interlocutor and an account of the circumstances of the conversation. I
have slightly abridged and edited each transcript for clarity, and rearranged a
few passages for chronological and thematic coherence. In the text (and, where
relevant, the translation)[22] I have tried to keep the conversational tone, inter-
rupting only to provide essential background and context. I have sent drafts of
each chapter, sometimes more than one, to the respective interlocutors, asking
1) does it represent their ideas fairly, 2) has their thinking changed since the
time of the conversation, 3) did they want to add anything, and 4) what are
they working on at moment? We have in each case resolved any issues by telephone or internet chat.

In many ways, this book is in the same mould as *Islam and Gender*, but
there are important differences. Let me point to two of them. The most obvious is that, in twenty-five years, my own perspective has shifted, and (I hope)
developed and matured. The second difference is that my main interlocutors
in the 1990s were clerics, and I was talking to them in Qom, the centre of
religious power in Iran. In order to open a dialogue with them I had to soft-
pedal my 'feminist' position; I took the position of suppliant rather than

---

22 Conversations with Kadivar and Vasmaghi were in Persian; with Lamrabet, partially in
French; the others in English.

interviewer – I asked for instruction, almost as a student, in their ways of thinking. With each of the scholars in this book, however, I have had no need to dissemble – we were already familiar with each other's work, some were friends of some years' standing, and we treated one another as equals, where necessary agreeing to differ.

1

The Issues at Stake: Shari'a, Justice, Gender Equality[1]

At least until recently, for Muslims justice was the business of the scholars (ulema). They defined what it requires and permits, its scope and its manifestation in laws, and examined its roots in Islam's sacred texts. As for gender rights, their conception of justice was determined by a strong patriarchal ethos. Take these two statements:

> The fundamentals of the Shari'a are rooted in wisdom and promotion of the welfare of human beings in this life and the hereafter. Shari'a embraces Justice, Kindness, the Common Good and Wisdom. Any rule that departs from justice to injustice, from kindness to harshness, from the common good to harm, or from rationality to absurdity cannot be part of Shari'a.[2]

> The wife is her husband's prisoner, a prisoner being akin to a slave. The Prophet directed men to support their wives by feeding them with their own food and clothing them with their own clothes; he said the same about maintaining a slave.[3]

Both statements were made by the same scholar, Ibn Qayyim al-Jawziyya (1292–1350 CE) – a reformist in his time and now a source of inspiration for some contemporary Islamist groups. The first statement, in my view, captures

---

1 This chapter, which summarizes my thinking and analysis on these issues since the early 2000s, draws from Mir-Hosseini, 2003; 2009; 2013b; 2015; 2019.
2 Ibn Qayyim, 1956, p. 1.
3 Quoted in Rapoport, 2005, p. 52.

succinctly what the Shari'a is about: justice, kindness, common good and wisdom. The second statement reveals Ibn Qayyim's understanding of what the Shari'a prescribes as just relations between men and women, reflecting the consensus in classical Islamic jurisprudence (*fiqh*).

Similar conceptions of justice and gender rights are to be found, of course, in other religious traditions. Gender equality is a modern ideal, which has only recently, with the expansion of human rights and feminist discourses, become inherent to generally accepted conceptions of justice. But what presents Muslims with a distinct problem is that the source of family law and gender norms is still classical *fiqh* rulings, expressed either in partially reformed and codified laws or in cultural norms and practices. These rulings uphold a patriarchal model of family, treat women as second-class citizens and place them under male authority.

I should note here that, although the term 'gender' (or equivalents in different languages) was not, until recently, familiar either to Islamic scholars or to the general public in Muslim contexts, I use the term here throughout as a convenient shorthand for the socially and culturally (as opposed to biologically) constructed roles of, and differences between, men and women.

PERSPECTIVES ON SHARI'A AND GENDER

The religious legitimation of patriarchy has been the subject of heated debate since the early twentieth century. This debate and the literature that it has produced continue to be tainted with the legacy and politics of colonialism and orientalist narratives of Islam. Broadly speaking, there are three competing discourses. The first, which I term 'Traditionalist', is premised on gender inequality as prescribed by classical Muslim jurists, and is still in operation in its unmodified form in a few Muslim countries, notably Saudi Arabia. The second discourse – currently dominant – developed in the early twentieth century and is reflected in the legal codes of many Muslim countries. It advocates 'complementarity' of rights, often referred to as 'gender equity', which, as we shall see, is a new defence and modification of the classical notion of gender inequality – hence I term this perspective 'Neo-Traditionalist'. The third discourse, which I call 'Reformist-feminist', emerged in the last decades of the twentieth century and is still in the process of formation; it argues for gender equality on all fronts. While the other two discourses take a protectionist approach to women's rights, reformist-feminists aim to democratize the dynamics of gender relations in law and in practice, both in the private sphere of the family and in society at large.

Gender Inequality

Traditionalists take a literal approach to the sacred texts, and their gender discourse is an ahistorical and simplified version of that of classical *fiqh* texts – those produced before the late nineteenth century. These texts take male superiority for granted, reflecting the world in which their authors lived. Biology is destiny; there is no overlap between gender roles; a woman is created to bear and rear children as her only contribution to society; her place is at home. Such a notion of women's roles and duties informs the ideology and practice of the most conservative Islamist political groups, which take it as the indisputable interpretation of the Shari'a. They are today a minority, but they often enjoy substantial financial support from Saudi Arabia and are active in propagating their views in many countries.

The gender discourse in classical *fiqh* was encapsulated in two sets of legal rulings (*ahkam*): those that defined the marriage contract and those that regulated women's dress and access to public space. In these matters, the various *fiqh* schools all shared the same inner logic and patriarchal bias. If they differed, it was in the manner and extent to which their conception was translated into legal rules. A brief examination of these rulings is in order here, as they are at the centre of debates about Islamic law and gender relations.

I must stress, I am concerned here only with the ways in which classical jurists understood and defined gender relations.[4] Whether these rulings corresponded at the time to actual practices of marriage and women's covering is, of course, another question, and one that recent research has started to answer. What this scholarship warns us is not to take the classical *fiqh* texts at face value. In pre-modern times judicial rules and court practices were quite different, and women had better access to legal justice than has been the case in more recent times; they frequented courts to negotiate the terms of their marriages and divorces and were present in public space.[5]

In classical *fiqh*, marriage crosses the boundary between its two main categories of rulings: those pertaining to *'ibadat* (ritual/devotional acts) and those

---

4 See Ali, 2010; Rapoport, 2005.
5 See, for instance, Sonbol, 1996; Tucker, 2000; Stilt, 2011.

pertaining to *mu'amalat* (social/contractual acts). In spirit, marriage belongs to *'ibadat*, in that Muslim jurists spoke of it as a religious duty ordained by God. In form, however, it falls under the category of *mu'amalat*, in that jurists defined it as a civil contract between a man and a woman such that any sexual contact outside this contract constitutes the crime of *zina* and is subject to punishment. In its legal structure, marriage is a contract of exchange with defined terms and uniform effects and is patterned after the contract of sale (*bay'*), which has served as a model for other contracts. Its essential components are: the offer (*ijab*) by the woman or her guardian, the acceptance (*qabul*) by the man, and the payment of dower (*mahr*), a sum of money or any valuable that the husband pays or undertakes to pay to the bride before or after consummation, according to their mutual agreement.[6]

With the contract, a woman comes under her husband's *'ismah/qiwama* (authority, dominion and protection), entailing a set of defined rights and obligations for each party, some with moral sanction and others with legal force. Those with legal force revolve around the twin themes of sexual access and compensation, embodied in concepts of *tamkin/ta'a* (submission) and *nafaqah* (maintenance). *Tamkin* (unhampered sexual access) is a man's right and thus a woman's duty, whereas *nafaqa* (shelter, food and clothing) is a woman's right and a man's duty. A woman becomes entitled to *nafaqa* only after consummation of the marriage, and she loses her claim if she is in a state of *nushuz* (disobedience).[7] The contract establishes neither a shared matrimonial regime nor identical rights and obligations between spouses: the husband is the sole provider and owner of the matrimonial resources and the wife is possessor of the *mahr* and her own wealth. The only shared space is that involving the procreation of children, and even here a woman is not legally required to suckle her child and can demand compensation if she does.

A man can enter more than one marriage at a time: up to four permanent ones in all law schools, and in Shi'i law also as many temporary marriages (*mut'a*)[8] as he desires, or can afford. He can terminate each contract at will: no specific grounds are needed, nor is the wife's consent or presence required. Legally

---

6 For a concise discussion of the terms of the marriage contract in classical *fiqh* texts, see Ali, 2008.

7 *Nushuz* means 'rebellion' and implies the abandonment of marital duties. Despite the fact that *fiqh* sources acknowledged that such abandonment can take place on the part of both spouses, they use the term *nashiza* (rebellious) only in the feminine form and in relation to maintenance rights; see Ali, 2007.

8 For this form of marriage, see Haeri, 1989.

speaking, *talaq*, repudiation of the wife, is a unilateral act (*iqa'*), which acquires legal effect simply by the husband's declaration. A wife cannot be released without her husband's consent, although she can secure her release by offering him inducements, by means of *khul'*, often referred to as 'divorce by mutual consent'. As defined by classical jurists, *khul'* is a separation claimed by the wife as a result of her extreme 'reluctance' (*karahiya*) toward her husband, and the essential element is the payment of compensation ('*iwad*) to the husband in return for her release. This can be the return of the dower, or any other form of compensation. Unlike *talaq*, *khul'* is not a unilateral but a bilateral act, as it cannot take legal effect without the husband's consent. If the wife fails to secure his consent, then her only recourse is the court's intervention and the judge's power either to compel the husband to pronounce *talaq* or to pronounce it on his behalf.

Unlike rulings on marriage, classical *fiqh* texts contain little on the dress code for women. The prominence of veiling regulations in Islamic discourses is a recent phenomenon, dating to the nineteenth-century Muslim encounter with colonial powers. It was then that we see the emergence of a new genre of literature in which the veil acquires a civilizational dimension and becomes both a marker of Muslim identity and an element of faith.[9]

Classical texts – at least those that set out rulings or what we can call 'positive law' – address the issue of dress for both men and women under 'covering' (*sitr*), in the Book of Prayer, among the rules for covering the body during prayers, and in the Book of Marriage, among the rules that govern a man's 'gaze' at a woman prior to marriage.[10] The rules are minimal, but clear-cut: during prayer, both men and women must cover their '*awra*, their pudenda; for men, this is the area between knees and navel, but for women it means all the body apart from hands, feet and face. A man may not look at the uncovered body of an unrelated woman; but a woman may look at an unrelated man. The ban can be removed when a man wants to contract a marriage and needs to inspect the woman he is marrying. The rules concerning covering during prayer are discussed under *ibadat* (ritual/worship acts), while rules of 'looking/gaze' fall under *mu'amalat* (social/contractual acts).

There are also related rules in classical *fiqh* for segregation (banning any kind of interaction between unrelated men and women) and seclusion (restricting women's access to public space). They are based on two juristic

---

9 Ahmed, 1992, pp. 144–168.
10 Many terms commonly used today in different countries for 'the veil', such as *hijab*, *parda* ('purdah'), *chador*, *burqa*, are not found in classical *fiqh* texts.

constructs: the first defines all of a woman's body as *'awra*, pudenda, a zone of shame, which must be covered both during prayers (before God) and in public (before men); the second defines women's presence in public as a source of *fitnah*, chaos, a threat to the social order.

These are, in a nutshell, the classical *fiqh* rulings on marriage and covering that the Traditionalists claim to be immutable and divinely ordained. They also claim that these rulings embody the Shari'a definition of gender relations, and thereby invoke them to legitimate male domination on religious grounds, closing the door to any constructive debate.

Gender Equity and Complementarity

Neo-Traditionalists take a more pragmatic approach; they recognize that a way must be found of responding to the challenges of the modern world, to changing social and economic conditions. While they recognize that classical *fiqh* conceptions of gender are untenable, they see 'gender equality' as an alien, 'Western' concept that must be resisted. Instead, they argue for 'gender equity' or 'gender complementarity', which, as we shall see, is set out in the laws of most Muslim majority countries.

The roots of this gender discourse can be traced to the Muslim encounter with modernity, which for many was a painful and humiliating encounter with Western colonial hegemony. In this encounter, 'women's status' and Islamic law became symbols of cultural authenticity and carriers of religious tradition – a situation that has continued ever since. The early twentieth century saw the expansion of secular education, the rise of modern nation-states and the creation of new legal systems inspired by Western models. In many such nation-states, classical *fiqh* provisions on the family were selectively reformed, codified and gradually grafted onto unified legal systems. With the exceptions of Turkey and the Soviet Central Asian counties, which abandoned *fiqh* in all spheres of law and replaced it with Western-inspired codes, and Saudi Arabia and other Gulf countries, which preserved classical *fiqh* as fundamental law and attempted to apply it in all spheres of law, most Muslim nations retained and codified *fiqh* only with respect to personal status law (family and inheritance). The impetus for, and the extent of, reform varied from one country to another, but on the whole one can say that, apart from the 1956 Tunisian Family Code, which banned polygamy, classical *fiqh* rulings on personal status were left more or less intact. Reforms were introduced by mixing (*talfiq*) and choosing (*ikhtiyar*) principles and rulings from different *fiqh* schools, and through procedural rules. These focused on increasing the age of marriage, expanding women's access to divorce, and restricting men's right to polygamy, which involved compulsory registration of marriages and divorces, and the creation of new courts to deal with marital disputes.[11]

The codification of *fiqh* provisions on family law transformed the interaction between Islamic legal tradition, the state and judicial practice. Codes and statute books replaced classical *fiqh* manuals in regulating the legal status of women in society; family law was no longer solely a matter for private scholars operating within a particular *fiqh* school, rather it became the concern of the legislative assembly of a particular nation-state. Once it existed in a codified form and was applied by the machinery of the modern nation-state, 'Islamic law' itself came to replace the Muslim scholars, the ulema, as the main source of legal authority, and fell within the jurisdiction of the state.

All this led to the creation of a hybrid family law that was neither classical *fiqh* nor Western, and a new gender discourse and genre of literature that is neither traditionalist nor modern. Though commonly subsumed under the label 'Modernist', I suggest that 'Neo-Traditionalist' is a better term, because this discourse upholds the classical *fiqh* rulings while providing a new rationalization for them. Hence the new genre of literature on "The Status of Women in Islam" that emerged in the late nineteenth century but proliferated in the course of the twentieth. Largely written by men – at least until mid-century – the stated aims of these authors were to shed new light on the status of women, and to clarify what they saw as 'misunderstandings'. They reread the sacred texts in search of solutions – or more precisely, 'Islamic' alternatives – to contemporary problems such as women's aspirations to equality.

Despite their variety and diverse cultural origins, what these rereadings have in common is an oppositional stance and a defensive or apologetic tone. Oppositional, because their concern is to resist the advance of what they see as alien 'Western' values and lifestyles; apologetic, because they attempt to explain and justify the gender biases that they inadvertently reveal in classical *fiqh* texts. However, they have problems responding to the voices of dissent within the Muslim world itself.[12]

---

11 For codification, see Anderson, 1976; for reforms, see Rahman, 1980b.

12 For a discussion of such writings in the Arab world, see Haddad, 1998; Stowasser, 1993. For Iran, see Mir-Hosseini, 2003. For a sample of texts in English, see Maududi, 1983; Mutahhari, 1991. For general critique, see Ali, 2003; Duderija, 2011; Mir-Hosseini, 2012.

Neo-Traditionalists do not see men's privileges in marriage, such as polygyny and the unilateral right to divorce, as discrimination but as an admission of the differences in male and female natures and sexualities, and between men's rational and women's emotional dispositions. They place their focus on the ethical and moral rules that marriage entails for each spouse, drawing attention to those Qur'anic verses and Hadith that affirm the essential equality of the sexes; ignoring the fact that these ethical rules, in effect, carry no legal sanction. They put forward no argument for translating them into law. As for *hijab*, they see it as a religious obligation whose function is to protect women and to safeguard public morality, while they keep silent on classical *fiqh*'s construction of the woman's body as 'awra', the sexual zone.

Unwilling to accept that aspirations for gender equality are not just imported from the West but part of twentieth-century reality, they find themselves in a contradictory position. On the one hand, they uphold *fiqh* rulings on marriage and gender relations; on the other, they are aware of and sensitive to current discussions of women's rights and to criticisms, from both secular and religious women, of the patriarchal biases in Islamic legal tradition. Education and employment, divorce laws and the question of hijab are the main themes through which they address issues of women's rights and define a range of positions. It is common to find a single scholar arguing for gender equality on one issue (for example, rights to education and employment), yet rejecting it on another (for example, divorce). In short, in these texts, the inequalities embedded in the classical *fiqh* construction of marriage and gender relations are defended and rephrased in terms such as 'equity' and 'complementarity of rights and duties'.

With the rise of political Islam in the second part of the twentieth century, these Neo-Traditionalist texts and their gender discourse became closely identified with Islamist political movements, whose rallying cry was 'Return to Shari'a' as embodied in *fiqh* rulings.

Gender Equality

Political Islam had its biggest triumph in 1979 when a popular revolution in Iran brought an end to the US-backed monarchy and introduced an Islamic Republic. It inspired Muslim masses and reinvigorated intellectual debates over the nature and possibilities of the Shari'a. The same year saw the dismantling of reforms introduced earlier in the century by modernist governments in Iran and Egypt, and the introduction of Hudood Ordinances in Pakistan.[13] Yet this was also the year when the United Nations adopted the Convention on the Elimination of All Forms of Discrimination against Women (CEDAW), which gave a clear international legal mandate to those advocating equality between men and women, and to the notion of women's rights as human rights.

These developments opened spaces for new forms of activism and debate. The Islamists' defence of pre-modern patriarchal interpretations of the Shari'a as 'God's Law', as the authentic 'Islamic' way of life, was now bringing the classical *fiqh* books out of the closet, exposing them to critical scrutiny and public debate. Socio-economic imperatives had already brought many more women than before into education and employment; a growing number began to ask whether there was an inherent or logical link between Islamic ideals and male dominance. A new phase in the politics of gender in Islam began. One crucial element of this phase was that it placed women themselves – rather than the abstract notion of 'the position of woman in Islam' – at the heart of the struggle between traditionalism and modernism.

By the early 1990s, in many Muslim contexts there were clear signs of the emergence of a new consciousness, a new way of thinking, and critical voices and scholarship that argued for gender equality on all fronts. Some versions of this new discourse came to be labelled 'Islamic feminism' – a conjunction that was unsettling to many Islamists and some feminists. I was one of the first to use this term for a new gender consciousness and discourse that emerged in Iran a decade after the 1979 Revolution had brought Islamists into power. I called this discourse 'Islamic feminism' because it was feminist in its demands and yet took its legitimacy from Islam. Women who articulated this discourse in Iran were those who in the early 1980s were 'Islamist', and some had played a crucial role in silencing secular women's voices. But by the late 1980s, many of them had become disillusioned with the Islamic Republic's official discourse on women and found an ally in feminism, and they were intent on resisting patriarchal interpretations of Islam's sacred texts.[14]

Islamic feminism, I argued, was the 'unwanted child' of political Islam; it did not emerge because the Islamists offered an egalitarian vision of gender

---

13 Hudood Ordinances were enacted in Pakistan in 1979 under the military rule of Zia ul-Haq, as part of a process of Islamization of law that had adverse effects on women. See Lau, 2007.

14 Mir-Hosseini, 1996; 2011.

relations. They certainly did not. Rather, their slogan and agenda of 'return to the Shari'a', and their attempt to translate into policy the patriarchal gender notions inherent in classical jurisprudence, provoked Muslim women to increased criticism of these notions.[15] Their voices started to draw the attention of media and academia, via publications, public meetings and workshops that provided a platform for scholar-activists. The challenge to patriarchal interpretations of the Shari'a can be traced to the late nineteenth century, but in my view it was only in the early 1990s that critical voices and scholarship emerged from within the tradition, in the form of a literature that deserves the label 'feminist', sustained and informed by a feminist gender analysis of religious knowledge.

Drawing their legitimacy from within the Islamic tradition, Islamic feminists question both the hegemony of patriarchal interpretations of the Shari'a and the authority of those who speak in the name of Islam. They have introduced gender as a category of thought and analysis to a tradition that until recently was gender-blind. Muslim feminist scholars have produced an impressive body of scholarship to tackle text-based sources of gender inequality, and to reclaim Islam's egalitarian message.[16] This literature is extensive and diverse in approach.[17] But they all agree that Islam's call for freedom, justice and equality was submerged in the norms and practices of Arab society and culture in the seventh century and the formative years of Islamic law. The genesis of gender inequality in Muslim legal tradition, these scholars argue, lies in a contradiction between the ideals of Islam on the one hand, and on the other, the male-dominated structures in which these ideals unfolded and were translated into legal norms.

CHALLENGING PATRIARCHY: THREE PRECURSORS

Let us now take a closer look at the development of arguments for gender equality in Islam by examining three texts that, in my view, mark the transition from Neo-Traditionalist to Reformist approaches to gender. I have chosen these texts for various reasons. First, the three authors have influenced my

---

15 Mir-Hosseini, 2011, 2020c.

16 For example, Al-Hibri, 1985; Hassan, 1987; Mernissi, 1991; Wadud, 1999, 2006; Barlas, 2002; Mir-Hosseini, 2003; Shaikh, 2004; Ali, 2006, 2010; Lamrabet, 2007, 2012; Abou-Bakr, 2013.

17 For recent assessments of this literature, see Seedat, 2013a & 2013b; Hermansen, 2013; Hidayatullah, 2014; Duderija, 2015; Reda & Amin, 2020; Sirri, 2021.

own thinking to a large extent, and their ideas and methodologies are referenced in the following chapters. Secondly, the texts tell us the state of play at three key moments in the struggle to redefine the nature of gender relations for Muslims. Finally, the issue of equality was central to the reform projects of all three authors; all three met a great deal of opposition in their own countries, where their ideas were declared heretical; and all three paid a price for going against official dogma – as is indeed also the case with all six reformist thinkers we shall meet in subsequent chapters.

The first text is the book *Our Women in the Shari'a and Society* (1930) by Tahir Haddad (Al-Tahir al-Haddad), written in the context of the early twentieth-century debates surrounding legal codification, when *fiqh* rulings were being grafted onto modern systems. The second is an article by Fazlur Rahman, "The Status of Women in Islam: A Modernist Interpretation", published in 1982 when a revived political Islam was at its zenith and Islamists were dismantling earlier reforms. The third text, Nasr Hamid Abu Zayd's "The Status of Women between the Qur'an and Fiqh", is an unfinished paper presented at a workshop on *New Approaches to Islamic Family Law* in January 2010, shortly before his untimely death; by this time, Islamic feminists were in conversation with reform thinkers such as Abu Zayd and were changing the terms of the debate over Muslim family laws, and at the same time women activists were making inroads in the process of law-making in Muslim contexts.

Tahir Haddad (1899–1936)

Tahir Haddad studied Islamic sciences at Zaytouna, the prestigious centre of religious studies in Tunisia, and qualified as a notary in 1920. He opted for journalism, and became involved in the movement for independence from France. He was active in the trade union movement and deeply concerned about the situation of workers and women and the injustices to which they were subjected. In 1927 he published a book on labour law, and in 1930 a second book, *Our Women in the Shari'a and Society*,[18] in which he offered a critique of women's treatment in Tunisia and argued that Shari'a, if properly understood, grants women equality on all fronts. The book caused an immediate uproar in Tunisia; Haddad was denounced, his degree revoked by his

---

18 An English translation by Ronak Husni and Daniel Newman appeared in 2007.

seminary colleagues in Zaytouna, and he was declared an apostate.[19] He died in 1936 in poverty and isolation at the age of thirty-six. But his ideas survived, and when Tunisia gained independence, they enabled the modernists to introduce the most radical reforms in the area of family law, which was codified in 1956, including the banning of polygamy.

Our Women in the Shari'a and Society is part of a nationalist and reformist debate on the 'status of women in Islam' that was ignited by the encounter with Western colonial powers.[20] Critical of fiqh rulings, reformists called for women's education, for their participation in society and for unveiling. One subtext in this debate was the repudiation of the colonial premise that 'Islam' was inherently a 'backward' religion and denied women their rights; another was the quest for modernization and the reform of laws and legal systems as part of the project of nation building. Without women's education and their participation in society, the modern, independent and prosperous state for which they were struggling could not be achieved.[21]

Haddad's book was distinctive in one major respect: it went beyond mere criticism and provided a framework for rethinking fiqh rulings. There are two related elements to Haddad's framework. First Haddad distinguishes between norms and prescriptions that are essential to Islam as a religion, thus eternal, and those that are contingent, thus time- and context-bound. In his words:

> We should take into consideration the great difference between what Islam brought and its aims, which will remain immortal in eternity, such as belief in monotheism, moral behaviour, and the establishment of justice, dignity and equality among people. Furthermore, we have to consider the social situation and the deep-rooted mind-set that existed in Arab society in the pre-Islamic era when Islam first emerged.[22]

The second element is what he termed al-siyasa al-tadrijiyya, the policy of gradualism, which, he argued, governed the process of legislation in the Qur'an

---

19 For the political context, reactions to al-Haddad's book, and the politics of family law in Tunisia, see Salem, 1984; Boulby; 1988; Charrad, 2001.

20 Amin (1899) was the most influential of this literature; for a critical discussion, see Ahmed, 1992, Chapter 8.

21 For the intellectual genealogy of al-Haddad's text, see Husni & Newman, 2007, pp. 1–25; for the intellectual and social changes that made women's issues central to politics, see Ahmed, 1992, Chapter 7; for the experiences of other countries, see Keddie, 2007.

22 Husni & Newman, 2007, p. 36.

and Sunna. In Islam the 'highest aim is equality among all God's creatures,' but it was not possible to achieve this aim in the seventh century and during the lifetime of the Prophet; 'the general conditions in the Arabian Peninsula forced the legal texts to be laid down gradually, especially those concerning women.'[23] 'Islam is the religion of freedom,' but it tolerated 'the selling and buying of human beings as goods, and their exploitation as animals for the duration of their lives.'[24] This toleration was a concession to the socio-economic imperatives of the time. It was not then possible to do away with slavery altogether, but the Qur'an and the Prophet encouraged the freeing of slaves, and made it crystal clear that the principle is freedom. For exactly the same reason, patriarchy was tolerated then, but again the Qur'an made it clear that the principle in Islam remains equality.

This framework enabled Haddad to offer different readings of Qur'anic verses 4:34[25] and 2:228[26] – the two verses that constitute the prime textual support for the institution of male authority over women.[27] He argues that both verses must be read in the context of the marriage and divorce practices of the time and the privileges that men enjoyed before Islam; the intent in both verses was to restrain these privileges and to protect women in the face of them. This becomes clear, he says, when we read these verses in their entirety and in conjunction with those that precede and follow them. In verse 4:34, a husband is required to provide for his wife, so that the continued growth of the world can be ensured; he is given the right to correct his wife's behaviour in order to

---

23 Ibid., p. 104.

24 Ibid., p. 48.

25 Verse 4:34 reads: 'Men are *qawwamun* (protectors/maintainers) in relation to women, according to what God has favoured some over others and according to what they spend from their wealth. Righteous women are *qanitat* (obedient), guarding the unseen according to what God has guarded. Those [women] whose *nushuz* (rebellion) you fear, admonish them, and abandon them in bed, and *adribuhunna* (strike them). If they obey you, do not pursue a strategy against them. Indeed, God is Exalted, Great.' I have taken this translation from Kecia Ali who leaves the **emphasized** words untranslated, pointing out that any translation of each of these key terms amounts to an interpretation (Ali, n.d.). I have inserted translations that approximate the consensus of classical Muslim jurists.

26 Verse 2:228 reads: 'Divorced women must wait for three monthly periods before remarrying, and, if they really believe in God and the Last Day, it is not lawful for them to conceal what God has created in their wombs: their husbands would do better to take them back during this period, provided they wish to put things right. Wives have [rights] similar to their [obligations], according to what is recognized to be fair, and husbands have a degree (*darajah*) [of right] over them: [both should remember that] God is almighty and wise.'

27 For how the link between these two verses was made through exegesis, see Abou-Bakr, 2015.

prevent a greater ill, namely divorce. This verse is not speaking about the rights and duties of spouses, but is about the course of action to be taken when there is marital discord, and it offers ways to resolve it. This becomes clear in the verse that follows (4:35), which reads: 'If you [believers] fear that a couple may break up, appoint one arbiter from his family and one from hers. Then, if the couple want to put things right, God will bring about a reconciliation between them.' Men are addressed because they are the ones who, then as now, have the power to terminate marriage, and the objective was to restrain this power and give the marriage a chance. Likewise, with verse 2:228, which the jurists read as evidence of men's superiority, Haddad maintains that it must be read in its entirety and in connection with the previous and following verses, which are all related to marital separation and the protection of women. The final part of the verse speaks of men's power to divorce, and this is what 'men having a degree over women' is about; divorce was in their hands.

With respect to marriage and gender roles, there are again two important elements in al-Haddad's approach. First, he rejects the argument that women are unfit for certain activities and that their primary role is motherhood. 'Islam did not assign fixed roles to men and women . . . Nowhere in the Qur'an can one find any reference to any activity – no matter how elevated it may be – whether in government or society, that is forbidden to woman.'[28] Yes, men and women are different; women give birth and are physically and emotionally suited to care for children, but this in no way means that Islam wanted them to be confined to the home and to domestic roles. The problem is not with Islam but with patriarchy, with reducing women to sex objects; it is 'primarily due to the fact that we [men] regard them [women] as vessels for our penises.'[29]

Secondly, Haddad breaks away from the transactional logic of marriage in *fiqh*, and places mutual affection and cooperation at the centre of the marital relationship:

> Marriage involves affection, duties, intercourse and procreation. Islam regards affection as the foundation of marriage since it is the driving force, as witnessed by the following verse:
>
> And among His signs is this, that He created for you mates from among yourselves, that you may dwell in tranquillity with them, and

---

28 Husni & Newman, 2007, p. 39
29 This phrase, which appears toward the end of al-Haddad's preface, is simply rendered by Husni & Newman as 'we regard them as an object to satisfy our desires' (2007, p. 31).

He has love and mercy between your (hearts): Verily in that are signs for those who reflect. (verse 30:21)

As for duty, this refers to the fact that husband and wife have to work together to build a life. In this sense, duty both preserves and enhances the emotional ties that exist between them and which enable them to carry out their duty wilfully.[30]

By shifting the focus from verse 4:34 to verse 30:21, Haddad could break the links, not only between maintenance and obedience as constructed in classical *fiqh* texts, but also between male authority over women (*qiwama*) as derived from verse 4:34, and male superiority (*daraja*), derived from verse 2:228. By contextualising these verses, he was able to offer an egalitarian interpretation of both. This also allowed him to make freedom of choice (*hurriyyat al-ikhtiar*) the starting point for regulating marriage. Love and compassion, Haddad argues, cannot develop in a relationship that is imposed; women, like men, must have the freedom to choose their spouses and must be able to leave an unwanted marriage, and this is what Islam mandates.

Haddad's ideas and proposals for reform were radical for the time, which to a large extent explains the harsh reaction of the clerical establishment to his book. He went much further than other twentieth-century reformers, even arguing for equality in inheritance, an issue that became a priority for Muslim women's movements only in the next century.[31] But in 1956, in a changed political context, when the modernizing nationalists had prevailed and Tunisia was an independent nation state, many of Haddad's proposals for reform were adopted. Under the leadership of Habib Bourghiba, the modernists embarked on reform of the judiciary, and among their first acts was the codification of family law. The new code made polygamy illegal and gave women equal access to divorce and child custody; though the inheritance laws remained unchanged. All these reforms were introduced from above – women were the beneficiaries of legislation, subjects of debate, not yet active participants in shaping them.[32]

---

30 Husni & Newman, 2007, p. 57.
31 A joint campaign by Moroccan and Tunisian women's organizations went public in 2006 with a two-volume publication: AFTURD, 2006.
32 For an overview and analysis of these reforms, see Kelly, 1996.

Fazlur Rahman (1919–1988)

Fazlur Rahman was another daring twentieth-century reformer whose ideas encountered a great deal of opposition in his own country, Pakistan, though his situation and background were different from those of Haddad. With a doctorate from Oxford University, Rahman taught at Durham and McGill Universities, but his intellectual genealogy is from reform thinkers in the Indian sub-continent.[33] The formation of his ideas belongs to the tail end of Western colonialism in Muslim contexts, when processes of nation building, modernization and reform of the judiciary, and codification of family law were well under way.[34] In 1961, he was invited by General Ayub Khan to help with reforming religious education in Pakistan, and became director of the Islamic Research Institute, an intellectual thinktank tasked with steering the path of modernization and reform in ways that would not offend the religious establishment.[35] However, his reformist ideas and critical approach to Islamic tradition faced much hostility in influential religious and political quarters. The fiercest opposition came from religious conservatives, and centred on the question of women's rights. Rahman began to receive death threats, and eventually decided to return to academic life in the West. In 1968 he joined the University of Chicago where he remained until his death in 1988, leaving behind an impressive body of scholarship. His work in turn has been the subject of scholarship, and played an important role in the development of Islamic studies in the USA.[36] But his vast output, all in English, remains almost unknown in traditional centres of Islamic religious learning, and his influence in his own country Pakistan is limited.

In his approach to Islam's sacred texts, Rahman shares with Haddad the ideas of historicism and gradualism in revelation and legislation. According to

33 Prominent among them were Syed Ahmad Khan (1871–1898) and Muhammad Iqbal (1877–1938). Iqbal delivered his reform agenda in a series of six lectures published in Lahore in 1930 (see Iqbal, 1934). These lectures, which did not receive much attention at the time, later became central to the formation of Muslim reform thought. For an illuminating exposition of Iqbal's lecture on the notion of *ijtihad*, see Masud, 2003.

34 For analysis of their impact on the rethinking of gender rights in Muslim legal tradition, see Moosa, 2001–2.

35 Major family law reforms in the sub-continent – the 1939 Dissolution of Marriages Act, and the 1961 Muslim Family Laws Ordinance – took place before Rahman's directorship. Women's groups were instrumental in pushing for these reforms.

36 For studies of Fazlur Rahman's work, see Sonn, 1991; Ibrahim Moosa's introduction to Rahman, 2000; Saeed, 2004. For his impact on American Islamic discourse, see Waugh & Denny, 1998.

Rahman, the Qur'an 'is the divine response, through the Prophet's mind, to the moral-social situation of the Prophet's Arabia, particularly to the problems of commercial Meccan society of the day.' Not all these solutions are relevant or applicable to all times and all contexts; but the moral principles behind them are immutable and permanently valid. These moral principles show us the way, the Shari'a, how to establish a society on Earth where all humans can be treated as equals, as they are equal in the eyes of God. This is at once 'the challenge and the purpose of human existence, the trust – *amana* – that humanity accepted at creation.'[37]

Muslims, Rahman argued, have betrayed this trust, since, in the course of the historical development of Islam, they distorted the moral principles behind Qur'anic laws; and the Shari'a, which is never mentioned in the Qur'an in the sense of a system of law, became the defining element of Islam. This distortion had its roots in political developments after the Prophet's death and in the subsequent decay and stagnation of Islamic intellectualism, which predate Islam's encounter with Western colonial powers. Muslims failed to create a viable system of Qur'an-based ethics, and from the outset jurisprudence in Islam overshadowed the science of ethics; in developing the latter, Muslim scholars relied more on Persian and Greek sources than on the Qur'an itself. The link between theology, ethics and law will remain tenuous as long as Muslims fail to make the crucial distinctions in the Qur'an and the Prophet's Sunna between essentials and accidentals, and between the prescriptive and the descriptive. They mistakenly view the Qur'an as a book of law, and take its legal and quasi-legal passages to be relevant to all times and places.

To revive the Qur'an's 'élan', Rahman proposed, Muslims needed two things. First was a fresh engagement with the Qur'an and a critical reassessment of the entire Islamic intellectual tradition: theology, ethics, philosophy and jurisprudence. The second was a realistic assessment and understanding of the contemporary socio-political context. Only then would Muslims be able to overcome centuries of decadence and backwardness and meet the challenges of modernity. The interpretative process that Rahman proposed for this revival came to be known as 'double movement', which entailed a movement 'from the present situation to Qur'anic times, then back to the present'. In the first movement, 'general principles, values and long-range objectives' of the Qur'an were elicited and separated from the socio-historical context of the revelation. In the second, these principles were applied to issues at hand,

---

37 Sonn, 1991, p. 128.

taking into consideration the current context and its imperatives.[38] This, in his words:

> requires the careful study of the present situation and the analysis of its various component elements so we can assess the current situation and change the present to whatever extent necessary, and so we can determine priorities afresh in order to implement the Qur'anic values afresh. To the extent that we achieve both moments of this double movement successfully, the Qur'an's imperatives will become alive and effective once again. While the first task is primarily the work of the historian, in the performance of the second the instrumentality of the social scientist is obviously indispensable, but the actual 'effective orientation' and 'ethical engineering' are the work of the ethicist.[39]

In "The status of women in Islam: a modernist interpretation",[40] Rahman suggests what 'effective orientation' and 'ethical engineering' entail when it comes to the issue of gender equality and family law. This is the only place (apart from his 1980 article on family law reforms) where Rahman focuses his attention on this issue; elsewhere he mentions it only in passing.[41] Published in 1982, the same year as his last major work (*Islam and Modernity*), this article can be seen as the application of his 'movement' theory in the area of gender rights and family law reform. Rahman begins by identifying himself as a 'Muslim modernist', one who pursues social reform through a new interpretation of Islamic sources and 'in contradistinction to the stance taken on most social issues by Muslim conservative-traditionalist leaders.' Islamic modernism, Rahman argues, 'developed under the impetus of modern Western liberalism but contains within it tangible differences on sexual issues, but is to be sharply distinguished from secularism.' He does not spell out the difference here, but in a later article he gives us a clue as to what he means when he states the position of a Muslim modernist: 'While he espouses the cause of the emancipation of women, for example, he is not blind to the havoc produced in the West by its new sex ethics, not least in the dilapidation of the family

---

38 Rahman, 1982a, p. 5.
39 Ibid., p. 7.
40 Rahman, 1982b.
41 For his views on gender rights and his impact on the development of a new Islamic feminism, see Part III of Waugh & Denny, 1998, especially Sonn, 1998.

institution.'[42] He is equally critical of social reform without reference to Islam, which he calls 'secularism (a la Mustafa Kemal Ataturk)', the 'apologetic aspect' of Islamic modernism that rationalizes and justifies gender inequality (p. 285).[43]

The legislation in the Qur'an regarding women, Rahman contends, is part of the effort to strengthen the position of the weaker segments of the community, which in pre-Islamic Arabia were the poor, orphans, women, slaves and those chronically in debt. Through reforming existing laws and practices and introducing new ones, the Qur'an aimed to put an end to their abuse and to open the way for their empowerment. Departing from the apologetic refrain on the position of women in pre-Islamic time, Rahman argues that the position of women was not altogether low, 'for even a slave woman could earn and own wealth, like a slave male, let alone a free woman. Khadija, the first wife of the Prophet, owned a considerable business which the Prophet managed for her sometime before their marriage, and after their marriage she helped him financially' (p. 286). But women could also be treated as property, as 'a son inherited his stepmother as part of his father's legacy and could force her to marry him or could debar her from marrying anyone else through her life, coveting her property' (p. 288). Women were also 'the central focus of the "honour" ('ird) of a man whose "manliness" (muruwwa) demanded that her honour remain inviolate' (p. 287). This, according to Rahman, was the distorted logic behind the practice of female infanticide, which was a way of preventing the eventual infringement of a man's honour.

What the Qur'anic reforms achieved was 'the removal of certain abuses to which women were subjected': female infanticide and widow-inheritance were banned, laws of marriage, divorce and inheritance were reformed. As with slavery, however, these reforms did not go as far as abolishing patriarchy; they expanded women's rights and brought tangible improvements in their position – though not social equality. Women retained the rights they had to property, but they were no longer treated as property themselves; they could not be forced into marriage against their will, and the customary marriage gift (mahr or sadaq) now went directly to them; they also acquired better access to divorce and were allocated shares in inheritance (pp. 286–289).

The essential equality between the sexes is clearly implied in the Qur'an; both men and women are mentioned separately 'as being absolutely equal in

---

42 Rahman, 1986, p. 160.
43 Page references here are to Rahman, 1982b.

virtue and piety with such unflinching regularity that it would be superfluous to give particular documentation' (p. 291).

> The Qur'an speaks of the husband and wife relationship as that of 'love and mercy' adding that the wife is a moral support for the husband (30:21). It describes their support for each other by saying, 'they (i.e. your wives) are garments unto you and you are garments unto them' (2:187). The term 'garment' here means that which soothes and covers up one's weakness (p. 293).

Rahman also rejects those sayings attributed to the Prophet that speak of women's inferiority and require them to obey and worship their husbands; they are clearly 'a twisting of whatever the Qur'an has to say in matters of piety and religious merit' (p. 292). Such sayings also contradict what we know of the Prophet's conduct from other sources.

> The Prophet's wives, far from worshiping him – with all his religious authority – wanted from him the good things of life, so that the Qur'an had to say, 'O Messenger! Say to your wives: "If you want to pursue this-worldly life and its good things, then I will give you wealth, but let you go in gentleness (i.e. divorce you)"' (33:29).[44] What the Qur'an required from a woman was to be a good wife, adding, 'Good women are those who are faithful and who guard what is their husband's in his absence as God wants them to guard' (4:34) (p. 293).

The Qur'an does speak of inequality between sexes. But when it does, it gives a rationale, which has to do with socio-economic factors.

> In 2:228 we are told, 'For them (i.e. women) there are rights (against them), but men are one degree higher than women.' That is to say, in the social (as opposed to religious) sphere, while the rights and obligations of both spouses toward each other are exactly commensurate, men are, nevertheless, a degree higher. The rationale is not given in this verse which simply adds 'And God is Mighty and Wise.' The rationale is given later, in verse 4:34 (p. 294).

---

44 [sic: should be 33:28].

This verse, Rahman goes on, 'gives two rationales for male superiority: (1) that man is "more excellent", and (2) that man is charged entirely with household expenditure.' But this superiority is limited to the socio-economic sphere (p. 294).

> What the Qur'an appears to say, therefore, is that since men are the primary socially operative factors and bread-winners, they have been wholly charged with the responsibility of defraying household expenditure and upkeep of their womenfolk. For this reason, man, because by his struggle he has gained more life-experience and practical wisdom, has become entitled to 'manage women's affairs,' and, in case of their recalcitrance, admonish them, leave them alone in their beds and, lastly, to beat them without causing injury (p. 294–5).

Having given his interpretation of verse 4:34 and the rationale behind the gender inequality in the Qur'an, Rahman then poses two questions: Are these socio-economic roles on which gender inequality is based immutable, even if women want to change them? If they are changeable, how far can they be changed? His answer to the first question is a definite no, these inequalities are not inherent in the nature of the sexes; they are the product of historical socio-economic developments. Once women acquire education and participate in society and economy, the 'degree' that the Qur'an says men have over women also disappears. But the answer to the second question, Rahman contends, is not that simple, and he is hesitant whether 'women should ask or be allowed to do any and all jobs that men do' – although he admits that 'if women insist on and persist in this, they can and eventually will do so' (p. 295).

But he has no doubt that law reforms must give women equality in all other spheres; classical *fiqh* rulings in marriage, divorce and inheritance can and must be reformed because 'it is the most fundamental and urgent requirement of the Qur'an in the social sector that abuses and injustices be removed' (p. 295). These inequalities are now the cause of suffering and oppression and go against the Qur'anic spirit, which is that of the equality of all human beings.

Nasr Hamid Abu Zayd (1943–2010)

Born in a small village in Egypt, Nasr Hamid Abu Zayd received a traditional religious education. He later studied literature at Cairo University, obtaining his doctorate in Islamic studies from the same university. In a compelling account of his engagement with Qur'anic studies, Nasr Abu Zayd traced the evolution of this engagement and his approach, starting with his memorization of the entire Qur'an as a child, his early sympathies with the Muslim Brotherhood, his entering the academic world and his vocal criticism of the dominant Islamic discourse in Egypt, which led to his exile. His aim was 'to achieve a scientific understanding of the Qur'an, and . . . to brush aside layers of ideological interpretation, in order to unearth the historical reality of the text.'[45] In 1990, he published a groundbreaking book: *The Concept of the Text* (*Mafhum al-Nass*), in which he brought to the traditional field of Qur'anic studies concepts and tools from other scholarly disciplines, namely modern linguistics and philosophical hermeneutics. His criticism of the instrumentalization of religion, and his challenge to the monopoly of interpretation of the sacred texts, made him the target of opposition by influential religious leaders in Egypt, who denounced him as an apostate and tried to annul his marriage. Forced into exile in 1995, he became Professor of Islamic Studies at Leiden University in Holland, where he remained until his untimely death in June 2010.

A deeply religious man, Abu Zayd defined himself as 'one of the Arab and Muslim adherents of "rationalism", a "rationalism" which does not exclude or despise religion as mere psychological phantom' (2011, p. 55). Equally at ease with popular Islam and with his deep knowledge of classical religious sciences, Abu Zayd engaged in international scholarly debate on Islam and human rights. In two books (both in Arabic), he addressed the issue of women's rights. His latest thinking on the issue is to be found in "The Status of Women between the Qur'an and *Fiqh*", a paper that he presented at a workshop in Cairo in 2010.[46]

Abu Zayd starts his discussion of marriage by quoting the Egyptian reformist Muhammad 'Abduh (1845–1905), who contrasts *fiqh* and Qur'anic conceptions of marital relations.

> Marriage, according to *fiqh*, is a contract which renders the female vagina the property of a male. The Qur'an's view, however, is that marriage is

---

45 Kermani, 2004, p. 175.
46 This workshop was organized by the Norwegian Centre for Human Rights as part of their project, New Directions in Islamic Thought, which I mentioned in the Introduction. It was published posthumously in the conference proceedings, Abu Zayd, 2013.

one of the Divine signs (*ayat*): 'Among His Signs is this, that He created for you mates from among yourselves, that you may dwell in tranquillity with them, and He has put love and mercy between you; verily in that are Signs for those who reflect' (30:21).[47]

The vast chasm between Qur'anic and *fiqh* conceptions of marriage, Abu Zayd argued, has to do with how, early in the history of Islamic sciences,

> [t]he worlds of the Qur'an, or its multi-dimensional worldview, were separated, in fact fragmented. Theology took over the world of divinity, i.e. the divine nature; philosophy took over the world of metaphysics, i.e. the cosmos, the grades of existence, nature, and so on; Sufism took over the ethical-spiritual world; and legal theory took over the legislative world.[48]

The high status of women in the Qur'an, which is part of its ethical and spiritual domain of meaning, became disconnected from the legalistic domain of meaning. The whole reformist project in Islam, from the onset, has been about how to deal with the consequences of this fragmentation, which has come to be felt more acutely in modern times. The gradual but steady marginalization of theology, philosophy and mysticism in the few past centuries, made 'the Shari'a paradigm, whether the legal theory or the substantive law (*furū'*) . . . the only representative of Islam. The two vocabularies, Shari'a and Islam, became synonymous.'[49]

'To reconnect the worlds of the Qur'an,' Abu Zayd argued, 'we need to approach the Qur'an differently,' which entails dealing with the tension between historicity and divinity, or between chronological order and the order in which the revelations are presented.

> The Qur'an was communicated as a series of oral discourses during the last 20 years of the Prophet's life (612–632); each discourse has its occasion, audience, structure, type, mode and message. These discourses were later collected, arranged and written down in the *muṣḥaf*. The difference between the *muṣḥaf* arrangement and the chronological order

---

47 Abu Zayd, 2013, p 154.
48 Ibid.
49 Ibid., p. 160

of these discourses is a well-known fact. The *muṣḥaf* gave the Qur'an the form of a book, which in its turn redefined the Qur'an as a Text.[50]

To transmit His message, God adopted a human language; the first addressees of the Qur'an were the seventh-century Arabs, whose language, which was part of their reality, became the language of the Qur'an. Like any text, the language of the Qur'an is not self-explanatory; it requires interpretation, which is the raison d'être of the Qur'anic sciences (*'ulum al-Qur'an*), whose task has been that of understanding and deciphering the language of the Qur'an. When we read classical Qur'anic scientific literature in the light of modern theories about textual analysis, they reveal that

> [t]he Qur'an, although recognized as a holy text, is a historically and culturally determined text. This historical text is the subject of understanding and interpretation, whereas God's words exist in a sphere beyond any human knowledge. Therefore, socio-historical analysis is needed for its understanding and a modern linguistic methodology should be applied for its interpretation. The Qur'an is a message revealed from God to man through the Prophet Muhammad, the Messenger of God and a human. The Qur'an is very clear about that. A message represents a communicative link between a sender and a recipient through a code or linguistic system. Because the sender in the case of the Qur'an cannot be the object of scientific study, the scientific introduction to the analysis of the text of the Qur'an can only take place through the study of the contextual reality and the cultural milieu of seventh-century Arabia.[51]

So, 'it will be always necessary to analyse and to interpret the Qur'an within the contextual background from which it originated' and 'being a unique text, the Qur'an employs a special linguistic encoding dynamics in order to convey its specific message.' He contends that it is here that the theories of modern linguistics and hermeneutics can come to our aid in reforming the tools of classical Qur'anic sciences.[52]

---

50 Abu Zayd, 2013, p 154. In Qur'anic studies the term *mushaf*, literally 'collection of pages', denotes the 'compiled, written pages of the Qur'an' as distinct from the term 'Qur'an', which denotes the specific 'revelation that was read to the Prophet Mohammad.'
51 Abu Zayd, 2011, p. 82.
52 Ibid., p. 83.

One main problem that has confronted the scholars of the Qur'an has been how to understand the 'phenomenon of contradictions' in a text authored by God.

As a revealed divine text, the Qur'an maintains that it has no contradictions (4:82). Yet the phenomenon of contradiction does exist. The theologians realised this, and took pains to solve it with the duality of clarity/ambiguity. So did the jurists, who tried to solve it by the doctrine of abrogation. In modern Qur'anic studies in the Muslim world, the solution proposed is to distinguish between two dimensions in the Qur'anic worldview: the 'universal' and the 'historical.' In all these efforts, the phenomenon is realised, acknowledged, but not fully solved.[53]

To understand what seem to be 'contradictions' with respect to equality in general, and between genders in particular, Abu Zayd contends that, apart from removing the layers of ideological interpretation, which entails consciousness of the historical reality of the Qur'an, we need to realize that the Qur'an 'was originally a series of discourses', and to analyse it as such.

For now, I propose dividing the worlds of the Qur'an – its multi-dimensional worldview – into five interdependent domains, each of which reflects one level that has been taken away and disconnected from the other levels in one of the Islamic disciplines, namely fiqh, theology, philosophy and mysticism.[54]

These domains are: 1) cosmology; 2) the divine–human relationship; 3) the ethical and moral dimension; 4) the societal level; and 5) punishment (2013, p. 155–156). To understand the Qur'anic view on gender relations, Abu Zayd maintains that we need to reconnect the different domains of meanings – or different worlds – of the Qur'an.

On the cosmological level, [human equality] is stated in the opening verse of the chapter 'Women' (Al-Nisa', 4:1), which addresses

53 Abu Zayd, 2013, p. 155.
54 Ibid.

humans: 'O mankind! Reverence your Lord Who created you from a single soul from which He created its mate and from them He emanated countless men and women; reverence Allah through Whom you demand your mutual (rights) and (reverence) the wombs (that bore you): for Allah ever watches over you.' It is quite significant that the term 'soul', *nafs*, is a feminine word, and that the mate created from it is named *zawjaha*, which is a masculine word that could be translated as 'twin' or 'husband'. The second meaning is highlighted in 7:189: 'It is He who created you from a single soul and made out of it its mate that he might dwell with her (in love).' As the chapter about women opens with absolute cosmological equality, the entire chapter, which contains most of the legal regulations concerning marriage, should always be connected to the principle of equality. Another point to support this proposition is the frequent reference to justice, *'adl*.[55]

Likewise:

On the ethical-spiritual level, equality is also sustained; both men and women receive the same reward for their righteous actions. In a cluster of verses [16:90, 16:97, 4:124; 40:40; 3:195] presenting a discourse of admonition, divine justice is put forward as the governing principle: 'Allah commands justice, the doing of good, and liberality to kith and kin, and He forbids all shameful deeds, and injustice and rebellion: He instructs you, that ye may receive admonition' (16:90). The admonition concludes: 'Whoever works righteousness, man or woman, and has Faith, verily, to him will We give a new Life, a life that is good and pure and We will bestow on such their reward according to the best of their actions' (16:97). See also 4:124; 40:40; 3:195; and 9:71–2, where the believers are presented as one unified community of males and females in mutual intimate guardianship . . .[56]

On the societal level, however, differentiation is acknowledged. In the case of religious difference, there exists a discourse of discrimination. Gender differentiation, however, is free from any discrimination.

---

55 Ibid., p. 161
56 Ibid.

Qur'anic gender differentiation developed into discrimination in the *fiqh* literature due to a certain cultural and socio-historical context.[57]

In deducing legal rulings on marriage and gender relations, classical jurists relied on the societal level in the Qur'an – in their milieu patriarchy was taken for granted; the embrace of gender equality had to wait until the feminist paradigm change in our own era. The existence of passages in the Qur'an that treat men and women differently, Abu Zayd stresses, is not an obstacle to an egalitarian construction of gender rights in Islam. He concludes with two remarks:

> It should be recognised that when the Qur'an sustains absolute equality in both the cosmological and the ethical–spiritual domain, this is the direction in which the Qur'an would like Muslims to upgrade the societal domain of inequality. Traditional law-makers failed to do so because there was no socio-cultural development in this direction ... The demand for gender equality is a product of our modern era of human rights. The challenging question is: are Muslims able to exert the same courage to upgrade the societal domain of meaning to the high level of the cosmological and the ethico-spiritual domains?[58]

I was a convenor of the January 2010 workshop in Cairo where Abu Zayd presented this paper, which I have quoted at such length. Although I was familiar with his work and we had crossed paths at a number of earlier meetings, it was the first time I interacted with him directly on gender rights. His paper clarified many things for me. This was less than a year since the birth of Musawah; I ensured that my colleagues Zainah Anwar, Mulki Al-Sharmani and Marwa Sharafeldin were also at the workshop, and we held a Musawah planning meeting immediately afterwards. While in Cairo I also made a tentative arrangement with Abu Zayd to interview him for my book project the next time we met – a plan unfulfilled because of his untimely death.

---

57 Ibid., p. 162.
58 Ibid., p. 164.

SUMMARY

Let me end by summarizing some of the issues to be discussed:

First, gender equality is a modern ideal, which has only recently, with the expansion of human rights and feminist discourses, become inherent to generally accepted conceptions of justice. In Islam, as in other religious traditions, the idea of equality between men and women was neither relevant to notions of justice nor part of the juristic landscape. To use an idiom from Muslim juristic tradition, gender equality is among the 'newly created issues' (*masa'il mustahdatha*) – that is, something for which there are no previous rulings. Simply put, gender equality is an issue that Muslim jurists did not have to address until the twentieth century.

Secondly, the idea of gender equality has confronted traditional interpretations of the Shari'a with a challenge that Muslims have been trying to resolve. Hence the debate over what 'true' Islam is, what Shari'a stands for, and the plethora of literature on relations between Islam and human rights, women's rights and democracy. This literature, in a variety of languages (and much of it now on the Internet), and ranging from sound scholarship to outright polemics, displays different positions and different gender perspectives, from those who endorse the classical *fiqh* rules, to those who seek their modification in the idea of 'complementarity of rights', and to those who advocate gender equality in all matters.

Irrespective of their position and gender perspective, all contributors to this literature agree that 'Islam honours women's rights', and that justice and fairness are integral to the Shari'a; they disagree on what these rights are, what constitutes justice for women and how to realize it within an Islamic framework. The intensity of the debate, and the diametrically opposed positions taken, are indications of a paradigm shift in thinking about gender rights, Islamic law and politics. We become aware of the old paradigm only when the shift has already taken place, when the old rationale and logic, previously undisputed, lose their power to convince and can no longer be defended on ethical and rational grounds. Feminist voices and scholarship in Islam herald the coming of an egalitarian legal paradigm that is still in the making.

The debate over gender equality continues to be entangled in the history of the polemics between Islam and the West, and the anti-colonial and nationalist discourses of the first part of the twentieth century. With the rise of political Islam in the second half of the century, and the Islamist slogan of 'Return to Shari'a', the debate became part of a larger intellectual and political struggle among Muslims between two understandings of their religion and two ways of approaching its sacred texts. One is an absolutist, dogmatic and patriarchal Islam that makes little concession to contemporary realities, such as the changed status of women in society. The other is a democratic, pluralist and rights-based Islam that is making room for these realities and values, including gender equality. The chapters that follow exemplify the latter approach, as advocated by six prominent Muslim scholars, coming from very different intellectual, social and cultural backgrounds, as we shall see, but converging in their views of the issues at stake.

2

Abdullahi An-Na'im

In order to be a Muslim by conviction and free choice, which is the only way one can be a Muslim, I need a secular state. By a secular state I mean one that is neutral regarding religious doctrine, one that does not claim or pretend to enforce 'Shari'a' – the religious law of Islam – simply because compliance with Shari'a cannot be coerced by fear of state institutions or faked to appease their officials.[1]

Abdullahi Ahmed An-Na'im is Professor of Law at Emory University Law School, and a renowned scholar of Islam and human rights. Born in Sudan in 1946, he studied law at the University of Khartoum and became involved in the reform movement of Mahmoud Mohamed Taha, an unorthodox and mystic visionary of Islam who had in 1945 founded the Sudanese Republican Party, also known as the Republican Brotherhood.

In 1970, on a scholarship from his university, An-Na'im went to the UK to complete postgraduate studies in law. Having obtained an MA and LLB from the University of Cambridge, and a Ph.D. from the University of Edinburgh, he returned home in 1976 and began teaching at the Faculty of Law of Khartoum University.

In 1983, when the military dictator Jafaar Nimeiri sought to consolidate his power by imposing Shari'a law, Taha and his supporters opposed these endeavours. There was a crackdown, and An-Na'im was among those arrested. Taha was convicted on charges of apostasy and was executed in January 1985; in April that year An-Na'im left Sudan. He had intended to go back, but subsequent political developments in his country brought Islamists into power and he realized that it would be unwise to return. After a stint of temporary

---

1 An-Na'im, 2008, p. 1.

academic and human rights posts, in 1993 he became Executive Director of Africa Watch, based in Washington. He resigned in 1995 to join Emory School of Law, where he has remained since.

Abdullahi An-Na'im's first book, *Toward an Islamic Reformation: Civil Liberties, Human Rights, and International Law*, received a great deal of attention when it came out in 1990. The book articulated an innovative and constructive approach to relations between Islamic and human rights law. Delineating in clear terms the areas of tension between the two, An-Na'im skilfully reworked Mahmoud Mohamed Taha's reformist ideas into a novel methodological approach to address these tensions. He was well versed in Taha's teaching, both as a close associate and as the translator of Taha's *The Second Message of Islam* – a book that contains his reformist approach and vision of Islam, which in 1982 Taha himself asked An-Na'im to translate into English.[2]

Reviews of *Toward an Islamic Reformation* were mixed. Its reception in academic and human rights circles was encouraging in general and led to constructive debates. For instance, in February 1992, the Norwegian Institute of Human Rights organized a seminar on "Human Rights and the Modern Application of Islamic Law" to discuss the book. Among the notable participants invited to critically engage with An-Na'im were scholars of Islam Mohammad Arkoun and Roy Mottahedeh, and scholars of Islam and human rights Ann Mayer and Bassam Tibi, all of them taking positions that differed from that of An-Na'im.[3]

An-Na'im's book and his writings on relations between Islamic and human rights laws shaped my own thinking profoundly. I found his critique of women's rights in Islamic law from a human rights perspective helpful, since he did not only criticize, but offered a framework for addressing the issue from within Islamic tradition. He also engaged with activism on the ground, speaking in different fora all over the world, and presenting papers at meetings organized by women's rights groups, including Sisters in Islam in Malaysia.[4] In a 1995 article, An-Na'im argued that in Muslim contexts not only is 'the apparent dichotomy between so-called religious and secular discourse about the rights of women in Islamic societies somewhat false or grossly

---

2 The first edition of the book was published in Arabic in 1967, followed by four further revised editions. An-Na'im's 1987 translation is based on the 5th edition.

3 For the seminar proceedings, with other commissioned articles, see Lindholm & Vogt, 1993.

4 For instance, the regional workshop organized in 1998 by SIS on 'Islam, Reproductive Health and Women's Rights'; see Anwar & Abdullah, 2000 – An-Na'im's paper is on pp. 33–57.

exaggerated, its implications are too serious to ignore in practice.' He then provided advice for forging an effective partnership between the advocates of the two camps. The essential tasks were: a) to challenge traditional so-called Islamic doctrines and dogmas about women's rights; and b) to develop and articulate Islamic justifications for the human rights of women.[5] What An-Na'im expressed in that article spoke to me so clearly; it captured what I was observing in the course of my own research on Islam and women's rights. It became a guiding light for me.

Then came an opportunity to work together in the context of the project "New Directions in Islamic Thought and Practice", initiated by the Oslo Coalition on Freedom of Religion or Belief (as described in the introduction). An-Na'im joined the advisory committee of experts, which met in London in June 2003 to prepare a platform statement and plan meetings. The first International Workshop and Public Forum of the project took place in June 2004 in Jogjakarta, Indonesia, in cooperation with State Islamic University (UIN) Sunan Kalijaga; the theme was "Exploring Issues of Equality and Plurality". An-Na'im and I were among the participants in the closed workshop, and both of us were speakers in the public forum, along with Zainah Anwar.

Then in late 2007, as Musawah was preparing the groundwork for our argument for equality from within an Islamic framework, Zainah Anwar emailed An-Na'im, explaining our vision, and invited him to contribute a concept paper on Islam and the human rights of women. To our surprise, he responded that he was done with this type of approach. I was curious to know what he meant by this response.

An occasion to follow it up came after the publication of his *Islam and the Secular State*, which received a great deal of attention in academia and beyond.[6] His earlier work was based on an elaboration of Taha's vision for an Islamic reformation. An-Na'im had argued that resorting to secular ideologies would not resolve the problem of human rights in Muslim contexts:

to seek secular answers is simply to abandon the field to the fundamentalists, who will succeed in carrying the vast majority of the population with them by citing religious authority for their policies and theories.

---

5 An-Na'im, 1995.

6 An-Na'im, 2008. *The Immanent Frame* features an online discussion of the book shortly after its publication https://tif.ssrc.org/category/book-blog/book-forums/islam-and-the-secular-state/ (accessed 20 May 2021).

Intelligent and enlightened Muslims are therefore best advised to remain within the religious framework and endeavour to achieve the reforms that would make Islam a viable modern ideology.[7]

Islam and the Secular State had a different tone and stance; it seemed no longer to be speaking to Muslims who are conflicted, unable to reconcile their religious tradition with human rights, and instead was making a case for a secular state as prerequisite to this reformation.

In January 2009, the Catholic University of Leuven awarded Abdullahi An-Na'im an honorary doctorate, and the occasion was marked by a conference to discuss his new book.[8] I was invited to present a paper, and I took the opportunity to repeat my criticism of An-Na'im for ignoring the epistemological and political implications of his refusal to make a distinction between Shari'a and *fiqh* throughout the book.[9] This was an issue that he and I had discussed in 2004 in Jogjakarta.[10] This time, by shifting the focus from theory to ethnography, to demonstrate the crucial place of this distinction I referred to the experience of political Islam in Iran, and to the emergence of Islamic feminism at the global level. I showed how the notion of Shari'a as an ideal had enabled reformists in Iran to argue for democracy, and Muslim feminists to challenge patriarchal laws enacted in the name of Islam.[11]

It was against this backdrop that our conversation took place. We were both invited to a symposium on "Reimagining Shari'ah: Theory, Practice and Muslim Pluralism at Play", organized by Shahin Sardar Ali of the University of Warwick and held in September 2009 at the university's conference centre in Venice. I used the occasion to record the first conversation for my new research project. I wrote to An-Na'im in advance, telling him about my project; he agreed to be interviewed, and we set a time to meet in the hotel lobby. When I arrived, he was having coffee with Lynn Welchman, a mutual friend (professor of Law at SOAS) who was also a conference participant. We invited her to stay for the interview, and she joined in at several points toward the end, when our conversation became heated.

---

7 An-Na'im, 1987, p. 28.
8 See Foblets's foreword to the edited conference proceedings, 2010.
9 See An-Na'im, 2008, p. 35; Mir-Hosseini, 2010b.
10 See the transcript of the discussion at that meeting, in Vogt, Larsen & Moe (eds), 2008, pp. 200–219.
11 Mir-Hosseini, 2010b.

Our conversation revolved around three main themes: An-Na'im's spiritual and intellectual trajectory and Taha's reformist methodology; his 2008 book, whether it was a departure from his earlier approach, and how he dealt with controversy surrounding his work; and finally the issue that divided us, namely the distinction between Shari'a and *fiqh*, which I insisted on and he rejected. As he repeated several times, however, we were united in our general perspective and analysis on the issue of gender equality and justice.

PERSONAL, SPIRITUAL AND INTELLECTUAL CAREER

I opened by asking An-Na'im to talk about his intellectual background, his education and the evolution of his thought.

AAN: In the name of God, I was born in a village on the Nile about 200 kilometres north of Khartoum, Sudan. I grew up in that village and went to school in a town further north called Atbara. While attending law school at the University of Khartoum in 1968, I stumbled by chance upon a lecture by Ustadh Mahmoud Mohammed Taha about the constitution of Sudan. Once I heard him speak in that and other lectures, I could not walk away. His clarity of thought, compassion and insight were so powerful that I felt his discourse in that and other lectures brought me home with myself. As a Muslim of that post-colonial generation at the time (I was born in 1946 and Sudan became independent in 1956), I was in a state of ambivalence and conflict, completely torn between the commitments I had to human rights, to liberal democratic values, on the one hand, and on the other, what I knew the Shari'a to be, as understood by the Muslims around me and by people I grew up with in my own community.

I followed Ustadh Mahmoud very closely and observed him frequently at home and among his followers while I lived in Sudan (except for five years of postgraduate studies in the UK from 1971 to 1976 and one academic year for a fellowship at Columbia University in 1981–82) until his execution in January 1985. He showed me a way to reconcile human rights and Shari'a in a very straightforward, systematic and coherent way, and the integrity of his approach is really what captured me. He lived the values that he preached, and he didn't wait for people to get persuaded in order to preach what he believed in, for example equality for women. Men and women participated equally in his movement: men and women wrote the pamphlets and books together, sold them in the street together and held discussion groups and public lectures together. We also equally led what we used to call 'delegations' throughout the country. We were taught to live in the moment, living immediately by the values that we were preaching, while being aware of the social and contextual limitations and ensuring that they did not inhibit or hinder our movement.

ZMH: You mention that you struggled with an internal conflict – a difficulty with Shari'a as people understood it and as it was lived – and that this conflict was resolved when you met Ustadh Taha and through your involvement with the movement. Can you elaborate on the nature of this conflict and how it was resolved?

AAN: The conflict was, and is, one which I continue to struggle and grapple with: the fact that Shari'a does not acknowledge the equal human dignity of women. When I say Shari'a, I mean Muslims' understanding of the Shari'a, I never mean Shari'a from God's perspective but rather as perceived from the human perspective.

I saw this as an opportunity to raise, right at the beginning, a major point of disagreement between us: the distinction between Shari'a and *fiqh*; and to clarify what he meant by 'Shari'a from God's perspective'. But An-Na'im did not take the bait, so I decided to let it go for now; we would come back to it later.

ZMH: When referring to Shari'a, I suppose you have *fiqh* rulings in mind, i.e. Shari'a as understood and defined in Islamic jurisprudence (*fiqh*)?

AAN: I am referring to the examples which you refer to yourself, regarding the legalistic approach to marriage, to the payment of maintenance for sexual access and so on and so forth. I studied these concepts both in grade school where we were taught religion as a course each year, and later while attending law school. What was being instructed and defined to us as Shari'a was in fact very regressive or patriarchal. To me that was unfair and jarring; I felt totally conflicted. On a personal level I struggled to understand how I could possibly be comfortable with treating my mother or my sister (I myself wasn't married at the time) – whom I loved and respected and knew to have as much value as men in the family – as inferior and subordinate.

The conflict concerned three matters, which Taha addressed in one stroke: relations between men and women, freedom of religion, and freedom to choose and live with one's convictions. That first lecture I heard him present was: 'Al-dastur al-Islami: Na'am wa La', meaning 'Yes and No to an Islamic Constitution.' Taha gave an affirmative 'yes' to the values of Islam and constitutionalism but a 'no' to the notion of an Islamic state. This was back in 1968 and to me it was very powerful, compelling, and persuasive. I simply could not walk away from becoming a student of Ustadh Mahmoud and part of his movement until he was executed for *ridda* [recanting belief in Islam – heresy] in January 1985 and his movement violently suppressed. I left Sudan and went into exile in April that year.

ZMH: What were the elements of Taha's methodology that you found so enabling in reconciling Islam and human rights laws?

AAN: Taha's methodology entails an evolutionary approach to religious experience, where individuals evolve in their relationship vis-à-vis religion and in their ability to use religion to liberate and to elevate themselves through many stages. Taha used to say that even pagan religions were appropriate and coherent for people in their time and that individuals were required to overcome that stage before evolving and acquiring a superior monotheistic religion which went from Judaism to Christianity, and finally to Islam.

Therefore, Taha viewed Islam as the culmination of the human story of religious transformation and evolution. Those of us who were fortunate enough, as he would see it – and I do see it – to be Muslims by the blessing of the Prophet's achievement and transcendent ability, were able to cover a lot of ground very quickly. That is one dimension of his methodology, as outlined in his book, *The Second Message of Islam*.

Taha held that there is a paradigm shift in the Qur'an between the verses that were revealed to the Prophet in Mecca and those revealed in Medina. For him, the real message of Islam is in the Meccan verses; they address humanity at large and contain the message of peace, freedom and equality. The Medina verses in effect are a historical adaptation of this message to the reality of life in seventh-century Arabia; they were directed not to the Prophet alone but to the community of the early believers. But inside the adaptation were the seeds of continuity for going forward, which did not repeal the fundamental and universal message of Mecca forever, but only postponed its realization until humanity was capable of living up to it. In his view, the entire process – living through Medina, the development of the Islamic civilization and religious thought, Sufism and religious practice – can all be viewed as a trajectory that prepared the scene for a return to the original message, which was postponed until the time was right.

He believed that the time was ripe, and that global humanity was now well positioned not only to appreciate but also to live up to the level of human responsibility that is required by the first and the original message of Islam. Here is where Taha could be wrong or right in his views about humanity today. Only time can tell; and we could have differing views as to whether humanity has yet reached this level.

The other dimension is that Taha believes that the Qur'an teaches you everything and nothing in particular, because it is the methodology of human transformation that enables us to comprehend and to transform every aspect of life, but it itself is not a code of law that give us rules. Rather, the Qur'an gives us moral guidance and then we struggle with it.

Taha used to say that because the Qur'an is the final revelation, it had to contain all that God intended to reveal to humanity; but it had to do it in a way that acknowledged the dignity of the human. So he says that the freedom to choose and to be responsible for our choice, equality between men and women, and between believers and non-believers, were in the Qur'an of Mecca, because that is the message that God intended humans to encounter, to appreciate and to embrace. So where and how we look for the sources of Shari'a will transform our understanding of the concept as Muslims. He cites specific examples, ranging from the questions of polygamy and veiling, to freedom of religion and Jihad, in order to demonstrate a paradigm shift in the Qur'an and how to understand the Shari'a. He called the understanding of the early Muslims al-shari'a al-salafiyya, i.e. the Shari'a of our righteous ancestors.

The object of Shari'a as a normative system is to assist and enable the individual to ascend to the divine. Taha used to say, 'We approach God and we come back to God not by covering distance, because God is not in place and time, but by bringing our qualities closer to the divine qualities.' He drew parallels and commonalities between the human and the divine: God is knowledgeable, we are knowledgeable, God is compassionate, we are compassionate. The qualities are shared but God's qualities are in the infinite while human qualities are at the very lowest level of achievement. The question of reverting back to God is not to cover distance or space and time but to align ourselves rather more closely with the divine qualities, and the Shari'a is the means to do that.

ZMH: I really can't see the social and legal implications. It's a very mystical and spiritual approach.

AAN: It is, but you have to understand the value and importance of social and legal institutions, neither of which is an end in itself. Taha used to say that we need the constitutional, legal, and various types of devices and institutions as a means to the end of enabling human beings to reach the highest levels of religious piety and to ascend to God through this internal transformation. One way he used to describe this methodology of internal personal transformation was to call it 'the approach of alternating between outward and inward': the combination of inner reflection and outward action based on the outcome of the reflection, though the two are interactive. We think and reflect, and we pray and fast, and, through this spiritual effort to clarify our thinking and purify our feelings, we act socially and politically, thereby coming to reinforce those values within ourselves. Therefore, inward and outward processes have to occur at an individual level, every person has to do this for himself or herself, and no one can do it for another. For Ustadh Taha, the Prophet was a living model of this process, so too were the instructive models – the guides or *murshids* – but they cannot take on and take over what we have to do for ourselves in order to achieve that model.

I believe in the value of this process and take it very seriously. Therefore, for me it is this ability to say that the original message of Islam lies in the Qur'an and the life of the Prophet, the example of the Prophet, his Sunna. He used the term Sunna not only as a source of *fiqh*, i.e., drawn on Hadith collections, but the lived example of the Prophet: what the Prophet did in his own life, the way he interacted with others and how he addressed questions of power, property, all issues that are the real test of living Islam.

ZMH: There are certain aspects in the lived example of the Prophet that could be seen as objectionable in our time. For instance, the Prophet practised polygyny and had nine wives when he died. If we go by Taha's methodology, does this make polygyny part of the original message of Islam? Isn't there a contradiction here?

AAN: I see no contradiction; the Prophet was a man of his time; he had to be in order to be persuasive and to be taken seriously by the community, he had to do things that were the norm. Now, we know for sure that there is something exceptional about the sort of polygamy practised by the Prophet, because he took up to nine wives, whereas the unanimous position in the traditional view is that the number should be four. One fact is that the Prophet was twenty-five when he married his wife Khadija, who was forty, and he remained in this monogamous marriage until Khadija's death.

The Prophet's practice contradicts the vulgar apologetic trope, that polygamy is necessary because men have greater sexual desire. If that were the case and the only justification, the Prophet would more likely have engaged in the practice as a young man than as an older man. The fact that he got married to a woman fifteen years his senior, remained married to her alone until her passing, and had all his children with her – with the exception of one child with Maria – is indicative of another dimension to this practice. In those terms, the Prophet's other marriages, which came later in his life, appear more like alliance-building and conformity to social norms, actions which he needed to take and to maintain in order to retain the support of his followers. Ustadh Taha used to say that the Prophet was the man of the future who came to the past in order to lead Muslims through the ages into the future. Inevitably, there are aspects of his practice which had to be consistent with his being of the seventh century in order to be able to lead his community forward. Only those aspects of the Prophet that are of the future can be part of the Sunna.

ZMH: I wonder if Taha or your group at large discussed this issue of whether men and women differ in terms of sexuality? I say this because, in traditional *fiqh*, part of the justification of unequal gender rights in general is premised on a difference between males and females in their sexuality and in their role in society.

AAN: No, he did not, and as a group we never talked in those terms. In fact, one of the aims of our group discussions and activism was to severely criticize the *fiqh* justification for polygamy as well as the whole question of hijab for women. Everything must be equal, and men and women have the exact same obligations, in every single respect. In fact, Ustadh Taha was often quite upset by the notion that men's sexual drive was just too 'overwhelming' to be tamed or controlled. This apologetic view was what I was referring to as the 'vulgar' notion used protect men's runaway sexuality and so on.

ZMH: I find it actually revolutionary that your group observed monogamy in the context of Sudan, where the culture endorses polygamy. Was this the group's ideology, the ideal? Did their practice conform to it?

AAN: Absolutely. Taha himself was monogamous for his entire life; he married one woman and remained with her until he was killed. While in prison in 1948, he wrote a will transferring everything that he owned to his wife in the event of his passing, and stating that she should have exclusive control of all the affairs of their children, and so on and so forth. That is the sort of person he was; he practised what he preached.

At the time, I was involved in a research project on *zina* laws (criminalization of sex outside marriage), which were being revived in some Muslim countries, such as Pakistan, Iran, Sudan and Northern Nigeria, as part of the Islamization of criminal laws since 1979. The project was initiated by Women Living Under Muslim Laws (WLUML), then the largest and most influential international Muslim women's network. The objective was to provide activists, policy-makers and civil society actors with a feminist analysis of *zina* laws, their current application and their impact on women.[12] During this research, in my attempt to understand the textual and legal pedigree of the concept of *zina* as part of the *hudud* laws in Islamic legal tradition, I had come to learn that Taha's conception of *zina* was very similar to that of classical jurists.[13] In his first book, An-Na'im outlined Taha's position without a critical analysis.[14] I was curious to know more.

ZMH: One thing that puzzled me when reading Taha's book was that he adhered to the traditional *fiqh* position when it came to *hudud* laws – for instance, defining any sexual relations outside marriage as *zina* – a crime punishable by flogging or death. Are those choosing to have a sexual relationship outside of marriage committing a sin, or a crime punishable by lashes or death? I think it matters whether such a relationship is defined as a sin or a crime.

AAN: Taha did not speak in terms of crime or sin. Taha was not a lawyer and was not talking about legal crimes or punishments, but about the principle of *hudud*. He cites only four *hudud*, those being *sariqa* (theft), *qata' al-tariq* (highway robbery and theft), *zina* (sex outside marriage) and *qazf* (slander). Three of them are related to two fundamental drives, which he referred to as *ghariza* (instinct): one of them being sexuality and the other being possession. So, it is about regulating sexuality and possessiveness or possession (property). This all goes back to the notion of needing to control and regulate two human drives in order to achieve the shift and evolution of the human from a lower level – one closer to the animal – to a higher dimension – one that is closer to the divine. For that, it is necessary to control and regulate human drives, especially in matters of sexuality; this is not a matter of respect for private choice. There is also a technical or

---

12 One of the products of this project was a book, Mir-Hosseini and Hamzic, 2010.
13 Taha, 1987, pp. 74–75.
14 An-Na'im, 1990, pp. 113–114.

methodological dimension. Taha's methodology for reforming or trans-forming our understanding of the Shari'a is premised on this notion of reversed abrogation: that certain verses about the status of women, non-Muslims, and peaceful persuasion were revealed in Mecca and were then repealed or abrogated by the Medina verses. The key to his methodology is to shift from one text to the other.

ZMH: Isn't this similar to the methodology of the *fuqaha* in the sense that they too privilege some texts over others?

AAN: In that sense it is, except that Taha is reversing what is commonly accepted, which is that the later verses repeal the earlier ones. Taha is guided by the rationale of abrogation, and rather than shifting from earlier to later verses, he proposes to shift from a verse or a text of the Qur'an that has exhausted its value to a text that serves our future value or the value of humanity today. However, that possibility does not exist with *hudud*; there are no verses in the Qur'an that he could rely on to repeal the verses of *hudud*.

ZMH: So, Taha's methodology has its own limitations and is not as 'comprehensive' as you just said.

AAN: Yes. It is limited in the sense that it is reliant on the Qur'an and it cannot just fly free. However, anything human has its own limits. 'Comprehensive' does not mean that it will give you what you want. To be comprehensive means to be coherent and consistent. So, his point is that from a methodological point of view there is no basis for abolishing *hudud*, because they are provided for by the explicit category of verses without counter-verses that we can use to repeal their application.[15] Therefore *hudud* – especially in matters of sexuality – has nothing to do with respect for private choice. By the way, there is the whole question of whether you are free to believe or not believe. You are free to choose but, if you do believe, this is what belief entails and prescribes. You can take religion on its own terms. Alternatively, you are free not to take it, as long as you have the choice.

I disagreed, but An-Na'im's response left no room for further discussion; I sensed that he didn't like my criticizing Taha's reformist methodology. His faith and his loyalty to his mentor Taha seemed so strong that my critical comments felt unwelcome.

---

15 See Chapter Five for Abou El Fadl's discussion of *hudud*.

For my own research, I relied on Fazlur Rahman, who demonstrates that *hudud* ('limits') in the sense of fixed punishment for specific crimes is not a Qur'anic concept.[16] The expression *hudud Allah* – from which *fiqh* rulings on *hudud* are derived – appears fourteen times in the Qur'an, but nowhere in the sense of punishment, fixed or otherwise; nor does the Qur'an say specifically what these 'limits' are.[17] In other words, defining crimes according to punishment must be seen as a juristic (*fiqhi*) development, thus not fixed but context- and time-bound and open to change. The argument that I eventually developed is that *zina* laws must be seen as part of a complex system of norms and laws devised by classical jurists to regulate sexuality, and I show how they are closely linked with two other sets of laws: those concerning marriage (*nikah*) and women's covering (*hijab*). All these laws are embedded in wider institutional structures of inequality that take their legitimacy from patriarchal interpretations of Islam's sacred texts, which must be challenged from within the tradition.

FROM *TOWARD AN ISLAMIC REFORMATION* TO *ISLAM AND THE SECULAR STATE*

ZMH: Let us now turn to your own work. Freedom of expression, gender equality and equal rights for Muslim and non-Muslims – the three themes that your encounter with Taha enabled you to reconcile with your faith in Islam – have endured in your writings. But there seems to have been a change in your trajectory. In your earlier writings, those from the 1980s and 1990s, you argue for bringing Islamic and human rights frameworks together, and you are critical of those pursuing a secular project in Muslim contexts. This is the stance that you take in your seminal 1990 book, *Toward an Islamic Reformation*. But your stance is different in your latest book, *Islam and the Secular State*, which came out in 2008; there you are arguing for a 'secular state.' I want to ask about this apparent change of stance.

AAN: You are right that in *Islamic Reformation* I explicitly state that I am opposed to secularism, but I also say that I am in favour of achieving the

---

16 Rahman, 1965.
17 Kamali, 1998.

benefits of secularism from an Islamic perspective – I am not in the least suggesting that I was clear about this then. To put it simply, back in the 1980s and 1990s, I was pursuing Taha's project, which is an internal transformation of Muslim understanding of Shari'a, which in Taha's view is a central notion and core of our collective identity and the anchor of our being in life. I was on this internal transformation and I saw it very much as my duty to persuade Muslims of this path. Therefore, my translation and writing of the introductory chapter for Taha's *The Second Message of Islam*, along with my own writing of *Toward an Islamic Reformation*, can be viewed as my efforts to reach out to Muslims and to offer them a methodology and a consistent, systematic approach. There were not many lawyers among Taha's students, and many did not concern themselves with the legal aspects at all. By virtue of my training, I saw it as my contribution to realize and to develop the legal dimension of Taha's vision, and that was what I did in *Toward an Islamic Reformation*. The book is an attempt to apply Taha's methodology and to present a model of Islamic constitutionalism, human rights and national law, which as a Muslim I feel committed to from an Islamic point of view.

ZMH: As someone who has followed your work, I feel that in *Islam and the Secular State* you have abandoned Taha's project of reform. Is this a departure or are you building on your previous work toward reform from within the tradition?

AAN: No, it is not a departure at all, in fact it is going deeper within the same approach that has two tracks. One is about the internal transformation of Muslim understandings of Shari'a and the practices of the Shari'a. This is an internal conversation. I hold that the universality of human rights arises from the internal transformation from within cultures and from the overlapping consensus among them, as I write in *Human Rights in Cross-Cultural Perspectives*.[18] The second track is the external conditions that enable this internal transformation and conversation to take place. In other words, I have to address the political, legal, constitutional and human rights dimensions not as ends in themselves but as means to the end, as what enables the internal conversation to go to its full extent and to challenge every aspect.

I need the external conditions to protect the space that I need in order to be as radical as I care to be in the internal conversation among Muslims

---

18 An-Na'im, 1992.

about Islam. Those two tracks already existed in my book, *Toward an Islamic Reformation*, because it contained the dimension of the methodological reformation of Shari'a and it also contained the constitutional and human rights dimensions. Although I was not explicit in the terms of the nature of the state, I personally believe that the two elements were there.

I'll tell you something interesting. I recently republished a book in Arabic regarding Sudanese criminal law, which I first published in 1986 just before I left Sudan. I wrote that manuscript in prison. Following Taha's arrest, some of us Republican Brothers were arrested. We were all released, but Taha was executed. I was in prison for a year and a half. Some of the guards were former students of mine in the Prison Officers College and so they were very helpful, allowing me to bring books and even a little desk.

I came back to that book because some people were asking me to republish it in Sudan. If you read the introduction that I wrote for the book in 1986, it becomes clear that what I said then is what I am saying now in *Islam and the Secular State*: that punishments, even *hudud*, should not be added into the penal code unless there is a democratic process, through public debate, not by virtue of being Shari'a. I was struck while rereading the proofs with my wife Sarah before republishing the piece. You know that the Republican Brothers in Sudan now attack me for calling for secularism, for departing from Taha's approach – the perception you were referring to, that I am abandoning Taha's mission, and so on. Sarah said, 'It's remarkable that in 1986 you were saying the same thing that you are saying today.' Of course, not in the precise words I am using today, or as developed a concept, but it is all there. It was implicit, as it was in *Toward an Islamic Reformation*, and it remained implicit throughout the 1990s. In fact, all along I was very suspicious of secularism, for very much the same reasons as Muslims tend to be, which is that we see it as anti-religious, as materialistic, as sort of making the human the centre of the universe, and so on.

ZMH: Also, because our encounter with secularism came on the back of colonialism and despotism, so our experience of secularism has been different.

AAN: Yes, that too. I used to say that secularism came to the region in the bad company of colonialism; we are suspicious of it. That is why, in *Toward an Islamic Reformation*, I was not willing to go for secularism, and still don't even today. I did not then see the difference between secularism and the secular state. I had my suspicions and did not want to use the term, and in fact I said, we don't want secularism, we want the Islamization of our laws and social order, etc. I gave a lecture in London in 1998 in which, for the first time, I came very close to what became the thesis of my book *Islam and the Secular State*.

LW: This was the Coulson Memorial Lecture at SOAS. That's the same series in which you, Ziba, also gave a lecture in 2003.[19]

AAN: The title is "Shari'a and Positive Legislation: Is an Islamic State Possible or Viable?" You can say that, from the mid-1980s until the late 1990s, I refused to acknowledge the secular factor, and I stayed within the language that has been familiar to me. Then, in 1998, I started using the term 'secularism', but even in the Coulson lecture I did not talk about the secular state, I simply said that Shari'a cannot be enforced by state law.

Something that I don't like, but have to live with, is the contradistinction that people make between the secular and the religious, in general conversation, in the media, as well as in academia. The assumption is that what is not religious is secular, and what is not secular is religious. In fact, I wrote a book chapter, still to be published, in which I try to challenge this dichotomy.[20] The point is that I see an interdependence and continuity between the religious and the secular. As I see it, the secular is of the religious too; religion works out, unfolds in real life and the whole Qur'an is both this life (*al-hayat al-dunya*) and the other life (*al-hayat al-akhira*), and of course there is a continuity. There is a need for the secular to test the spiritual, the transcendental, because as human beings we are in the physical, we cannot escape the secular, and our religion makes sense in the secular.

But I reject secularism as a life philosophy. What I mean by using the term is that we need a state that is non-Islamic, one that is neutral vis-à-vis religion. So, what I do in the book is to start with defining what I mean by 'secular state', a state that is neutral regarding religious doctrine; and for the rest of the book I use the term as I defined it, and repeatedly I come back to note that I am not personally in favour of secularism as a belief system. Whatever term you use you have to explain, because it may carry different connotations for different people. I am not invested in language and terms, I am invested in persuasion.

ZMH: But persuasion also is very much related to language. Certain terms and ways of saying things do create knee-jerk reactions.

---

19 Lynn Welchman, as Chair of the Centre for Islamic and Middle Eastern Law at SOAS, had invited both of us to give Coulson lectures. An-Na'im, 1998–1999; Mir-Hosseini, 2004.
20 An-Na'im, 2015.

AAN: Yes, I agree. When I say I am invested in persuasion I mean that I am happy to change my language so long as it does not change the content of what I want to say. But language cannot be adapted at the expense of what I am saying. That is the point about secular and secularism.

ZMH: The same goes for the distinction between Shari'a and *fiqh*, which you dismiss. You have used the two terms interchangeably in your work. We need to discuss this in more detail, but for now I want to ask whether you have developed any new ideas or any new language when it comes to gender rights. Is there a shift or evolution in your approach from that which you had in the 1990s?

AAN: To answer this, we need to go back to what I call the 'two tracks approach'. As I said, one track concerns the internal transformation within cultures and the contestation process, and the second track deals with creating the space and securing the conditions for the contestation or transformation to take place. My approach remains the same regarding the internal conversations, which I take from Taha and elaborated within *Toward an Islamic Reformation*. In *Islam and the Secular State*, I note that there are two aspects to the issue of reforms – one concerns the internal conversations among Muslims and the other concerns the external conditions. This book is about the external conditions, not the internal conversations. I wish to reach a wider audience – including non-Muslims – and I seek to persuade my readers on the values being discussed in the book without needing to invoke Qur'anic authority in their support.

In fact, one criticism that I am receiving from my Republican Brother peers is that I do not use Qur'anic sources to support my arguments. But this is an intentional and deliberate omission on my part. I hope that this book achieves its purpose of being an exercise in civic reason. That is why it addresses both Muslims and non-Muslims, because we all need to cooperate in order to create the conditions for Muslims to engage in an internal conversation.

There are two aspects to my thesis. First is a separation between Islam and the state. The second concerns the connectedness of Islam and politics. I made this distinction because I hadn't come across it in many places; and it is a difficult distinction to make because the state is a political institution. But what I propose is for us to at least try to separate religion from the state, and to regulate the connectedness of politics and religion in a way that does not overcome, overshadow or destroy the separation between religion and the state. I also call it a 'paradox', as we are attempting to engage in these topics in a way that allows individuals the opportunity to promote their religious values through civic institutions, but not to rely for support on religious arguments, because those are conversation killers. For example, if you claim that we should punish this crime and ban this practice because God said so, there is not much room for discussion.

ZMH: Similar kinds of debates have been taking place in Iran. Some of the religious thinkers who had supported the merger of religion and politics came to question the very idea of an 'Islamic state'. They have developed religious arguments for the necessity to separate the institution of the state from that of religion, which in the case of Iran is the clerical establishment.[21] In my view it is important to make the case for reform, for change, from within the tradition, which is what you did in *Toward an Islamic Reformation*. But reading your latest book, *Islam and the Secular State*, I get the impression that you are no longer engaging in reform conversations. There is a finality there; in the first line of the preface you say that this book is 'my final statement'[22] . . . whereas I think reform has always been a process.

AAN: I agree, reform is a continuous and ongoing process, but in order for it to be effective, it must be purposeful, with a sense of direction and a framework. I think what I am saying in this book is that for me personally, at my personal responsibility, this is my direction. I am open to challenge and I am, inshallah, ready to change my mind if I am shown to be wrong.

ZMH: I think we need to engage with Islamic legal tradition; there are both the potential and mechanism within *fiqh* to address these issues.

AAN: Not if you accept the *usul al-fiqh* framework that precludes the possibility of any change that contradicts a text (*ijtihad ma fih al-nass*), unless you are arguing for replacing *usul al-fiqh* with a new *fiqh*. In *Islam and the Secular State*, I make an Islamic argument in a fundamental sense when, in the opening sentence of the book, I note that in order to be Muslim and for me to remain a Muslim by conviction and choice – which is the only way that I can be Muslim – I require the state to be secular.

ZMH: This a faith-based statement and declaration.

ANN: Yes, but what I am trying to convey is that I believe that I am making a fundamentally Islamic argument by stating that my sole concern is the existence of a secular state ('secular' here meaning neutral regarding religion) in order for me to be able to exercise my religion freely and with

---

21 See, for example, Chapters Six and Seven.
22 An-Na'im, 2008, p. 1.

conviction. This is not a hermeneutical nor an exegetical argument, because if I argue on those bases, I exclude non-Muslims from the discussion. I would like my framework to be equally persuasive to both Muslims and non-Muslims, and for us to invest in a shared understanding of the world. Through these means, a space can exist for individuals to be what they want to be – irrespective of their religious beliefs.

When I say this is my ultimate or final statement, I don't mean that there is nothing else to say, but rather that it is now clear to me that my future trajectory is along this path. I will keep unfolding, explaining and responding. In any case, my point is that my position remains the same, I continue to hold the same views that I did on gender and on freedom of religion, opinions echoed from Taha's *The Second Message of Islam* and my *Toward an Islamic Reformation*, along with other writings. I keep working on it whenever the chance arises. *Islam and the Secular State* does not replace this effort but rather facilitates this position. That is, to be able to continue that work, I need to invest to create the necessary conditions, including the creation of a secular state. Ustadh Taha used to say that in the future we will come to write about Islam and Islamic values without citing a single Qur'anic verse. The Qur'an is a means to an end, Islam is the means to an end, the end is the human and everything else is a means to it. He said that humans are predisposed to tend toward text-worship – like *shirk*, idolatry – because we are incapable of dealing with the abstract, we always look for an embodiment. The text is an embodiment of meaning; we become attached to the text because we cannot swim with the meaning without clinging onto something as an anchor. So, there is a very problematic question about the text and how we relate to it; it is more about the person than the text, every time.

Now, to turn to your observations on Iran. As I mentioned before, the first lecture that I heard from Taha, "Islamic State: Yes and No", concerned the fact that we were and are talking about an Islamic constitution in terms of the essence of Islam, not in the name of Islam and that the issue of an Islamic state is that it is in the name of Islam while at the expense of Islamic values. Part of my point is that there has never been an Islamic state. I used to say that the Prophet's experience was exceptional because he was the Prophet, meaning that he was the ultimate arbiter of religious issues. In contrast, everyone who succeeded the Prophet lacked that authority; they could only try to persuade, without having the categorical authority to say, 'This is the *din* (religion), this is Islam.'

ZMH: Taha was definitely proved right, and paid with his life for speaking truth to power. But his work has been controversial, construed by some as abandoning parts of the Qur'an by privileging the Meccan verses. You have followed Taha's project, pushed boundaries and provoked many debates, thus you have met with resistance from some Muslims, especially in the religious centres of learning. What do you believe drives such harsh reactions toward your work, and how do you deal with them?

AAN: To start, I would like to make a general comment that I have no problem with being controversial. I have no option but to be controversial when going up against something deeply troubling about our communities, societies, and ourselves as Muslims. The question is whether or not I am consistent and honest about my position. In fact, in the preface to the Arabic translation of *Islam and the Secular State* (*Islam wa dawlat al-madani-yya*), I write that I do not mind if people disagree with what I do say, even if all of humanity disagrees with me, but I do mind when people disagree with what they think I am saying when I am in fact not.

It is the very old story of power, of people who are undermined and threatened by someone who challenges the structures of power. And you know, for women and other causes, in order to discredit the message, the messenger is discredited. Knowing that it happened to Ustadh Taha, and knowing how his work was distorted, I have seen it so many times. People who tend to dismiss someone in that way, do not actually read what they say. I have met many intellectuals and lawyers who have never read my book on Islamic Reformation, but have only read a review. When asked, some even say, 'We do not read you,' as if I were a heretic.

Ustadh Taha himself lived fifty years of his life preaching what he believed in, and for that he was killed. If there is a single Muslim that I have encountered throughout my life who was Muslim in the most supreme way, it was that man, Ustadh Taha, the best Muslim I have known in my life, yet that man was condemned and killed as a heretic. To say, 'Taha is a heretic and he is overthrowing half of the Qur'an,' is nonsense, because, as I was mentioning about *hudud*, his point was always, 'I have to rely on one verse to challenge another verse. It is not an arbitrary exercise that allows me to just swim out of the entirety of the Qur'an.' So, he was very explicit and specific about which verses we were referring to, which Hadith, and what their consequences were. It is not rejecting 'half of the Qur'an' to address just these three issues: equality for women, equality for non-Muslims, and freedom of religion and expression. The Shari'a remains intact, and this is absolutely critical.

As I mentioned yesterday [in the Reimagining Shari'a symposium], I do not expect much from the faculties of Islamic or theological studies because they are trapped in a certain paradigm and have a vested interest in it. I have greater hope and faith in 'secular' and civic Muslims than in theological Muslims. My hope rests within and among Muslims like you; sort of, so-called 'civic', or 'secular', 'Western-educated', modern professionals whom I view as transformative societal forces.

SHARI'A AND *FIQH*: LANGUAGE AND STRATEGY

The last part of our conversation focused on our disagreement over the distinction between Shari'a and *fiqh*, which we had discussed twice before (2004 and 2008) when we coincided in conferences. Just the day before this conversation, I had raised the issue again when I presented my paper in the symposium. I began by giving a brief account of the launch of Musawah, using it to highlight women's participation in the family law reform movement and claiming that the Shari'a/*fiqh* distinction was central to our arguments. An-Na'im and one other academic participant had rejected the distinction. This had led to a debate that continued after the session ended.

ZMH: Now I want to turn to our differences over the distinction between Shari'a and *fiqh*. Can I ask why you dismiss this distinction; for me it is crucial; what people claim to be 'Shari'a' or 'Islam' is so often nothing more than a human *fiqh* interpretation or ruling.

AAN: And Islam is more than Shari'a. It's true, it's a point of difference between us, but let us talk about it now. The way I see it is this: Islam, Shari'a and *fiqh* are all means to the human. Therefore, I see a sort of hierarchy in terms of access, not necessarily in the sense of for better or for worse. Taha used to say, 'Everything in the universe is a means to the end of the human, the human is the object.' That is, the human is God's focus in the universe.

ZMH: This sounds like humanism.

AAN: No, humanism is a substitute for religion. Here, the human individual is the object and everything else is the means to that object. This view can be supported by verses 3 and 4 of Chapter 43 of the Qur'an, which can be translated as follows: 'We have rendered the Qur'an in Arabic for you to understand. Yet the essence of the Qur'an is with God, beyond human comprehension.' As I see it, this verse confirms that the Qur'an is beyond human understanding, but that does not mean beyond human experience, because human understanding is only one aspect of human experience.

The point is that the Qur'an is rendered in Arabic, which is a human language, therefore requires a methodology in order to understand it. However, that methodology is not the end, it is a means to the end of comprehending the Qur'an, and comprehending the Qur'an is the means to the end of experiencing the Qur'an, and experiencing the Qur'an is the means to the end of bringing the human closer to God. When I use the term *fiqh*, I mean that the historical *fiqh* or the idea of *fiqh* is required in order to better comprehend and to comply with the Shari'a and to bring oneself closer to God. Therefore Shari'a is divine from God's perspective; but for us to understand it we need a way, a methodological lens, in order to be able to better resonate with human experience.

ZMH: So if we always get to Shari'a through a methodological lens, i.e. a *fiqh* – which literally means understanding – then why do you say that Shari'a and *fiqh* are the same?

AAN: I am not saying that, I am saying that the distinction is not useful, because whenever you talk about Shari'a, you need to present a *fiqh*. Yesterday you said that when you talk to women, you do not say that Shari'a is unjust but that the problem is with the *fiqh* rulings. But they immediately ask: 'What do you mean by Shari'a? What is the rule on this question?' When you talk about Shari'a as something distinct from *fiqh*, you are postponing the issue, you are not resolving it, because as soon as you gain their confidence, they say, 'Okay, we agree that the Shari'a is divine and perfect and that human understanding is not; but what is the rule regarding inheritance? Does a girl inherit the same as a boy?' So, you have to come to a *fiqh* level. The point is, there must always be a human understanding of the divine.

ZMH: This is not how I talk about Shari'a; I do not see Shari'a as a set of rules and laws but as a transcendental ideal whose essence is justice, and I say that this justice must be reflected in laws that are made in its name. As an activist, a believer, and an individual wishing to communicate all of this, I begin by claiming this justice, so I tell them that Shari'a is just; it has to be just because God is just; in this way I can be critical of *fiqh*-based family laws, and frame the demand for change from within. But if I conflate Shari'a with *fiqh*, then I have no argument, no room for contestation.

AAN: But when you say the essence of Shari'a is justice; then what is this justice?

ZMH: It's not my task to define justice, but to cry out when I see injustice. That the essence of justice is Shari'a is a foundation of Muslim belief; but justice can only be understood through actions, that is why we say that an action must be just. The point again, surely, is that if we don't 'know' for sure what Shari'a is, we can only seek to describe what justice requires in our context and time – and attribute our understanding of this to Shari'a guidance.

AAN: How does the distinction help feminist objectives?

ZMH: It helps in two ways. First, if I conflate Shari'a with *fiqh*, in effect I am saying that the possibility of legal justice does not exist within Islam. As I said yesterday in my talk, because religion and culture always interact, the religious legitimacy of patriarchy needs to be challenged from within, and this is what Islamic feminism is about. So, it keeps our demands for equality within the tradition, which is very important for women in contexts where gender inequality is so embedded in understandings of religion and is justified through Islam.

Secondly, a secular state does not necessarily bring gender equality. The separation of religion from the state – a state that is neutral on religion – on its own is not necessarily going to be bring about justice and equality for women; a secular state is not devoid of patriarchal power relations. In other words, the secular state will not solve the problem for us women without addressing patriarchy, culture and religion. That is why I, along with some other feminists, believe that we will not attain meaningful and sustainable change until we tackle the issue of inequality within a religious framework; we need to engage critically with patriarchal *fiqh* rulings and understandings of the textual sources. And that is why it is important to maintain a conceptual distinction in the terms.

AAN: Ziba, we see eye to eye on all of these issues. We don't need to say this to each other. Everything you said just now, I not only completely agree with it now, but I have been working with it for forty years of my life, so it is not new to me or something that I have a problem with. Yes, the secular state, as I see it, is not a guarantor of gender equality and justice; rather, it creates the groundwork for us to struggle for them. In my book I don't claim that the secular state is an alternative to religious discourse, but rather that religious discourse is a necessary condition for the legitimatization of the secular state; that an internal transformation of the Muslim understanding of Islam must take place in order for a conversation about what it is to be Muslim to continue or to even exist.

ZMH: But we do need the language, as well as the conceptual and analytical tools, for us to begin a conversation about the internal transformation. I see the problem in this way: as soon as we voice our critique of *fiqh*-based laws, we are silenced by a Qur'anic verse, by a Hadith, by a *fiqh* ruling. Therefore we – women's rights activists and Muslim feminists like myself – see the distinction between Shari'a and *fiqh* as a necessary precondition for any conversation. And you are telling me that this distinction is false.

AAN: It is not helpful, it is not useful. We don't need to repeat to each other what we both accept, which is that you need this conversation; you need a way of challenging this dominant understanding, all of that is correct. My point is that whatever it is you do, it is a form of *fiqh*; it is a *fiqh*. Now, part of the confusion is that we assume that the *fiqh* today embodies what was historically accepted as *fiqh*, whereas I believe that there is a *fiqh* that is appropriate to our particular time and condition. Therefore, the challenge and struggle are about defining the terms, the framework and the concept of *fiqh* that best enables us to engage in that conversation and struggle. That is why my position, following Taha, is to say that we need to transform *usul al-fiqh* because it was man-made and is therefore open to challenge and change.

Taha's *The Second Message of Islam* and my *Toward an Islamic Reformation* are efforts to transform the framework or the methodology of *fiqh* in order to engage in the conversation that will help us say, and persuade the Muslims, that the embodiment of justice in Shari'a is equality for women. Because someone may argue – using the *usul al-fiqh* framework – that the embodiment of justice in Shari'a is complementarity, not equality.

ZMH: That is what we are doing in Musawah; we say that justice in our time and context mandates gender equality; we seek to change the patriarchal assumptions that inform and underpin the construction of gender rights in *fiqh*; we show the injustices resulting from those *fiqh* rulings.

AAN: If we shift to the other track of my dual track approach, the internal argument, are you able to make the internal argument without challenging the earlier *usul al-fiqh*?

ZMH: In effect we are challenging it by making the distinction between Shari'a and *fiqh*, and saying that, in our time and context, the *fiqh* rulings are not just. We need to appeal to a higher authority in order to change *usul al-fiqh*.

AAN: But you need to proceed to the next step and to present an alternative formulation of *usul al-fiqh* in order to supplement, correct or modify the old. That is where the struggle lies: spell out what you view as the new *usul al-fiqh* and the different means by which you are challenging the assumptions. Ultimately, the question is whether feminists, individuals like Asma Barlas and amina wadud,[23] have articulated an alternative *usul al-fiqh*. Or have they made a call for it but not presented what it is? I think it has been like the call for *ijtihad*, which has been repeated for the past 200 years, but not many people have done an actual exercise of *ijtihad* that gives us an outcome that we can consider. I think what you are saying, what Asma is saying, what amina is saying, is emphasizing the need to change *usul al-fiqh*. However, having followed your work, neither you nor your colleagues have actually proposed an alternative *usul al-fiqh*.

ZMH: It is not our task to propose an alternative *usul al-fiqh*, but rather to be critical and expose the patriarchal assumptions of conventional *usul al-fiqh* and the injustices they lead to. The work of amina wadud and Asma Barlas concerns the hermeneutics of the Qur'an and ontological issues; questions surrounding the notion of the human and of the gender perspectives in the text. This is important, the Qur'an is the main source of authority and the main source in *usul al-fiqh*.

I believe that legal theory often follows practice, and that once the reality on the ground changes there will be pressure on the jurists. I can now see the beginning of a new *usul al-fiqh* taking shape. New approaches have been developed; a trend in reformist thought that we can call 'neo-rationalism' is reviving rationalist elements dormant in Islamic tradition. I view the work of Abdulkarim Soroush, Nasr Abu Zayd, Khaled Abou El Fadl and some others in this regard. I personally have been influenced by Soroush, who argues that in order for a new *usul al-fiqh* to be developed, we must first have a new *kalam* [theology] ... I would be suspicious of anyone who claims to have come up with a new *usul al-fiqh*, because it must develop organically, as part of the tradition.

AAN: As I said before, I agree with you fully. However, I believe it is still someone's job to complete the task, meaning that if individuals such as Asma Barlas, amina wadud or yourself are making the case for the need to reform *usul al-fiqh*, someone must lead the way. When you say that theory

---

23 Both these scholars have written pioneering books on women and the Qur'an: Wadud, 1999; Barlas, 2002.

follows practice, I partially agree. However, there is a dialectic between theory and practice, because we need to know where we are going in order for our energy to be channeled toward that specific purpose and direction. Therefore, we require an alternative articulation of *usul al-fiqh*. The term itself means the science of jurisprudence, or the parameters of how you interpret, and to what end.

In spite of Na'im's repeated insistence that we were in agreement, we were clearly talking across each other. I still did not accept his dismissal of the distinction between Shari'a and *fiqh* as 'not useful'. I was also dismayed by his appraisal of the contribution of feminist scholars to the reform project. Those he mentioned (wadud and Barlas) focused on the Qur'an as the highest source of textual authority in Islam. But there are both veteran scholars, such as Aziza Al-Hibri, and younger ones, like Kecia Ali, who have done important work on *fiqh*. I found it unreasonable that he expected us to offer an alternative *usul al-fiqh*, while not hinting what he considered it might look like.

At this point Lynn Welchman saved the conversation by saying, '*usul al-fiqh* is a methodology.'

AAN: Exactly, it is a methodology. Now my position is that Ustadh Taha's methodology makes a case for an alternative *usul al-fiqh*. Therefore, individuals like Khaled Abou El Fadl, Asma Barlas and amina wadud are performing a valuable function of making the case for an alternative methodology. I am not placing the burden on women but rather arguing that someone must make the case for it, in order for it to be able to move forward.

To be frank, there is one dimension that I find very important regarding your own work, Ziba, and Lynn will agree with me on this issue. The way I see it is that the methodology has to be consistent, because if I engage in the arbitrary selection of certain scholars and verses without providing a comprehensive framework or rationale for my approach, it will result in counter-selectivity. The value of Taha's thinking and methodology is that it offers a comprehensive and systematic approach that confronts the problematic aspects, as well as celebrating the liberating parts of the tradition.

However, the missing link arises when you make the faith-based assumption that Shari'a is the embodiment of justice, and you are met with questions by the general public as to what solutions you are able to offer as a way out of their predicament. I believe that the missing link is fulfilled through

Taha's vision, and I seek to share the struggle and to make a case for an alternative *usul al-fiqh*. I believe that Taha has provided the necessary alternative methodology, which will enable us to move, for example, from the position that polygamy is unjust to the alternative, which is that monogamy is just.

We were back to Taha's methodology, which al-Na'im saw as an 'alternative' *usul-al-fiqh*, a legal theory that can resolve all the tensions between Islamic and human rights laws. So this time I decided to be more explicit by saying that I saw it as limited in potential, by comparison with other reformist thinkers.

ZMH: But Taha's methodology does not address the question of *hudud*. I see all laws as interconnected. You cannot address one part of a legal system without addressing another. Criminal law is as important as family law. I am more convinced by Fazlur Rahman's methodology, which separates the essential from the incidental, the essence and spirit of Qur'anic verses and injunctions from their historical context and legal forms, that the Qur'an does not give us the law, it gives us the ingredients for making a just law; the direction and the principles. More contemporary thinkers such as Nasr Abu Zayd, Abdulkarim Soroush, Mojtahed Shabestari and Khaled Abou El Fadl provide better answers for Muslim feminists like me to understand how a verse like 4:34 in the Qur'an is not in contradiction with the idea that Islam mandates essential equality between men and women. The context is embedded in the text; the Qur'an unfolded in a particular context where patriarchy and slavery were part of the social fabric . . .

AAN: You are again repeating what we previously agreed on. Taha takes the same stance as Fazlur Rahman. That is the whole point about the distinction between the Mecca and Medina verses; it is about the context. When you say Fazlur Rahman distinguishes what is essential and what is incidental, how do we make that distinction? It is true there are the essential and the incidental, which Taha calls *al-usul* and *al-furu'* – that is, the original and the incidental. But Taha goes on to elaborate on how to make the distinction; Fazlur Rahman does not. Fazlur Rahman does not address the question of *hudud* and has no answer to it. Neither does Nasr Abu Zayd. When you say that your objection to Taha is that he does not resolve the problem of *hudud*, tell me who else did. Or alternatively, let us look for a person who will do it and accept that position on that point. I believe that it's unfair to claim that you will not take Taha's approach on gender and freedom of religion because he does not equally address the *hudud* question. If you say that he has certain advantages, take them and work on supplementing what is missing.

I realized that I had touched a sensitive point. A critical discussion of Taha's reformist methodology, which was premised on a shift from the Medinan to the Meccan verses as the source of law, was a no-go area, as was invoking Fazlur Rahman's or Nasr Abu Zayd's approach to the Qur'an. So I moved the discussion to another level – that of strategy.

ZMH: Of course, Taha's methodology is important. But as a feminist and as an activist, I need to work with the powers that be, with the structures and centres of learning, because I am trying to bring change from within. So, I need to have allies, to engage in a kind of dialogue with those in the Qom seminaries, or Al-Azhar.[24] We need to engage them and have a dialogue with them. As an intellectual, as a reformist, as someone inspired by Taha's vision, you can afford to stand by his methodology. But as a feminist scholar, as part of Musawah, I cannot afford that. The reality is that we live in a context where the ulema and institutions like Al-Azhar define what religion says. We need to find a discourse for engaging with them, as well as with political Islam and the state.

I also wish to expand the debate and further my own arguments. I am very much influenced by Abdulkarim Soroush, whose work I have been following since the early 1990s. I had a conversation with him in 1995 regarding the implications of his approach for rethinking gender rights, a conversation that continued on and off for over ten years. I felt frustrated because he was not interested in feminism and gender rights, and always stayed at the level of *kalam* – that is his project, and it is an important one; but my project is *fiqh*. But I find his approach and arguments extremely enabling in the 'desanctification' of *fiqh*, a process that is currently taking place. I firmly believe that we need to remove the veil of sanctity from *fiqh*. Laws are man-made, social constructions and therefore there can be no immutable law, or any such thing as 'Shari'a family law', but rather certain bases and values given to us through the Qur'an

---

24 Al-Azhar in Cairo, founded in the tenth century, is one of the oldest centres of religious learning and education. In the 1960s it was re-established as a university. Today it is regarded as the main source of Sunni religious knowledge and power.

such as *'adl* (justice), *insaf* (fairness), *ihsan* (goodness). That is the project we are pursuing in Musawah.

AAN: We see eye to eye on all this. But as you said earlier, it is an issue of the division of labour. I understand why Abdulkarim Soroush does what he does, because he feels that that is his mission and calling. I do what I do because I think it is mine, and you do what you do because it is yours. That is not the problem in itself, but we should be able to tell each other about whether what we are doing is effective or useful.

The point is, with all due respect, it is futile to engage with Al-Azhar. You must realize that they too have issues of power relations, issues of privilege, and advantage. Maybe that was my main disagreement with Sisters in Islam; they thought that they could co-opt the government to carry out their mission without creating a grassroots movement in support of their position.

I have known Sisters in Islam since 1992, when I first travelled to Malaysia at their invitation and as part of their work, and was a part of their work since then. I noted several times that expecting them to be able to co-opt the government to their objectives sounds expedient and fast, but in fact it is not; instead the government will co-opt them. Because the government talks about hard laws, realities, power and privilege; who is the government, what is their objective? What I argue is that feminists like Sisters in Islam must create a grassroots political movement.

ZMH: They do now work with the grassroots. Apart from grassroots, we need to open up the public space for dissent.

AAN: I am glad to hear it. You must cultivate political movements and social movements. It is a longer-term investment, but it is a secure investment. Because when you rely on tactical alliances, they will let you down when you need them most.

We were getting nowhere. An-Na'im must have felt it too, as he turned to Lynn Welchman:

AAN: Any final word, Lynn?

LW: No, but this last half an hour has helped me understand your position, Ziba, and your need to make that distinction between Shari'a and *fiqh*. I have seen you in conferences, but I really didn't previously understand your explanations, Ziba, and why you need to make that distinction. I hadn't realized that you were so tied to engaging, feeling that you have to be in the mainstream in order to effect the changes that you wish.

ZMH: No, it is not about being in the mainstream. It is about not closing the door to the mainstream, to keep a conversation going, because it's the mainstream that sets the agenda, the laws. We must therefore engage in a dialogue with them. There are moments when we need to push and challenge them and moments when we need their support as well. We cannot afford to cut ourselves off from the mainstream, because we are engaging in the realm of politics as well. Do you think like Abdullahi that we should abandon the mainstream entirely?

LW: Well – to be fair – I don't want to speak for Abdu, but I don't think that is what he is saying.

AAN: I am not saying 'abandon'.

LW: He is talking about the different ways of affecting the mainstream, with longer-term strategies. There are always more people in the street than there are in government. Perhaps what Abdullahi is saying about a longer-term strategy is a different way of influencing them.

When you begin your dialogue, and if your ultimate aim is subversion or the achievement of some sort of radical change, then you are going to need that space for protection in order to establish that dialogue; you need what Abdu is arguing in his latest book, *Islam and the Secular State*. In a sense you are actually going to be reliant on what you see as his longer-term vision, because you need that space if any of your arguments are to be implemented beyond the dialogue.

ZMH: Yes, but meanwhile we have to do something, because we cannot wait for the longer-term vision, i.e. the secular state, to emerge. There are pending and pressing issues in the realm of family law that we must address today.

LW: Absolutely. But I do think Abdu has a point. When you make these arguments, whether you are talking about a certain verse, law or form of state, people will very quickly respond by saying, 'Okay, then what?' You require a longer-term strategy for change, so that you can engage in those more abstract debates at the same time as proposing particular changes. Don't you think?

AAN: You need the methodology that gives you an alternative answer. I think my point about power is this: you are right that scholarship is tied to power. However, what I am saying is that you need to create your alternative base of power to challenge the powers that be. When we talk of the 'mainstream', such as Al-Azhar, they have their power because they have an established discourse which the generality of the public accepts. You need to create an alternative discourse that captures that popular support, that will give you the power base from which you can challenge the establishment, but you can't expect Al-Azhar to turn around and destroy itself.

ZMH: That is what we aim to do in Musawah, but we also need to bring together different groups of women – from those who work within human rights to those who work within a religious framework – to publicly create a voice for women's demands, and at the same time to build the scholarship to support that voice. Later, with this unified voice, we will be able to go to Al-Azhar and others and say, 'What you are saying cannot be Shari'a, because it is not just.' That is why feminist voices and scholarship in Islam are important.

AAN: Yes, they are crucial. But the view that Lynn and I share is that you must take the next step as well. That is, when you create the powerbase, they will ask you, 'Okay, we are persuaded by your arguments, but what do we need to do next?'

AN UPDATE

I share An-Na'im's humanistic vision of Islam, and continue to admire his scholarship and activism, which have been trailblazing. However, as our conversation ended it was evident that we diverged on two issues. One was An-Na'im's continued rejection of the distinction between Shari'a and *fiqh*, terms that he uses interchangeably in his work. For him it was a futile strategy for opening space for debate. The other issue was engagement with traditional ulema and centres of religious learning and power, which he also saw as futile. I consider the distinction between Shari'a and *fiqh* as essential for challenging patriarchy from within, and engagement with ulema as vital to the internal transformation of Muslim understandings of Shari'a.

On the first issue, I now see how we talked across each other. Our disagreement was not over principles but over semantics. Although I didn't realize it at the time, the differences between our approaches and strategies for reform were clearly at least in part due to differences in terminology and our understandings of key concepts. An-Na'im did distinguish Shari'a from *fiqh*; but we had rather different understandings of the terms. In a way, what he called Islam, I called Shari'a; what he called Shari'a, I called *fiqh*: then, as now, I understood *fiqh* as applying not only to the process by which jurists derive rulings from the Qur'an and the Sunna, but also to the rulings themselves; in other words, the vast corpus of juristic scholarship and jurisprudential texts covering methodological discussions and legal theory (*usul-al fiqh*). What An-Na'im called *fiqh* I would term *ijtihad*: novel or original solutions, efforts in searching for and deducing correct laws.

An-Na'im must have felt this discordance. I sent him my edited transcription of the conversation (May 2020) to ensure that I had reproduced his views correctly. When he sent back his edits (which were minor), he added this paragraph to his response to my first question:

> In the name of God, the Merciful and Compassionate. Shari'a is the outcome of intergenerational consensus among Muslim communities, each in its own context. As a Muslim I do believe in the binding authority of Shari'a as the normative system of Islam, but also believe in my right and obligation to contest what I find to be objectionable interpretations of Islam. More specifically, I believe that certain aspects of Shari'a, regarding the rights of women in particular, are no longer valid or binding. In those instances, I believe that alternative interpretations of Islam are appropriate and binding in the modern context of present Islamic societies. These are what Ustadh Mahmoud [Taha] calls 'the Second Message of Islam', which were postponed at the beginning of Islam, because they were not appropriate for the context of the early societies. Now that the Second Message of Islam is appropriate and binding on present Muslims in the modern context, it is the obligation of Muslim scholars to elaborate and propagate this view of Islam among Muslims at large.[25]

* * * * *

In spite of my admiration for his groundbreaking theoretical work, I believe An-Na'im was so in thrall to Taha's methodology, so convinced that it was the only way to bring change, that he overlooked the work of other, more recent, reformist thinkers. I see the inclusion of women's voices, their ways of knowing sacred texts and their lived realities, to be integral to the production of a new religious-based knowledge. And as for the need to distinguish Shari'a and *fiqh*, I still hold to what I wrote in my paper for the Leuven conference on An-Na'im's work:

---

25 In a footnote he added that Ustadh Mahmoud's main thesis is explained and substantiated in Taha, 1987.

[T]he very possibility of changing and reforming the mandates of the Shari'a depends on the contestedness of the concept and disputes over its correct interpretation through *fiqh*. Absent a distinction between Shari'a and *fiqh*, those who are struggling for democratic and feminist interpretations of the Shari'a have little to work with. Given the deep connection between religion and law in Muslim societies, I suggest that denial of the distinction not only impedes the reception of An-Na'im's great theory where it most needs to be received, but makes it unusable in contexts where Islamists have the loudest voices in defining the terms of political and gender discourses among Muslims.[26]

---

26 Mir-Hosseini, 2010b.

3

amina wadud

God created women fully human. Anything, anyone, or any system that treats them privately or in public as anything less than that is destroying the potential harmony of the entire universe.[1]

Amina wadud is among the first scholars to offer a gender-inclusive interpretation of the Qur'an. Born in 1952 into a Christian African-American family, she converted to Islam in 1972 while a student at the University of Pennsylvania. She did postgraduate studies at the University of Michigan, which included a year of advanced Arabic at the American University in Cairo, Qur'anic studies at Cairo University and philosophy at Al-Azhar University, and obtained a Ph.D. in Arabic and Islamic Studies in 1988. Between 1989 and 1992 wadud worked as an assistant professor in Qur'anic Studies at the International Islamic University Malaysia (IIUM). It was during this time, when she met with a group of women and co-founded Sisters in Islam, that she became involved in activism for reform.

After her return to the US in 1992, wadud taught Islamic Studies at Virginia Commonwealth University (VCU) until 2007, when she took early retirement as Professor Emerita. Subsequently, among other commitments, she was Visiting Researcher at the Starr King School for the Ministry, and a researcher in 'Sexuality, Diversity, and Human Dignity in Islamic Primary Sources', and has travelled widely across the world to lecture.

Wadud's first book, *Qur'an and Woman: Rereading the Sacred Text from a Woman's Perspective*, has become the seminal text of feminism in Islam. The book, a revision of her Ph.D. thesis, was published in Malaysia in 1992; it has

---

1 Wadud, 2006, p. 254.

now been translated into over a dozen languages. In 2005 she led a mixed Friday prayer in New York. The event was widely reported in the media – it provoked a heated debate among Muslims in which wadud did not take part. Though she gave no interviews then, she did write about the event in her second book, *Inside the Gender Jihad: Women's Reform in Islam*, published in 2006; there she also traced the route of her gender-inclusive theology into social action and policy reform:

> My life experiences as a believing Muslim woman, and Islamic studies professor, have been intimately connected with Islamic reforms. As a participant in these reforms, I struggle to knit together intellectual discourse, strategic activism, and holistic spirituality. I did not enter Islam with my eyes closed against structures and personal experiences of injustice that continue to exist . . . I entered Islam with a heart and mind trusting that divine justice could be achieved on the planet and through-out the universe.[2]

In 2007 she was the subject of a documentary film by Ellie Safari, *The Noble Struggle of Amina Wadud*.[3] Then, in 2012, appeared the book *A Jihad for Justice: Honoring the Work and Life of Amina Wadud*, edited by Kecia Ali, Juliane Hammer and Laury Silvers, containing 32 contributions by well-known scholars, a list of her publications and a select list of academic works engaging with her work.[4]

I first met amina wadud in Kuala Lumpur in 2001 during a conference on family law reform organized by Sisters in Islam. I had already read *Qur'an and Woman*, which had just been republished by Oxford University Press with a new preface in which she adamantly rejected the label of 'feminist', something that I found puzzling. As I became more involved in the work of Sisters in Islam, we often crossed paths at events leading to the launch of Musawah in 2009, and became friends. I came to admire and was touched by her deep faith, her spiritual way of relating to the world and her deep commitment to gender justice. I saw her as the key feminist theologian in Islam – though she did not call herself feminist at the time and had a complex and ambivalent relationship with feminism.

---

2 Ibid., pp. 2–3
3 Safari, 2007.
4 Ali, et al., 2012.

I was keen to engage her in conversation for my book. The opportunity came in November 2011 when Musawah organized a workshop in Amman, Jordan, that brought activists and scholars together as part of its first research project: to rethink *qiwamah* and *wilayah*, two central juristic concepts that we argue lie at the basis of the unequal construction of gender rights in Muslim family laws.[5] Wadud had already agreed to the conversation, which started on the evening of 26 November (the final day of the workshop) and continued the following day in the airport lounge. She talked about her childhood, her conversion to Islam, and her spiritual, personal and intellectual development, moving from a conservative position to becoming a theologian of gender justice in Islam. We resumed our conversation three years later, on 11 December 2014, in Kandy, Sri Lanka, this time on the last day of one of Musawah's courses for South Asian activists.[6] We focused on two topics that I had not raised in 2011: her leading a mixed public prayer in New York in 2005, and her evolving relationship with feminism.

In the following edited transcript of these conversations, I have kept the chronological order as far as possible, and provided some context when necessary. I began by asking about her spiritual trajectory and what brought her to Islam.

COMING TO ISLAM AND THE QUR'AN

aw: My spiritual journey is largely intertwined with my experiences growing up with my father, a Methodist minister. He was a very gentle man, in contrast with my mother who was quite violent, and he invoked the name of God in whatever he did. I adored my father and had a very ambivalent relationship with my mother. The vision of life that my father shared with me was, first of all, a vision of incredible honesty and integrity; in my mind he never did anything that was apart from his perspective of an intimate relationship with God.

His story is quite interesting and has had a great influence on my relationship and understanding with both society and the sacred. When my father was about seventeen, he walked out onto a field in Georgia and had

---

5 For this project, see https://www.musawah.org/knowledge-building/qiwamah-wilayah/
6 Islam & Gender Equality and Justice (I-nGEJ), https://www.musawah.org/capacity-building/ingej/

a profound personal experience that impacted the rest of his life. Whatever that experience was to him, he understood it to be that he should dedicate himself to God and therefore sought to become an ordained minister.

When I was little, I was frightened of thunderstorms and I took the fear to my own divine level, so when the thunder came, I thought it was God giving me a message about whatever shortcomings I knew I had in my little life. I once took this fear to my father; I must have been six or seven. He sat me on his lap and told me the story in the Bible about how God promised never again to destroy the world by water, and the symbol of that is the rainbow. I had my first transcendental experience at that time. From his story and the consistent integrity of his life and, of course, the comfort and poise that I experienced with him sitting me on his lap and telling me the story, I opened up to this God who was not going to destroy the world again by water, to this infinite and awesome possibility right there in my heart on his lap.

We were very poor, and my father's devotion to God, and his poor level of education, caused him not to pursue paths sufficient to provide money to meet our needs. When I was ten, we were evicted from our home, which my father had built, being himself a carpenter like Jesus. Our mother abandoned us, and my father took me and my younger siblings, and we lived in a trailer for the summer months, and he worked diligently until we eventually moved to the city. Living in that sort of poverty meant that the correlation between the divine and materialism was not at all self-evident. It wasn't a mandate. I never disbelieved my father, even when homeless and wandering in this moveable home. However, I saw that his vision did not come to fruition.

Our move to the city caused me to go into a kind of internal retreat as I tried to battle different challenges, from experiencing hormonal changes to encountering dishonest people. By the time I entered middle school I did not feel that my family valued education, and I stopped producing. One of the school counsellors noticed that I was testing in the upper ninetieth percentile nationwide while being less than average for grades. This led her to apply for scholarships, under the scheme that took 'economically disadvantaged' youth who had also proven to be intellectually advantaged, to try to get them a better education. It was called 'ABC' ('A Better Chance'); it was summer intensive study, where we went away for six or eight weeks and they would prepare us, basically, to go to private schools or to some other type of school alternative. They eventually took me out of my family home and local school to put me in a high school in an all-white neighbourhood. I was fourteen when I left home and moved to New England, surrounded by very wealthy, white families. I realized that my path was not the same as my birth family's. I went to high school between 1967 and 1970, which was the time of the Black civil rights movement. All this offered me opportunities that broadened my vision, although I had to embrace some alienation and isolation. This early experience had an impact on my ability to put into practice certain ideas in terms of Islamic reform.

When I began college at seventeen, I intentionally studied Eastern traditions: culture, dance, music, art and religion.[7] At eighteen, I became a Buddhist and I lived in a kind of Buddhist ashram. I was a vegetarian, and meditated for an hour in the morning and in the evening. Buddhism has a non-theistic sacred orientation and this freed me from the God the Father that I had been raised with. It didn't clarify other questions that I had, but the nature of the practices was very harmonious, very good for the stripping of the ego, not in an exaggerated pietistic way of abstinence, but in a simplistic and holistic way. I slept on a mat on the floor; life was very simple and focused on the inner.

In Philadelphia, there is a vibrant Black community in terms of arts, politics and spirituality; on campus, there was a vibrant Muslim student population that was mostly immigrant but obviously also Muslim converts. I began to hear about Islam, so I took my usual route, which was to read. I started reading about Islam.

In November [1972] on Thanksgiving Day I decided to go to the mosque which was around the corner from my mother's house in Washington D.C. I had already, as part of my own consciousness transformation, stopped wearing short skirts, so I wore long skirts. I still wore pants, and I had started covering my hair with a different kind of hair wrap, so when I walked into the mosque, there was a bunch of guys and I think they were impressed that I got the dress thing; they assumed I was ready for Islam, so they said, 'If you believe that there is no God but Allah, and Muhammad is His Apostle . . . then just take the *shahadah* [declaration of faith].'[8] So I did. I had no idea what I was getting myself into, but I started to read more. The only thing I had from them was a small booklet with transliterations of the prayers and instructions on how to pray. My routine

---

7 Wadud began her studies at the University of Pennsylvania in 1970, and graduated in 1975.
8 See also Wadud, 2006, p. 9.

was that I would go to the library, occasionally going to D.C. to visit my mother, so I could go to this mosque on Friday; then I would return to the university to read more books.

Five or six months after I had taken my *shahadah*, one of my neighbours gave me a copy of the Qur'an and that was it. I fell in love with the Qur'an in just English – in fact it was the Yousef Ali translation, which I can no longer accept. I fell so in love with it that I could not stand the impediments to reading it on my own, so I began learning Arabic.

I learned the Arabic alphabet in two days; I sat down with the sound sheet, practising the writing and pronunciation. When I started Arabic, every single word that I learned was a word that was in the Qur'an some-where; it was like unravelling a mystery and all of the steps that led to this personal relationship with unravelling. When you struggle with the Qur'an there is a *baraka* (blessing power) in that. I had a visible and palpable mani-festation of that *baraka*; every single step began to open up this universe to me.

I slowed down a little when I got married, because then I wanted to identify in a very subjective way with my husband, who was also a convert and also very motivated. He was also a learner – a self-motivated learner – and we were in the kind of Muslim communities in America that deferred so much to the Arabic-speaking world, the Middle East as the heart of Islam. My husband was Tablighi[9] in his orientation and then more Salafi[10] in his training, so I kind of went into another inner world.

That is why, when I got married, I started wearing the *niqab* (face cover). He didn't want me to, I did. I wanted a barrier between myself and all this craziness that is out in the world. The *niqab* was perfect for me because I would be non-visible in the way in which, in my youth, I was visible only on the basis of the body.

ZMH: You mean, you wore the *niqab*, but not as an Islamic obligation?

aw: I never thought it was an Islamic obligation, but I thought it was the better Islam. I thought women who wore the hijab were following what was

---

9 Tablighi Jama'at (lit. a society for spreading the faith) is a conservative Sunni movement that defines its primary aim as reaching out to ordinary Muslims to practise their religion as it was done during the life of the Prophet Mohammad, with the emphasis on matters of ritual, dress and personal behaviour.

10 Salafi (lit. follower of pious ancestors) is an anti-modernist movement in Sunni Islam advo-cating return to the tradition: contemporary Muslims, in order to understand how to practise their religion, should go back to the 'pure' traditions of the first three generations of Muslims.

a mandate, and women who wore *niqab* were a just little bit better. I was among a crowd of Tablighi women in the DC mosque with whom I took the *shahadah*, who also wore the *niqab*. We were fervent and the idea that there could be multiple understandings of Islam had not even occurred to me. I did have my arrogance. I don't need to pretend that there wasn't a kind of self-righteousness in it, but I became slightly agoraphobic. I was in a city and to this day I am still overwhelmed by the city. I was more cloistered within myself. I did not need a world outside the small cluster of my Muslim friends and my husband, except that I was still reading. The *niqab* provided me with a separation from an external world or society with which I already did not identify.

ZMH: I can't fathom what was in that interpretation of Islam that persuaded you to cover your face. To be honest, I find it difficult to imagine you as a *niqabi* and Salafi Muslim!

aw: The conservative representation of Islam is often appealing to converts. Whatever level of identity crisis converts are going through, they see that as a mark of distinction from what it is to be mainstream Western. So, one way not to be mainstream Western was to be this overly symbolized *niqabi* – I mean, this was in the seventies, I was wearing *niqab* in Philadelphia in the United States. Already being an individual who had always experienced a sort of isolation-alienation, since high school, the notion of not being *with* America was fine with me. The way to not fit into America was the kind of Islam where the guys would go on thirty-day retreats, and they were fervent in their *'ibadah*, reading the Qur'an, reading Hadith, doing *zikr* and isolation in the mosque. I wanted that too, but they didn't take the women anywhere, so I had to recreate that experience in my home or with the women with whom I associated.

ZMH: This is fascinating! When and how did you emerge from that mode of understanding Islam and being a Muslim?

aw: My outlook started to change when we moved to Libya in 1975, when my husband received a scholarship from Muammar Ghaddafi. As we started our life in the Arab world, I began to engage with the Arabic language in my day-to-day life and with the people. It made me question the relationship between Arabic as it is used and understood by the people and what is written in the Qur'an.

What I began to see there was that Muslims, in Muslim majority contexts ... yes, they had this thing that I called Islam, but they did not aspire to the ideal at the level of practice – which I thought all Muslims did.

In fact, they lied and cheated. I guess they were regular people, but at the time, it shoots a hole in your illusion; reality comes in and I didn't know how to synthesize it, so in Libya I chose friends who were also very Salafi. I met another *niqabi* from Egypt, we hung out together; we were flamboyant in our *niqabiness*. This was real Islam; the rest was something else. The whole idea of experiencing something different all the time was very unnerving.

At the same time, my marriage was not what I wanted it to be. We had no conversations about my own growth in learning about Islam; once the husband starts learning, that is supposed to be all. I assume I was supposed to learn vicariously through him or through his recitations to me. I did not agree with everything that he said. It simply didn't make sense to me when, for example, he would say, 'In Islam, women can't drive.' I responded, 'In Islam a woman can do anything she wants.' What I perceived to be Islam and what he was telling me and was available to me as a Muslim woman – those two stories already were not jiving.

By the time I was pregnant with my second child, I started to move out from the location of dependency on the reception of knowledge and began to feel more with my own gut. I applied for a job in the same institution in Libya where my husband was a student – I had already finished my first degree but he had finished only a year of college and then, in his Muslim journey, not only did he not finish the degree, he did nothing else but read about Islam. I started to teach creative writing and a basic English course. I was still wearing the *niqab*, although going to work every day and taking off the *niqab* to teach put me in a place where I started to have a split identity. I was teaching male and female students, but you can't teach English without a face and I knew that, so I responded to that appropriately. I took off my *niqab* when I went to work, but put it on again when I went home. Already there were starting to be holes in the bubble I was living in. None of this was negative; not covering my face did not cause me to lose anything of my own motivation, direction or relationship with Allah.

After having my second daughter and leaving Libya, I was clear that my husband was not the centre of my existence, and I asked for a divorce and left with the children. I then had to make my way in the world of earning a living and that kind of thing. I didn't feel that this 'retreat Amina' could do that. I had to visualize some way to be in the world and not be completely of it, whereas before I did not want to be in the world, I wanted to be in this space-bubble called Islam. My first degree was in education, so I was certified to teach, I had something that I could use.

Once I got back to America, with no husband, two babies, literally by myself, I had to find a place to live and to get a job. I started substitute teaching. Something happened to me in that first year of teaching. First of all, the community in Philadelphia, where I was living before, learned that I was not wearing the *niqab* any more. Sometimes I tied my scarf back and they started talking about me, saying, 'Now that she's not with her husband, she's not going to be Muslim.'

I really had to think about that. Why am I a Muslim? Am I Muslim for my husband? And because this was between me and Allah, I could not lie about the answer. I was not Muslim because of my husband, I was Muslim because I really loved Allah, and I did not know what that meant but I really wanted to be Muslim. I also was not going to be Muslim just because of the stream. Whether my scarf was tied in the back or the front, I was still a Muslim; whether I wore a *niqab* or not, I was still a Muslim. So I gained an affirmation of my identity as a Muslim that was not attached to all these other things that I myself had attached a great deal to before; but I still did not have a path, so I decided to go to graduate school and study journalism.

I had a friend – a white convert to Islam – who said two things to me that became rather prophetic. The first was, 'You should go to school for Islamic studies, because no one has a love for learning about Islam the way you did.' The second thing he said was, 'People listen to you better when you have a Ph.D.' I went to a summer programme just for Islamic studies [in 1980] where I started to learn about Islam at the university graduate level; I was already really smitten with the Qur'an, and I knew my goal was understanding the Qur'an, and I stuck to it.

THE JOURNEY TO QUR'AN AND WOMAN: READING THE SACRED TEXT FROM A WOMAN'S PERSPECTIVE

aw: When I started [my graduate studies], I was single, divorced from my first husband. After the first year I applied for the Center for Arabic Study Abroad programme and I returned to the Arab world to polish up my Arabic; I even took a tutorial course on the Qur'an with a male professor from the University of Cairo. Reading the Qur'an with him was an interesting experience. We would read and he would tell me what it meant. At first, I was okay with that, because I was getting my Arabic language up to university level, and I hadn't yet entered the stage of critical thinking.

However, when we read the verse in the Qur'an that said, 'Do not force your girls [meaning slave girls] against their will,'[11] he told me that it meant, 'Don't put them into prostitution, but you can have as much sex with them as you want because they belong to you.' I said, 'What?!' Not just what, but *how* do you come to that conclusion when the words just say, 'Don't force them if they don't want.' I don't understand how it means you can do what you want, isn't that force too?

When you are raised Black in America, the media already puts a slant on stories of Black people. When you are Black and you live with Black people and love Black people, you know those stories not to be true. Just because somebody writes it, doesn't make it true. I'm reading the Qur'an and having no problem understanding the words; so when this man comes and tells me they mean something different, and I ask him on what basis he does so, and he can't tell me, then my brain tells me he is wrong and my being will not accept it.

We could not resolve this dispute, and it became a big issue. Eventually it required the programme director to intervene in order to change the format of the class. After that, instead of him telling me what the verses meant, we simply read a survey of *tafsir* (exegesis) literature. From that moment on, I said that there is nobody who can tell me what this means, because if they tell me what it means and they cannot show me their methodology for achieving that meaning, they could be telling me anything!

As we shall see, this encounter proved to be formative at the beginning of wadud's search for the methodology that she went on to develop in her thesis.

aw: When I got back to the United States in 1982, my previous advisor had left the University of Michigan, leaving a void in the area of Islamic studies. Fortunately, a Pakistani professor, Mustansir Mir, whose area was Qur'anic studies with a focus on Islahi's methodology, joined the faculty.[12] He was the one who made it clear to me that all of the scholars from the classical period who wrote *tafsir* did so based on how they understood the Qur'an

---

11 Qur'an 24:33.

12 Amin Islahi was a Pakistani scholar who promoted the idea of thematic and structural coherence in the Qur'an. Two important aspects of his methodology, in his influential Urdu exegesis of the Qur'an – *Taddabur-i Qur'an (Pondering on the Qur'an)* (Islahi, 1979) – are the use of reason and the focus on the text of the Qur'an itself rather than on the traditional *tafsir* literature.

and what they thought it meant, even though they were different from each other. All of a sudden, I knew that no one person has it; that everybody does the best they can based on whatever, and that maybe they were not saying things that spoke to me as a woman. In fact, it was clear to me as a woman that, after all the surveys of *tafsir* that I had to do, and all the classes I had to take, nobody was speaking from my reality. My reality was an African-American woman of poor background. I didn't see this voice in any of the *tafsir*. I would read and I would look at their methods and conclusions, and I would look at the Qur'an and I realized that the answer for me was not going to come from them; the answer for me would come from the Qur'an.

By the time I got to the dissertation phase, Professor Mir was introducing the idea of *nazm* or Qur'anic coherence: that the Qur'an was not randomly organized. I didn't get everything from Islahi, because I didn't read Urdu. I was really interested in the idea that there were different ways to understand the Qur'an, rather than this atomistic study of verses and chapters, and I was looking for that in others. Of course, Mawdudi and Sayyid Qutb had a social justice component in their work. But it had absolutely nothing to do with gender. I used those two and Zamakhshari as the basis for developing my argument about gender inclusive reading, but I had no guideposts.

ZMH: What about Fazlur Rahman? He has had great influence on my own thinking; Tamara Sonn, in her article on "Fazlur Rahman and Islamic feminism", which focuses on developments in the US, says that Muslim feminists have been among the main beneficiaries of Fazlur Rahman and his methodology.[13]

aw: Fazlur Rahman was the favourite of my second husband in terms of his philosophical orientation, and his idea of modern Muslim education. We both loved Fazlur Rahman's work on Muslim education and began to problematize formulas of production of knowledge. My second husband was also a convert, and much more Afro-centric than my first husband, much more politically astute and in tune with African-American Islam. We were here in America as Black people, not trying to be Middle Eastern. What we liked in Fazlur Rahman as a philosopher was the seeds of the idea of the production of knowledge in Islam. He helped us to see what that means in our time and in our location. That marriage was good for me intellectually,

13 Sonn, 1998.

we were good company and he challenged my thinking. He was also much more attuned to hermeneutics, and I began to study that in the graduate courses.

Once I started reading Gadamer, Lacan, Derrida, I understood what was happening with that guy in Egypt. People view the world through different frames. When they are looking at language, language acts or texts, or when they are hearing texts, because text is more than just something written, they are responding to that, they are responding on the basis of some type of experience that they have had; and it became very clear to me that none of the men who wrote *tafsir* experienced what it was to be a woman. The idea of female experience as an aspect of textual reality was nowhere in sight for them. I had to figure it out, because it was not simply linguistic tools but the whole idea of the hermeneutical location, because you, as a reader, were as legitimate a reader as anybody else. My understanding of religion, that there is no intermediary between a person and God, means that I do not have to agree with anybody's opinion of what is Islam or who or what is Allah if I do not have a way to follow their logic in saying what it is. I have the right to have my own opinion and to develop the validity of that opinion, including the affirmation that it makes in my experience of God.

That's why I could say, before I had done any study of feminism, that I had done a reading that comes from my own prior text and that was legitimate, because as far as I was learning about hermeneutics, everybody was doing it anyway. They may not have said they were doing it but that is what they were doing. And to be able to understand that that was a legitimate way to address the Qur'an, that was what I had to communicate to my department and my advisor, who was also a Qur'anic scholar, but somehow, for him, a gender sensitive reading was totally irrelevant to understanding the Qur'an. I had nobody on my committee who led me somewhere with the specifics of Qur'an and women, reading with a gender lens, gender as a category of thought; there wasn't any literature. The best I could find was something like Fazlur Rahman. What Fazlur Rahman did in the introduction of his book, *Major Themes of the Qur'an*,[14] was not *tafsir*. He talks about the methodology of understanding the Qur'an as an articulation in its seventh-century Arabian context. One that is inspired by God in the Prophet, that somehow had to mediate between that seventh-century

---

14 Rahman, 1980a.

Arabia and its patriarchal context and its transcendent message of guidance; as soon as I saw that, it meant that I could negotiate with anything that was there.

ZMH: Your first book, *Qur'an and Woman*, based on your dissertation, offers a women-inclusive reading of the Qur'an, i.e. gender as an aspect of textual analysis. So how did you come to develop this methodology? What were your main questions?

aw: My initial dissertation question was trying to understand how, and why, the Qur'an is at some points generic, addressing human beings, and sometimes inclusive, addressing both male and female, or women and men, and sometimes exclusive to men in its address. Therefore, it was very much like the Umm Salama enquiry. When she asks the question ('With all these verses addressed to men, what about women?'), then we get the famous verse *'al-mu'minin, al-mu'manat'*, for believing men and believing women, surrendering men and surrendering women ... fasting, chastity and so on.[15]

Other aspects of reading for gender in the Qur'an had to do with simply interrogating the questions in terms of application. Is this equally as applicable to women as it is to men, and why or why not? Sometimes in reading for gender, I am simply asking about the application. Why does the Qur'an always address the masculine plural form? Is this both exclusive of females and also inclusive of them? Because there is no distinct form unless you say them both, so the masculine form also applies to females in an audience.

For example, if the Qur'an says something with regard to *azwajukum*, 'your partners', it is not clear from the English who the 'your' is. It could be male or female. Nor is it clear who *azwaj* are, because it could be male or female. However, when it says *nisa-u-kum*, 'your women', and your women are not just women in the community but actually it's a juxtaposition that can mean not all women but your marriage partners; when that is said, the purview for application cannot be equally for women as it is for men because the language itself is too gender specific.

I was also interested in the idea of gender neutral, and what it means to be gender neutral in a language that is stratified by gender markers on everything: animate and inanimate. That was important because I was

---

15 Qur'an 33:35. Regarding this verse, one account relates that one of the Prophet's wives, Umm Salama, asked him: 'Why is it that we are not mentioned in the Qur'an as are the men?' See Nasr, 2015, p. 1030.

interested in removing this reaffirmation of the 'maleness' of God which so many parts of my being just could not accept. But Arabic is a gender-specific language, and this is why, for people who speak Arabic, Allah is only referred to as *huwa*, and is meant literally 'He'. So they often cannot fathom how I could choose to say 'She' in English. I could also say 'It', but of course Arabic does not have 'It.'

I was interested in that, because subjecting God to human categories, for example of sexuality, giving God gender, did not abide with my notion of a transcendent, holy, ultimate essence or reality. In the dissertation, I did not resolve this. If you notice, in that book, I never refer to Allah as 'She'; but I began to do so later, and now I do it all the time. In Arabic, everybody is either male or female, which actually causes people to think in such binary terms, but the grammarians also decided that the male form is the generic. For example, the generic form for one who is pregnant, *hamel*, is in the male form, even though men never get pregnant. So it's a function of grammar and language, maybe even of syntax; but it is not a function of God. Although I did not resolve that within *Qur'an and Woman*, I resolved it later; but that is also an aspect of reading, it is to understand whether or not the language, which reifies the explicit and separate gender, is open to the possibilities of any sentient being. People will read the Qur'an to exclude females on certain things, simply because the language is in the male form.

I believe that any time the divine is subjected to human language, there is going to be a limitation on divine expression; in other words, it will be constrained by the language itself, and this is certainly what I learned by studying hermeneutics and language. But I did not want to have the divine restricted by those language limitations, especially in excluding by gender, so when I first started doing research for *Qur'an and Woman*, I would call it a 'gender inclusive reading'; now I say 'gender as a category of thought'. In other words, interrogating the gender and applied meanings and possibilities of the language of any text to see whether it is inclusive or not. Therefore, another aspect of reading for gender is this ability to see the power relations happening in the language. Men speak from the position of privilege all the time.

ZMH: And often without being aware of it!

aw: All the time, and we have to call them on it. It's okay to have a bad opinion if you own it as your opinion. But don't put it out there as if it is sacred. This is what happens in terms of Islamic discourses. Therefore, that was another aspect of reading for gender and it is now clearer to me regarding the '*tafsir* of praxis', that is, to interrogate justice as one who is supposed to be experiencing that justice. Working with activists who have actual case study information, real women are experiencing certain things and even abiding by certain things because they are truly dedicated to their identity as Muslims and they would not want to move away from it, so they don't know. For example, they ask themselves, 'How much would I have to take on in order to still be Muslim?' I really want to get some clear articulation that the inability to experience justice is justification for the impracticality, in fact the illegality and immorality of applying certain practices, so I call that, like Saʿdiyya Shaikh, *tafsir* of praxis.[16]

ZMH: Any other further insight . . .

aw: There is another thing about reading for gender that I have not done a lot of work on, which is ambiguity. As you know, the Sufis have done it, not exclusively regarding gender but they allow space for ambiguity. People connected to religions are often so keen on right and wrong; they don't want to be wrong and they don't want to do wrong, but the implication is that they want to do right and they want to be right. Eventually they become so much invested in the rightness of the thing that it makes them inflexible, and they become unable to see that perhaps there are other possibilities, and they are not just right or wrong, they are just different perspectives. To be able to engage with ambiguity in meaning yields an opening in the mind and heart to more possibilities of meaning coming out of a thing, and not just, 'This is right and this wrong.'

I haven't developed that as much as I would like, also because I would like to go back and discuss examples. However, all of these issues – apart from *tafsir* of praxis – are not relevant to gender reform, in fact they are abstract, philosophical, and at the moment I haven't felt the luxury of being able to deal with them; but there are certain aspects that I would like to see some clarity about. I've been engaged with the Qur'an from the beginning, and I'm not done. So, if I am at one place, I do the best that I can at that place, and I stumble over something, and I write about stumbling, and then I get to another place and I write about that. I mean, I do analysis of the Qur'an, and I know it is a work, or in some ways it's a discourse, it's a text, but I am only concerned with the Qur'an as the divine self-disclosure.

---

16 The term 'tafsir of praxis' was coined by Saʿdiyya Shaikh (2007) in an article based on in-depth interviews with eight battered women in Cape Town to understand how they grappled ethically with Qur'an 4:34 in the light of their own experiences. It is now used for drawing theological arguments from experience rather than texts.

Not everybody opens up the Qur'an and gets transformed. Once I picked it up, I never travelled without it. For many, the Qur'an is Islam and Islam is this patriarchic, hegemonic, domineering teacher that cracks you on the knuckles if you do not learn. I was blessed with something else, I was blessed with an opening that came from Yusef Ali's translation. If I could spend the rest of my life just in that kind of relationship with the Qur'an, with students, that would be paradise on Earth. Instead I have had to deal with politics, gender, and I mean, it is real, but my ideal is to sit in some school and lead people into their own hermeneutical space with the Qur'an.

INVOLVEMENT IN ACTIVISM, AND
THE TAWHIDIC PARADIGM

Between 1989 and 1992, when wadud taught at the International Islamic University of Malaysia (IIUM), she met with a group of women advocating reform of family law; together they founded Sisters in Islam (SIS) – the first women's organization to work within both Islamic and feminist frameworks. I asked her what took her to Malaysia and how she came to be involved in activism.

aw: Malaysia at that time was the perfect place to go; I had a skill, I had a degree, a contract for at least three years. Had I stayed in America I would have succumbed to any one of the sub-disciplines of Islamic studies to get a job. I might have been a historian, a Middle East specialist of Islam. The next level of transformation, that is from the ideas of gender sensitive reading to the idea of transformation into society and policy, I don't know whether it would have happened. I met a couple of women through Rose Ismail[17] who had been at Michigan as a journalist to do a two-month course and had been working with SIS. Rose told me about Salbiah Ahmad, who was also teaching at IIUM, and that she had been coming to SIS meetings. I went to meet Salbiah, and one month later she took me to their next meeting. They had not yet achieved a cohesive form. They had just suffered a setback because they tried to go to the courts and encounter the judges, and they were ill-equipped to do it, and so they had been thrown back.

---

17 Another of the founding members of Sisters in Islam.

They were strategizing to move forward and I said, 'You should read the Qur'an.' I mean, you come to a Muslim majority situation, from a Muslim background, of course you know that the Qur'an is the book of Allah, revelation to the Prophet, the guidance, you know that stuff but you don't have a sense of how it relates to what you are doing or to your being. That is how we began reading the Qur'an once a month; meanwhile there was a public debate about polygamy, and they wanted to make a position statement, as a letter to the press, for which they needed to refer to what was in the Qur'an. I was trying to explain to them that if you look at the language – just what is in the Qur'an and the language – it is not a *right* for men. And that became the main argument of the SIS booklet *Polygamy is Not a Right for Men*.[18]

ZMH: While you were in Malaysia you revised your dissertation and published it as *Qur'an and Woman*. It has had a lot of impact on activism, as a defining text in empowering Muslim women to challenge patriarchy from within.

aw: I was not out there to have an impact. I was not there to challenge patriarchy, I was searching for meanings in the Qur'an, and I was also hoping, by writing the dissertation and then getting it published, to join the community of people who were also searching for that meaning. For me it was about meaning-making in the context of divine revelation. I didn't see any link between my work and the law; I believed that it was there, but I did not know how to establish that link on my own. I mean I could see the coherence, I just could not figure out the steps. So, you mediate in some ways, because you actually understand my work and can see its implications for law reform – before you, Salbiah Ahmad did, she was the one who took me to the Sisters in Islam meeting in 1989. I felt that there were connections, but I just couldn't make those steps. You know I have a friend who is an artist; she has taught art to others and when she describes how you produce a piece, literally starting with a blank slate, it is interesting how many people can see the finished product and can see the whole material but cannot fathom the steps to get there. I believed in the finished product, that is policy and law reform, but I couldn't get the steps and couldn't mediate between vision and practicality.

ZMH: For me, it came gradually and through a process, first in the course of fieldwork in family courts in Iran and Morocco in the 1980s, then with my

18 Sisters in Islam, 2002.

conversations with ulema in Iran in the 1990s. It was clear that we were talking about Islam and gender at three levels.[19] The first was the diverse and often conflicting interpretations of the Qur'an and Sunna; the second was national gender ideologies, laws and legislations, and the third was 'lived reality', the lived experiences of individuals and their understandings of gender rights in Islam. I could see that change was happening, and conventional understandings of gender in Islam were being challenged at all three levels – you were doing it at the theological level through engaging with the Qur'an. I mean, in the late 1980s and the 1990s we were all thinking and writing, but our ideas were not yet formed as to how to intervene at each level to bring change. For me, this formation began to take shape after I went to Malaysia in June 2001, when Zainah invited me to write a paper for an SIS regional workshop on Islamic Family Law and Justice for Women. It was there that I met you for the first time, as well as Amira Sonbol and several Indonesian scholars. This for me was a new experience, in fact we can say that meeting was the starting point for what eventually became Musawah.

As part of the activities leading to the launch of Musawah, in early December 2007 we held a 'Conceptual Meeting' in Cairo on "Equality and Justice in Muslim Family Law". Drafts of the commissioned papers were presented in this meeting; their implications were debated and teased out by activists from diverse contexts, as we shaped the document that eventually became the Musawah *Framework for Action*. In her paper, amina wadud proposed her '*tawhidic* paradigm' of reform, making a strong case for 'the legitimacy of women as actors on the basis of Qur'anic analysis', as well as offering a theological basis for gender equality to underline 'the horizontal reciprocity between any two human beings, especially between male and female humans.'[20] I asked her how to explain how she came to this paradigm.

aw: After years of studying Sufi traditions, especially Sachiko Murata's book *The Tao of Islam*[21] – where she has all these lovely conversations about the Pen and the Tablet and how this works out, but every time she places that over the social reality of men and women, I kept thinking about the arguments and the model set forth in the text and felt that the female had no

---

19 Mir-Hosseini, 1999, Introduction.
20 Wadud, 2009, pp. 107–109.
21 Murata, 1992, for instance, pp. 12–13, 152–167.

direct contact with Allah in that model; and I felt the need to create a model that enables that interaction, and there it was: the *tawhidic* paradigm.

At its most fundamental level, *tawhid* refers to the oneness of Allah. Allah is one and unique. And this is the principal theological foundation for my claim that Islam does not oppress women. Islam is based on the ultimate reality of *tawhid*, or monotheism, or the unicity of God. The word *tawhid* comes from the second form of the verb *wahhada*, a dynamic term emphasizing the divine power to bring all things into unity or harmony.

A fundamental idea in Islam is that Allah is the greatest, *Allahu akbar*. The Qur'an makes it clear that whenever two persons are together, Allah makes the third, or when three are together, Allah makes the fourth, and so on (Qur'an, 58:7). As long as Allah is the greatest and is unique, according to *tawhid*, then there can be no other relationship between any two persons except the one of horizontal reciprocity. The horizontal plane is mutually cooperative because the role of the one can be exchanged with the role of the other with no loss of integrity. This is how patriarchy is a kind of *shirk*. It places men and women in a relationship that is not capable of reciprocity because one person is always 'superior' to the other. Under *tawhid*, this is not possible, because the presence of Allah must remain as the highest focal point.

It's funny, I first talked about the *tawhidic* paradigm at the 1997 American Academy of Religion meeting in San Francisco. In a conversation with another professor about the *tawhidic* paradigm he asked, 'How do you put this into law?' I said, 'Look, I have the theology and the theory, can't you guys put it into law?' I just had no way to equate it to social action, which then has strategic implications with regard to policy and law reform. It wasn't that I did not see that it was a necessary component, or feel that mandate. I believed it, but I couldn't see it then. From that year forward, I would talk about it theologically, but when in 2007 we started talking about this as a lived reality, which I thought is key, I started to see the steps that linked them together.[22]

LEADING A MIXED PRAYER

In December 2014, when we were both in Sri Lanka for a Musawah I-nGEJ course, we resumed our conversation. I began by asking her to talk about her

---

22 Wadud, 2006, pp. 24–32.

personal experience of breaking a taboo by leading a mixed Friday prayer in public, which had been assumed to be a male prerogative.

aw: My experience started with an invitation to a conference in South Africa in 1994, which was followed by a two-week lecture tour throughout the country. I was still in the process of articulating my understanding of Islam and my reading of the Qur'an. I did so through the lens of affirming the particular experiences of women and emphasizing the nature of the feminine as an important element in textual analysis. I was consistently *hijabi* and I wore my scarf all the time, and even though I would say in public that I didn't think it was a requirement, people would not hear me because I always wore it; they would even point out that contradiction: if it were a choice, why was I always wearing it?

The evening after the conference we had a dinner, and the Imam Rashid Omar from Claremont Main Road Mosque kind of stopped me and said something rather vague about the mosque's interest in deconstructing some of the gender binaries. He proposed that I deliver what they called the 'pre-*khutbah*', which precedes the Friday Prayer; it is delivered in the local English vernacular and is followed by the Arabic *khutbah* itself. I told him I was in agreement; we wanted to move forward, but I didn't know the details and I didn't anticipate everything.

I had no time to prepare the *khutbah* beforehand, and I decided to go from what I knew instinctively and most intimately through experience, which was Islam as an engaged surrender from the perspective of delivering a baby. I was fortunate that they recorded it and that one of the women who worked with either Muslim youth or gender affairs transcribed the entire *khutbah* and put it in the paper, *Al-Qalam*. I am glad that she transcribed it all, because I had only a few notes and I liked what I said. But I had not planned it. I just spoke from my heart. Later, when I analysed it, I did so by using it as the particular experience of women, as a public discourse on the meaning of what is Islam – all of which is documented in the fifth chapter of *Gender Jihad*.[23]

---

23 Ibid., pp. 158–186, 'Public Leadership and Gender Inclusiveness'. In an illuminating foot-note, she writes: 'Throughout this chapter, as elsewhere in the book, I refer to some individuals, real people with life-expectations and capacities. I mention them only to facilitate my construc-tion of a narrative, even while acknowledging that no one is reduced to a mere facility in my construction in real terms ... It is especially important how a prism of paradoxes bounce between me and my intention and outcome, and these various characters. That they configure differently, in my telling the story, than they configure in another telling, leads to two inevitable

ZMH: Did you lead the prayer after *khutbah*? And were men and women praying in the same room?

aw: No, I did not; on this occasion I did the *khutbah* and Imam Rashid went ahead and led the prayer. Then I went to where the ladies were standing. In that mosque, women prayed on the balcony floor above the main prayer floor where males prayed, but they came down for that particular Friday; but after that, they said women never went back to the balcony. I think the arrangement is side by side. Events for the rest of my time in South Africa were all shaped by that.

That experience was emotionally very moving for me and it also led to a great deal of debate and conflict. A number of protests took place at the mosque the following Friday and there were many who took to public forums to call me all kinds of heretic. This all came as a shock for me because, while my thinking was not at all mainstream, it also was not revolutionary and I conducted myself quite privately through an introverted stance; I am much more extroverted today. At the time, I was focusing on raising my children while quietly plugging away at gaining a personal understanding of Islam; so, when the controversy arose, I felt quite exposed.

It's important to contextualize this in the political developments of South Africa at the time. The country was still in the first few months of the Mandela presidency and still celebrating the successful defeat of apartheid. There were divisions within the Muslim community as well; on the one hand there continued to be an ambivalence on the part of the minority Muslim community (i.e. the main architects of the protests) who took a quietist approach and chose not to engage in anti-oppression on the basis of race as they did not associate with that particular struggle. On the other hand, there were certain parties who were completely engaged in the intersection of race, class and religion associated with the struggle, and in doing so, they *intentionally* invoked the element of gender and, as such, they questioned the standardization of male privilege in ritual. It was not a new experience for them; but, as in most places today, it remained in the form of small gatherings of Muslims who collectively agreed to allow a woman to be the imam. Inviting me to lead the pre-*khutbah* was their attempt at making that event public: to do it in a mosque and to do it on a Friday when other people got news of it. I was told that the reason they selected me was in part

hermeneutical considerations: whose version of this story is true? Or how are *all* versions of this story true?' (footnote 12, p. 275).

because I was leaving, and therefore they could take up the challenge without my being in any particular focus or danger.

ZMH: You were an outsider. What made you feel that you could take up
this role?

aw: Yes, an outsider to the local context. It was a novel idea for me, and I was
swept up by the momentum. This coincided with my engagement with the
tawhidic paradigm in terms of my construction of the reality of Islam. At
the time I realized that it doesn't matter who fulfils that role, if the person
does so with sincerity toward the ritual itself – that is, to honour it as a
formal set of ceremonious actions, the purpose of which is to realign
ourselves with Allah, a ritual affirmation of our alignment with Allah,
standing, bowing, prostrating. After that, I no longer felt that that role
needed to be fulfilled only by men. It was simply a function that needed to
be performed in order to organize a highly stylized ritual that was done in
a group, therefore that role could be filled by either a man or a woman.

However, when the backlash came, I went into a much deeper kind of
internal inspection, where I could not determine if my interest in it was about
my ego or about some greater political cause, i.e. gender equality, or whether
or not it was about my relationship with Allah. This last factor held me back
for another eleven years. Whenever I was approached and asked whether I
would lead the *salat* – be it in small groups for men and women on the same
lines, or for women as imams – I always declined. By the time the 2005 prayer
came along, I had resolved it within myself, without a shadow of a doubt.
Before that, I was still working with some uncertainty, and part of the conflict
was whether or not I was trying to make myself to be better than other
women or men by standing in the role that I envisioned for myself as leader
and therefore, because I had studied certain things, I deserved to be in front.
I battled with *nafs al-lawamah* (the self-accusing *nafs*)[24] for a long time.

ZMH: How did the idea of that March 2005 prayer come about?

aw: There was an attempt in 2004 to establish a 'Progressive Muslim
Organization' in the United States, where I was asked, alongside a group of
academics, to be part of its advisory committee – I had no direct engagement or involvement with the organization. They had initially desired to
plan a weekend-long conference at Harvard University, commencing with

---

24 *Nafs* means 'self', but has also been translated as soul, psyche or ego. In Sufi wisdom and on
the path to spiritual maturity, *nafs* goes through three stages: *nafs al-ammarah* (the inciting
nafs); *nafs al-lawwamah* (the self-accusing *nafs*); and *nafs al-mutma'innah* (the *nafs* at peace).

me leading the Friday prayer. At the time, I was completely ready to accept the responsibility; but the conference did not take off, due to what I perceive were internal disagreements.

Then in March 2005, I was invited to speak at the Auburn Seminary in New York City; Asra Nomani and Ahmed Nassef (leader of the online magazine *Progressive Islam*), two of the main architects for the 18 March Friday service, knew that I was going to be in New York, and asked that I stay over a bit longer and perform the *jumah* [Friday prayer] there. I agreed and the organizers started with a religiously neutral place – an art gallery; but after a bomb threat they were forced to pull out. In the end they settled for Synod House, at the Church of St. John the Divine in Manhattan.

ZMH: Did they approach mosques?

aw: I believe they asked many of the mosques in New York but didn't receive an acceptance. I really don't know how they went about it. After the lecture, Asra Nomani came into my room and said that the *New York Times* wants to interview me. I said, 'I am tired, I have just given a lecture and I am not interested in giving an interview.' And she said, 'But it is the *New York Times*!' and I said, 'That does not change me from being tired.' So, we were not on the same page as to how much press there should be, but they had *a lot* of press.

ZMH: Yes, and they had planned for it to be a media event.

aw: Yes, and the press responded and was interested. There were as many cameras as there were people for the ritual prayer, so the organizers in my estimation were not very familiar with what you would call the *fiqh* of *jumah* (ritual laws governing Friday Prayers). Some of the things that I mentioned to them, they didn't even know how to carry through. For example, there are two calls to prayer; one of them is actually supposed to take place when the imam comes in. They didn't even wait; they had a woman make the *adhan* (call to prayer) and of course they wanted to celebrate that, and it didn't matter if it fell into another type of formula when I stood in front of a congregation of people.

ZMH: Was it solely prayers and no *khutbah*?

aw: There was both *khutbah* and prayer. In fact, Juliane Hammer happened to get her hands on a copy of the entire tape recorded by one of the news agencies when conducting her research for her book, *American Muslim Women, Religious Authority, and Activism*.[25] It is funny because I talked so

---

25 For a comprehensive and insightful analysis of this first public, woman-led prayer and the debates that it gave rise to, see Hammer, 2012, pp. 13–55; see also Elewa and Silvers, 2010–11.

slow back then and wanted to articulate the *tawhidic* paradigm. While reading Juliane Hammer's book, I realized that Asra Nomani had been getting impatient with the length of my sermon and that our visions for the event did not overlap. All of this information is in her book,[26] but I did not know it at the time, so when I finished the *khutbah*, I turned to face the direction of *qiblah* – and they had put the press in the *qiblah*!

ZMH: Oh my God!

aw: Yes, that is exactly what I said, only for a minute I forgot who my God was! I was like, 'Why are these people at this spot, why would you put people at that spot?' Then I realized that I can't think about them, that I have to think what I am doing, and that I was fulfilling the same role that I fulfilled even when I was praying alone, doing remembrance of Allah.

I left immediately afterwards, even though they insisted on hosting a press conference before and after, and I told them, 'I don't give press conferences before or after I pray, so don't mind me if I don't participate.' I had one conversation with the press before the prayer and I didn't do any more, even when they started calling me and e-mailing me, I just didn't participate further.

ZMH: It was all over the papers.

aw: It was everywhere, so in a way the fact that I wasn't a participant in the media aspect makes my role even stranger, because it made my goal more ambiguous.

ZMH: Yes; why didn't you talk to the media?

aw: I just don't like the media. At the time, my life was divided between my work at the university – teaching students, grading papers – and my family. Therefore, the spiritual identity needed to be balanced between those things. The notion of engaging with the media as a public intellectual or leader, and being recognized as such, did not correspond with my life, and was absolutely foreign to me, and I was not at all comfortable to even assume such a role. I eventually had to make peace with it, but it took a number of years to achieve that peace, and required me to leave my job at the university and to go off and live somewhere else, where I was less known.

ZMH: In 2007, the year after the prayer, you did quit your post at the University of the Virginia; why?

aw: There were rumours that I had received death threats, which I had not. However, there were apparently concerned parents who called the

---

26 Hammer, 2012, p. 29.

university and said that they didn't want their children to be collateral damage for any particular threat, and the university listened to them. The university arranged for my physical classroom to be conducted virtually, and so I continued my teaching at home without a physical presence on campus, with the exception of one class whose students insisted on a physical classroom and so the class was moved to a location unannounced. That gave me a lot of time at home and the university gave me leave from some summer teaching, and I didn't go back to the classroom regularly until September.

ZMH: By then the controversy had died down.

aw: Yes, of course. It was about six months of not having to teach but at the same time receiving the same income. It was then that I realized that my location did not embrace my person. I filed for a leave of absence from the university, but I didn't know back then that I would no longer be in US academia, because I didn't think of it as such, but that's what it turned out to be, because almost fifteen years has passed now.

ZMH: Many Muslims believe that women are not supposed to lead public and mixed prayer; what you did was somehow unprecedented, and by virtue of that, the backlash shouldn't have come as a surprise, correct?

aw: I knew my act was unprecedented; the purpose was to have an impact on the public, and I did not see it as contrary to Islam in any shape or form, as I essentially understood and understand the religion itself; that still remains true today. Because of that, and the fact that I had no public ego, I did not anticipate the kinds of reactions I would receive. You need to understand that I am not socialized within a Muslim culture. I am *acculturated* to Islam as a theological ideal that has the potential to organize culture, society, community, family, but there was nothing about me that is acculturated through custom or in any way that would persuade me to measure the smallness of people's minds above the way in which I conceptualize and continue to strive to be in a relationship with Allah. Therefore, if there is a system that we understand on the basis of a relationship with Allah, i.e. a *fiqh*, then I was in accordance with that system to the best of my understanding, and to the purest of my own intentions.

ZMH: It's interesting, because when you first took on this role in South Africa, it came with a particular social and political dimension and goal: some Muslims there wanted to break barriers, one of them being gender. In 2005, gender was again a barrier, because up until then women were excluded – not from the ritual space, but from the positions of leadership within that space. However, there are those Muslim women who believe either that leadership in this particular space does not belong to them or that achieving equality or gaining a foothold in such a role is not a salient issue or priority. For example, I know some women who argued then that there were more concrete and urgent issues, such as equality in marriage and before the law, that should have taken precedence over the goals which you were espousing; that in fact this act was making things more difficult for women and so they strongly opposed its continuation.

aw: The issue of gender equality in the ritual space was an issue that I precisely had in mind. By that time, I had begun to look at feminism and religion in the discourse over why we want to deconstruct gender hegemony in every field and every discipline, every social, economic and political area, but we leave gender hegemony in religion totally up to the male perspective. I realized that this question cannot be complete if we leave that arena unchallenged – if we accept and sustain it and, even within ourselves, support the idea of exclusive male ritual leadership. What we have basically said is that at some teleological or cosmological level, men and women are not equal; that in fact men are preferred, and they are preferred by God, and that the same kind of rigorous analysis that we were giving to deconstruct the hegemony in the disciplines in the academy – politics, society, economy and culture – that same kind of analysis was lacking in our conceptualization of the Divine.

That latter part, I emphasized intentionally. However, I can confess that I was ignorant and not sufficiently informed on all of the important overlapping issues concerning society, culture and politics, and had some catching up to do. I was really naïve; I wasn't steeped in the academic backgrounds of sociology, law, anthropology or political science, but rather witnessed them unfold. I lived within the metaphor of the potential of an exclusive relationship in the world and with the Divine on the basis of an individual internalization of the reality of the presence of God. By virtue of my exclusion within those circles and my departure from the university, I virtually isolated myself and began to appreciate the kinds of relationships with members of the community who were not bothered by the relative position of the female in matters of faith and God. I therefore had a better chance at actions and interactions that nurtured the nature of the God–Human relationship that I believed in, but I also realized that it was a very small minority. At the time, I believe that the majority of Muslim women had never examined for themselves what the role of *imama* (female prayer leader) was, its purpose, and their relationship to that role and to the God that is supposed to be the focus of that ritual in the first place, even if the ritual is performed out of rote.

ZMH: You did it from a place of total conviction, your relationship with God, and your own place in that ritual space. Your action started a conversation that would not have begun *but for* your action, and that significantly altered the landscape of conversations and public opinion. Before that event, the issue of women as leaders in ritual space was not an issue, there was no debate, so no one was yet in agreement or disagreement. That event opened space for other women to lead public prayer.

aw: Yes, it was a challenge to the presumption that what was normative by consequence of patriarchy was in fact divinely necessary – that the ritual itself was *contingent* upon male hegemony. I simply hadn't this logic, that the imam is closer to God; that has never been our theology, we never had the notion that the individual who stands first in the line is somehow closer to God in relation to others. The notion that God is on some type of horizon? No – God is everywhere. And this was the message that I wanted to articulate to the public, that this movement is not about me, it is not about amina wadud. In order to do so, I had to decline invitations to lead prayers.

It doesn't matter what line I am standing in while performing the prayer, Allah is everywhere and everyone is equal in Allah's eyes. That is why I like praying with Muslims who line up in mixed gender lines, that you simply stand and perform the prayer, no matter who is standing next to or in front of you. When that happens, you truly start to deconstruct certain essential aspects of gender differentiation, as you come to observe that here, we are all simply servants before God.

ZMH: The common rationalization used to justify the separation of the sexes within the ritual space is that men and women get distracted when in close proximity to one another and that therefore separation is necessary to prevent that outcome.

aw: Yes, the same problematic notion that sexuality and the spirit cannot co-exist, that somehow sexuality transcends the spirit.

AN EVOLVING RELATIONSHIP WITH FEMINISM

In the preface to the 1999 edition of *Qur'an and Woman*, wadud declined any identification with feminism – despite the fact that, by then, her book had become one of the inspirational texts for the emerging 'Islamic feminism'. While appearing supportive of 'the definition of feminism as the radical notion that women are human beings', she went on to say: 'That I never refer to myself with this title – no matter what definition – does not prevent others from calling me out of my name – whether positively or negatively applied, as though I do not count as a human being.'[27] I found her statement paradoxical and ambiguous. In the mid-2000s, when we often coincided at meetings, we discussed this statement and her position on feminism. I used to point out that when it came to her scholarship and her approach to the Qur'an, she was definitely feminist. While she admitted that was the case, she would say 'I am not feminist but rather "pro-faith and pro-feminist".' But then her position gradually began to change, and she no longer declined to be called a feminist.

ZMH: My last question relates to the general topic of feminism, and Islamic feminism. I know you have experienced a personal evolution in this respect because, back when we got to know each other in the early 2000s, you definitely did not identify with feminism.

aw: Yes. It wasn't until 2009 and the launching of Musawah that that happened. In the 1990s, I was also very much into continually growing and transforming in my identity as a Muslim, and the notion of the secular divide over gender discourses simply did not resonate with me. Actually, in this particular case I was more familiar with the conversations and the critical analysis by African-American women about the imperialist location of mainstream feminist discourses, scholarship, activism and the like. In the United States, the Civil Rights Movement was focused primarily on race; gender was looked at only in the context of the white majority and white supremacy, allowing equality to their women. It wasn't about all women. The title of the book I always refer to captures this: *All the Women Are White, All the Blacks Are Men, But Some of Us Are Brave,* by Akasha Gloria Hull, Patricia Bell-Scott and Barbara Smith.[28] Barbara Smith coincidentally was my residence counsellor in the ABC programme when I was fourteen years old, which was the first time I left home; afterwards we kind of kept up, and then fell away from each other; she wrote that book at a time when we were not writing to each other.

---

27 Wadud, 1999, p. xviii.
28 Hull, et al. 1982; an anthology that became a landmark in Black Women Studies. Among the first books to provide a potent critique of feminism for leaving out women of colour, it paved the way for the concept of intersectionality as developed by Kimberlé Grenshaw (1989).

I was aware of the idea that somehow race and gender had not been resolved for the intersectionality of oppression, that every time I tried to invoke a conversation that was true to my location, the dominant feminist framework was still complicit in white supremacy. For me an articulation of a feminism that affirmed my spiritual identity was as problematic as my racial identity. At the time, most Muslim women whom I met and who identified as feminist were essentially secular; they did not wish to engage in any discussions about God. So, I just stayed away.

ZMH: How about groups like Sisters in Islam and people like Zainah Anwar?

aw: When I arrived in Malaysia in 1989, Sisters in Islam did not identify as feminist. The only exception was Norani Othman, who identified as a feminist but was much more secular in orientation.[29] As a political scientist, she had actually done analysis of discourses on oppression politics, and we engaged in discussions attempting to observe the structures through her methodological lens; meanwhile, as a collective, we remained in a sensitive and uncertain place where we were struggling with our own identities as Muslims who were seeking the means to achieve gender equality. She was the only person who overtly identified herself as feminist in the early years of Sisters in Islam. Go back and check out the literature, there's nothing in our literature from the 1990s that talks about feminism. It wasn't even an issue in those years. I left Malaysia in 1992, but I would go back and forth.

ZMH: And Islamic feminism as a concept, the way we talk about it now, did not exist then. It was only later that the very term 'Islamic feminism' began to be used in the literature.[30]

aw: No one had yet discussed Islamic feminism in the way we do today; when they did, they used terms such as 'Islamist-feminist', which I would still consider to be an oxymoron. Not because they are trying to capture the most public articulation of faith: devotion and feminism – personally, I wanted to capture those two things. But I understood the term as using Islam as an adjective, as one woman said, 'if Islam is the motivation for your feminism, that's Islamic feminism.' On the other side, I understood a 'Muslim feminist' to be a person who is Muslim and believes in a feminism that is uninterrogated for some of its own problematics but is the only

---

29 A founding member of Sisters in Islam, and Professor of Sociology at University Kebangsaan Malaysia.
30 See Badran, 2002.

articulation available that affirms equality on the basis of gender. But examining what feminism means in relationship to Islam, what Islam means in relationship to feminism, is not a part of most Muslim feminism. The fact that they benefit from those of us who do interrogate it is fine.

I became aware of the tension between these two perspectives on gender among Muslims when I went with members of SIS to the 1995 Women Conference in Beijing (that was after I had returned to the US from Malaysia). There were these two separate discourses by Muslim women, and both of them claimed something; and the only reason that they could claim an opposition to each other was that they claimed that you couldn't have Islam and feminism together. One side would take Islam, even though Islam was not interrogated, to be irretrievably patriarchal and just recapped all of the patriarchy. The other side took an Islamist stance and projected itself as the most viable stance to Western hegemony, that there could be no liberation for Muslim women without faith, but Islam had to be accepted without question as a mark of faith and identity.

I continued to struggle with the two discourses led by Muslim women who argued that feminism and Islam are irreconcilable. The best way I can describe this period is that it was when feminism was not wide enough to embrace Islam and Islam was not universal enough to embrace feminism. It was a living reality for many people including myself, who weren't willing to give up one for the other. I just had to take them both.

The launch of Musawah in 2009 was really transformative for me. It was there that I began to see the political, social, cultural impact of this gender-inclusive analysis of Islam. And I said, well there it is. That's what Islamic feminism is and I was more comfortable with it. I actually have a T-shirt that says 'feminist' that I was wearing at the launch in February 2009, and Fatima Seedat[31] saw it and said, 'No! Don't say you're going over to that side.'

Today, I am no more my African-American identity than I am my Muslim identity, or my feminist identity, I am all those identities which now live in *tawhidic* harmony within me. There's not a place where I give up race, Islam or feminism as an aspect of identity and struggle. I am now united in all those beings. I was not so in the past, and the three were not suddenly united through the use of a label or term. I had to take complete possession of each of those terms before I could identify myself with them.

---

31 Seedat has written on different approaches in Islamic feminism; see Seedat, 2013a, p. 404; and 2013b, p. 29.

ZMH: So, this shift and transformation came about during the launch of Musawah in 2009. But you had been involved for many years with Sisters in Islam, who in fact gave birth to Musawah; in 2007 you wrote one of its concept papers. Can you elaborate what occurred during that launch?

aw: Well, I felt that I was a part of a global community. This didn't mean that everybody agreed on all sets of issues, however we were all in universal agreement that there was oppression occurring in the name of Islam, that we did not experience Islam in that way, and therefore felt the imperative to affirm our experience by unifying our forces in order to bring about a much more publicly realized articulation of Islam. Clearly, the battle is not over, but that launch was a moment of collective awareness on those issues.

AN UPDATE

Since her retirement in 2007, wadud has been travelling widely. In 2018 she moved to Indonesia, where she is currently Visiting Professor at the Post Graduate Centre at the National Islam University Sunan Kalijaga Jogjakarta. She will also be teaching at Gadja Mada University at the Indonesian Consortium for Religious Studies, an interfaith international centre. She says she has been warmly welcomed and highly respected at these institutions, and has plans to develop a Centre for Queer Islamic Studies and Theology. She misses her family but she is more than content in Indonesia, and intends to take up permanent residence.

She also has an active social media presence, recently using the avatar 'The Lady Imam' for all her online activities, including on the Patreon platform.[32] In June 2020, wadud created 'Friends Along the Way' on her Patreon page, where she interviews her network of friends sharing the path to gender justice in Islam. She opened the series with a conversation about Islamic feminism with Margot Badran and myself.[33] Another conversation, in September, was with Zainah Anwar,[34] who talked of wadud's role in shaping the activities of Sisters in Islam. Anwar gave a first-hand account of the clash between political

---

32 https://www.patreon.com/TheLadyImam; Patreon is a membership platform that connects 'content creators' with fans and supporters – a modern take on the concept of patronage.
33 https://www.youtube.com/watch?v=TXc0Oravhfo&t=3184s
34 https://www.youtube.com/watch?v=e4b0N1QEVQU&t=525s

Islam and women's rights in Malaysia that gave birth to SIS in 1989; her narrative affirms the crucial role of feminist scholars of the Qur'an like amina wadud on the ground – something dismissed by An-Na'im in the previous chapter.

4

Asma Lamrabet

[T]his new feminine perspective questions the alleged male superiority but not on the basis of rivalry between the sexes. It is a new perspective which can only be enriching and which takes into account the spiritual experience of women, so often absent from Islamic references. Spirituality has no gender, but there is a given lived relationship to God which is perceived differently by women and men . . .It is here that the inclusion of female perspective can be an essential addition to the human spiritual experience.[1]

Asma Lamrabet is a Moroccan medical doctor and author with an active presence in public and on social media. She has worked as a haematologist at Avicenna University Hospital, Rabat, and is also Gender Studies Chair at the Euro-Arab Foundation for Higher Studies in Granada, Spain, and a member of the scientific committee of the Moroccan Driss Benzekri National Institute for Human Rights. She was born in 1961 in Rabat but, after her father became a political exile, she was schooled in France, Algeria and Lebanon, before returning to the University of Rabat to complete her medical studies, specializing in pathology. She married in 1982, when she was still studying and her husband had begun his diplomatic career. Between 1996 and 2003 they lived in several countries in South America, where she did voluntary work in public hospitals. In 2008 she co-founded the International Group of Studies and Reflection on Women and Islam (GIERFI). Between 2010 and 2018 she was Director of the Centre for Studies and Research on Women's Issues in Islam at the Mohammedian Council of the Ulama. She has been a member of the Moroccan National Committee on Education and Culture since 2015 and is

---

1 Lamrabet, 2016, pp. 7–8.

also a founder of the Fatima Mernissi Chair at the Mohammed V University in Rabat, established in 2017.

Her debut as a writer came in 2002 with *Musulmane tout simplement* (*Simply Muslim*).[2] This announced the distinctive voice of a woman who both opposed Islamophobia and patriarchal readings of Islam, and reclaimed her feminist and Muslim identities – a voice that was amplified and nuanced in her many subsequent publications on the theme of women and Islam, all written in French, mostly also translated into English, Arabic and Spanish. In 2013, she received the Organization of Arab Women's Sociology Award for her book, *Femmes et hommes dans le Coran* (*Women and Men in the Qur'an*).[3]

From 2006 I visited Morocco several times for a project on the trajectory of family law reforms in Iran and Morocco, building on my earlier research in family courts in the late 1980s. In May 2008 I came across Lamrabet's work; I bought her recently published book *Le Coran et les femmes: une lecture de liberation* (later published in English as *Women in the Qur'an: An Emancipatory Reading*).[4] I was intrigued by the foreword, in which the author reflected on a meeting, in a Paris suburb, with a group of Muslim women to whom she dedicated the book. These women were struggling to be both Muslims and equal citizens 'in an environment that is increasingly hostile to their need for spirituality, to struggle against all forms of discrimination, to assert their right to be fully fledged citizens, to denounce the politics of marginalization which consistently relegates them to an eternal sub-culture.'[5] Evidently the author identified with these women who 'have moved beyond the stage of identity crisis which means one feels torn between two apparently irreconciled cultures. Through their faith, they have already reconciled the two and wish moreover to define their own culture, diverse, fertile, open to all universal values.'[6]

The book's tone and style reminded me of Fatima Mernissi's later writings, and I was keen to meet Lamrabet. We were introduced through a mutual friend, and I visited her at her home during that trip. She knew of my work and we found that we had a lot in common in our approach to the politics of gender rights in Muslim contexts, and in our vision for change. After that first meeting, we met again every time I was in Rabat, and I arranged to interview her when she became director of the first ever centre for women's studies in a religious

---

2 Lamrabet, 2002.
3 Lamrabet, 2012.
4 Lamrabet, 2007.
5 Lamrabet, 2016, p. x.
6 Ibid.. p. xi.

institution in Morocco, Rabita Mohammedia des Oulémas (the Mohammedian Council of Ulema; henceforth referred to as Rabita). Established in 2006 by a royal decree (*zahir*), with a mandate to promote values of moderation in Islam, the council was headed by Dr Ahmad Abbadi, who had a reputation as a reformist and broad-minded scholar of Islam. Appointed by the king, he was charged with bringing 'various factions of Moroccan thinkers to the table with the purpose of developing a vision for the country'.[7]

The first conversation I recorded with Asma Lamrabet took place on 25 March 2010, shortly after she officially took up her post there in February as director of women's studies. We met at Rabita's headquarters, where I also had a short meeting with Dr Abbadi, whom I had first met in 2008 in Marrakech, at one of the Oslo New Directions Project meetings. I asked her to talk about her personal and intellectual trajectory, from secular to Islamic feminism, and about her appointment in Rabita, as well as her approach to the Qur'an.

FROM SECULAR TO ISLAMIC FEMINISM

ZMH: Let us begin with your own personal, spiritual and intellectual trajectory, from practising medicine to the study of women in the Qur'an.

AL: It all began for me as a spiritual quest rather than a search for women's rights. I was 'Westernized' so to speak, in that, for me, Islam was merely a religious tradition that I viewed as very discriminatory regarding women. When I was young, I wanted to change things, but from a perspective that was inculcated in me through school and university, which was very Westernized. But there came a time when I started to rediscover my faith and asked myself whether it really was incompatible with my belief in women's rights.

This is the classic question – and it could have created a real problem for me regarding my relationship with God, with myself, and my faith. That is when I decided to act. I thought: I am an educated woman, a physician, I can read in several languages – Arabic and French among them – and religious knowledge should not be the monopoly of the scholars. As a Muslim woman, I told myself, I have the right to see what the textual sources really say about me as a woman. I wanted to find out for myself.

---

7 Gray, 2013, p. 161. Gray includes an informative discussion of the council's mission and Abbadi's reformist approach (pp. 161–167). There is also a brief account in Tripp, 2019, pp. 166–167.

That was the starting point, and it has remained a daily process of discovery for twenty years. I came to realize that throughout the centuries we have been fed lies about the status of women in Islam. I believe that Islam was pioneering in giving women rights, and I am saying this as a twenty-first-century woman. This is not an apologetic discourse, and I don't wish to preach; I say this because I am convinced of this fact; it is what I believe. There are plenty of things to be found in the Qur'an and the Prophet's Sunna that – if we know how to read, reinterpret and recontextualize them – we can say constitute an avant-garde discourse. This discourse is universal in its principles but not in its interpretation, which changes depending on the context.

ZMH: Was there any particular experience or event that triggered or incited this transition, your change of perspective?

AL: Yes, of course. It was during the 1990–91 Gulf War. I felt a sense of betrayal by the West – it was not so much a break but a re-evaluation and recalibration of my relationship with myself and the West. I began to ask myself what part of my identity was so offended or alienated by what I saw as an act of Western aggression. Well, surely the answer was that it was the Muslim side that was hidden up to that point. I should confess, this was the beginning of my personal struggles with my identity. This was when I began to rediscover my faith.

ZMH: For me too, the first Gulf War was a turning point; I was so angry with what was happening then, the double standards and injustice of it all; it's interesting that we felt the same. Was it then, I mean when you began to reclaim your faith, that you took up wearing hijab?

AL: No, that came much later.

ZMH: I am actually curious to know why you did that – as a marker of your new identity or as an Islamic obligation? How does it relate to your emancipatory reading of the Qur'an?

AL: My answer may astonish you. I am *against* hijab; it is oppressive to women. I consider it an absolute anathema to female liberation. It is not hijab but *khimar* [headcover][8] that I choose to wear. For me the *khimar* is a spiritual conception of my belonging to Islam and responds to a Qur'anic *recommendation*, not an obligation. I don't find it to be a religious priority. I want to write an article about the distinction between these two. The

---

8 The word *khimar* comes from the root *khamara*, meaning 'to cover'. The term refers to a piece of cloth which is used by a woman to cover her head.

Qur'anic concept of covering has nothing to do with hijab. When the Qur'an speaks of the ethical conduct of women, it speaks of *khimar* – as in 24:31 when it says that women should draw their cloaks (*khumurihina*) over their bosoms.[9] You know Fatima Mernissi was the first to write about this matter, but she never went into details in this sense.[10]

In Qur'anic terminology *hijab* means to separate, to hide, to respect the private space. The term itself appears in the Qur'an seven times and always in the sense of a barrier – its root word in Arabic is *hajaba*, meaning to hide, to veil; nowhere does it refer to women's dress or the covering of hair.[11] The verse that has been used as an argument for women's seclusion is 33:53, which states: 'O believers do not enter the dwellings of the prophet unless you are invited ... When you ask the Prophet's wives for something, do it from behind a curtain (hijab).' This verse is about the proper conduct with the Prophet's household, to meet a politico-cultural necessity of that period; it was needed to preserve the privacy of the Prophet and his private life. In any case, it does not correspond to a model of clothing or a particular dress code. The spirit of this prescription was mainly to educate the Arabs of the time to respect people's privacy and to introduce them to good manners.

We know from the Qur'anic commentaries that this verse was revealed at the Prophet's wedding with Zaynab Bint Jahsh; on this occasion he invited a large number of people for a festive meal organized in his small house. After the meal, three men remained talking to each other late into the evening, while only the Prophet and his bride remained in the room. The Prophet, known for his courtesy, could not ask them to leave and found himself extremely embarrassed. The revelation of this verse was in response to this situation. It also definitely allowed the Prophet's wives to attain the special status of 'Mother of Believers' and to be respected and honoured by all members of the community.[12]

My point in engaging with the notion of *khimar* is to evoke modesty and decency in manners and behaviour, both internal and external. What is important is that we must correct this conceptual error: the covering of the head or any form of modest dress should not be called *hijab* but *khimar*, as it is called in the Qur'an. This semantic slip has caused women to be secluded;

9 For this verse and *khimar*, see Nasr, 2015, pp. 875–876.
10 She is referring to Mernissi, 1987.
11 These verses are: *al-Ar'af*, 7:46, *al-Isra'*, 17:45, *Maryam*, 19:17, *Sad*, 38:32, *Fussilat*, 41:5, *al-Shura*, 42:51, *al-Ahzab*, 33:53.
12 For the occasion of the revelation of the verse, see Nasr, 2015, p. 1035.

it is symbolic but very important, as it runs against the Qur'anic concept of modesty and dress for women. Therefore, I reject the Arabic term 'hijab' and I refuse to use it in English or French. When Westerners say a veiled woman is an oppressed woman, I respond by saying. 'Yes, she is oppressed when she is "veiled" or secluded.' And when Muslims say 'hijab' is important, I say, 'Yes, it's an important tool for keeping women in seclusion.'

What is certain is that the so-called 'hijab verses' are among those Qur'anic verses that have to do with interactions and moral issues. I believe that they were intentionally left open, not at all rigid, in order to allow women and men of every society to interpret them as they wish. In every context there is a different notion of modesty; in every socio-historical context, human beings have dressed differently.

Now, going back to your question, I adopted this *khimar* a long time after those personal experiences. It was not really an identity crisis, but after I had fully imbibed this new Qur'anic vision, I thought to myself, 'I have the right to choose!' It came to me as an act of liberation, and I find no contradiction between being liberated and wearing the headscarf.

This whole debate is false from the start, because we haven't chosen the true meaning of the Qur'anic concept to build it on. That is what I am trying to tell all the women I meet, that they are not wearing a hijab, but rather the *khimar*, so at least be aware of what you are wearing. Because if hijab is what you are wearing, then you should not be out in public at all. And this is the tragedy of our society; we carry a message and concept that we are not even aware of, that are totally false, whose meanings are not what we think they are, but which we still claim. This is why the debate is wrong from the outset.

The fact is that in the Islamic legal tradition the concept of hijab in the Qur'an was distorted and misinterpreted in such a way as to give rise to the concept of harems, and then served to exclude women from society. But that is a total distortion of the original meaning. I really believe that the existing discourse on women is a diversion, somehow a convenient subject for some of our ulema today to focus on, rather than on their indigenous autocracies and deviations from Islam's discourse.

I did not understand then why Asma was so much invested in using the term *khimar* instead of hijab, but I decided to let it go and to turn the conversation to Islam and feminism, which was a contentious issue at the time in Morocco. But my question, or the way I framed it, provoked another strong reaction.

ZMH: Asma, you have no qualms with calling yourself a feminist; it is also evident in your approach to the Qur'an and in your addressing women's rights from an Islamic perspective. This is something that is seen by many as a contradiction in terms. How do you define your feminism?

AL: Ziba, I accept this question because it comes from you. I had an experience with Canadian feminists. The first time they engaged with me, their first question was: 'What is feminism for you and what is equality for you?' They asked me this question because I came from the South, from a Muslim country, and given that, they supposed that for me equality is to be in the kitchen where I belong, serving my husband! I accept the question coming from you, Ziba, but not when it comes from Western journalists and the like. I tell them that if I were an American or a European or without a *khimar*, you would not have asked this question at all. They ask me this question to ascertain if it is really their kind of feminism and their kind of equality. There are some racist feminists out there.

ZMH: But Asma, we do need to talk about what feminism means to us; there are many feminisms . . .

AL: Yes, for me generally and roughly, whenever there is discrimination against women and there are women speaking up and struggling against it, it is feminism, period; I do not add any adjective. I believe that feminism has existed since the dawn of humanity: Eve was the first feminist. The term itself saw the light in a certain Western context, and was consequently given a specific definition; but the question for me is: 'What about the feminism before Western feminism, what should we call that?' For me, it's a term that transcends the history of the Western context. I should admit that it is this very Western history that gave it its language, its claims and its validity as a concept. But I believe that women's struggle throughout history should not be denigrated and scorned because they were not born into this Western context. Nowadays, when I refer to myself as a Muslim feminist, I say it is because I live in an Islamic context, speaking from values that are Islamic, and I do not see any contradiction in this whatsoever.

Therefore, I claim both positions without any hesitation. I have been a feminist my entire life and I want to remain a feminist. But I do take offence with the attitudes of those Western feminists who are ethnocentric and think that feminism is their private property, and I have a problem with Muslim women who reject feminism as a Western construct. I think we should not waste our time in such a sterile debate; if taken as universal values, both concepts are quite clear. I believe that all women should rally toward this cause; despite our specific contexts, backgrounds and discrimination, we share a common denominator that we should work from.

ZMH: I agree with you; but at the same time, words have histories and also have a different baggage and impact for different people. There are many Muslims who say that we must put feminism aside because it has been so much implicated with colonialism and Western ethnocentrism.

AL: It's like with medicine, have you ever heard of someone who says that I will not be using this cure for such-and-such an ailment because Westerners have discovered it? I am a doctor, and we use drugs manufactured in the West daily, because today wealth and technology and scientific discovery are in the hands of the West. Should I avoid these drugs because the geostrategic and political environment they were made in are hostile to Muslims? That is ridiculous! We should get over this. You know, the more you debate a subject and the more you use a word, the less dramatic it becomes. Even if one opposes a particular term, its recurring usage frees it of its controversial nature and connotations.

When I was doing field research in Morocco in the late 1980s there was no talk of 'Islamic feminism' – the concept was not yet born. The frame of reference for all the women's groups I encountered was feminism and human rights, and all centred on reforms of the family law code – *Moudawana*. At the time I shared the same perspective: it was during my stay there, while befriending women's rights activists and being mentored by Fatima Mernissi, that I became a feminist. When I returned in 2006, the politics of women's rights had been transformed: the *Moudawana* had been reformed, and there were now women and organizations that argued for women's rights from within an Islamic framework.[13] These women were mostly from the lower-middle classes; some were part of political Islamic organizations, but many others were independent. The veteran Moroccan feminists whom I knew from before were suspicious of this emerging discourse, seeing it as another Islamist ploy to subvert the hard-won gains of the feminist movement. To them, Asma Lamrabet was a puzzle, an upper-class feminist who identified with the cause of 'Islamic feminism', which for many Moroccan activists was a contradiction in terms. Asma's appointment as director of the centre for women's studies in a religious

---

13 On the politics of women's rights in Morocco, and the tension and evolving relationship between feminism and Islam, see Salime, 2011; Gray, 2013; Tripp, 2019.

institution made her discourse even more of an enigma.[14] I was curious to know Asma's own take on her situation.

ZMH: In February 2010, you became director of the first centre for women's studies ever established in Morocco in a religious organization, Rabita. How did this come about?

AL: It all started with my book about the Prophet's wife Aisha, who for me was the first model of Muslim feminism. I found her way of being in seventh-century Arabia very avant-garde. She had her room open onto the Prophet's mosque, and pupils came to her while she supposedly should have remained behind her hijab. The so-called hijab verse did not prevent her from getting involved in the politics of her time, and waging a battle on Imam Ali; even though this proved to be unwise, she still performed a political act. Aisha narrated approximately two thousand Hadith, and, as the Prophet said, 'Take half your knowledge from her.' Her relationship with the Prophet was extraordinary. Even her alleged child-marriage is now being questioned by many historians and thinkers; she apparently didn't get married at the age of nine, as people have said, but at the age of eighteen. It is important to stress that.

I wrote a book about all that and I called it *Aïcha, épouse du prophète ou l'islam au feminine (Aisha: The Prophet's Wife or Feminine Islam)*[15] because, in my opinion, Aisha wasn't very much known as the feminine incarnation of Islam; we only cite her as a narrator of Hadith, unaware of the crucial role she played. In 2006 the Cultural Centre of Mexico organized a meeting to discuss the book and invited Dr Abbadi to introduce it, since he had read it, and so he did, and that is how our relationship began. We stayed in touch and when I finished writing *The Qur'an and Women* I passed it to him to read and comment; I acknowledged his editorial assistance in the book. When we started GIERFI[16] [in 2008], I asked him to give a talk in his capacity as a religious scholar, an '*alim*, since his presence is very symbolic. At that time, there was not much about Islamic feminism, there were no Francophone publications or organizations. Abbadi was very happy about this organization and I remember that he said we should hold our first

---

14 Doris Gray gives an incisive analysis of Asma's position, and how she was viewed; Gray, 2013, pp. 151–161.

15 Lamrabet, 2003.

16 GIERFI (Le Groupe International d'Etude et de Réflexion sur la Femme en Islam); see Gray, 2013, pp. 151–155.

meeting in Rabita – you know it was a scoop, a feminist organization hold-ing a meeting in Rabita; it was 2009, the event was in all the media – the Francophone media – it was like a coalition between feminist and orthodox and official Islam. In Morocco, everybody was talking about Islamic femi-nism, which was new in the French context; and it was then that Moroccan feminists began the war against me, because of GIERFI, and my working with the Rabita.

After the event Dr Abbadi requested that we officially form a partner-ship with the Rabita Mohammedia des Oulémas, and told me about creat-ing a centre for women's studies in Rabita, asking me to be its director. I began in February 2010.

ZMH: Do you personally see any conflict in your public persona as a feminist and working with a religious institution like Rabita? I ask this because in Morocco, like many other Muslim countries, a large majority of feminists and women's rights activists choose to keep their distance from religion; for them religion is a matter of the private rather than the public realm. They say: 'We are all Muslims and entitled to our beliefs, but when we come to the realm of law and society, we put our religion aside.'

AL: They are out of touch with the reality on the ground. They are a small portion of Moroccan society, the bourgeois, well off and 'cultured' elite centred in Rabat. Islam is inescapable for the masses in both the private and the public realms. Islam cannot be ignored, it is integrated into the histori-cal DNA of this nation, we cannot go forward and evolve if Islamic concepts do not evolve with us. You see, there are secular values that I think are not entirely incompatible with Islam; sometimes adopting a secular approach can be a way of protecting religion. The fact is that family laws have always pertained to the domain of religion. Society cannot advance if these laws do not evolve and if women are not aware; and when one engages in religious discourse, it has a greater impact and it reaches the heart. Religion and spirituality after all are very important. I believe that even in Western socie-ties today we are witnessing a revival of spirituality, but it is even more conspicuous in Muslim countries. Orthodox Islamic discourse is not work-ing any more, neither with the youth nor with adults. Religion must be put in contemporary terms, and then it can change the mentalities of women, as well as those of men.

But we must not be deluded into thinking that all problems will be magically resolved with our reading of the Qur'an through a feminine lens; it is part of our equation, not all of it. Our real problem is the lack of democracy; without democracy and political liberty, we cannot achieve anything. Part of our renewed understanding of Islam is to understand that Islam requires that we live in a country where justice, equality and rights exist. It is worth noting that the issue of women in Islam is now exploited for political ends. Women are granted rights so that the international community, when they look, will be distracted by those rights and forget that general and basic political rights are still missing. I can't see how I can have my rights as a woman when my basic political rights are not secured; the two must come together and women must be aware of this dimension and claim the whole range of rights, political and otherwise.

ZMH: I agree that in countries like ours, the route to women's rights, human rights and democracy inevitably goes through the door of Islam. But the problem is the ways in which both despotism and patriarchy are being justified and sanctified in the name of Islam; in many ways, they constitute each other. Without a democratic political structure and freedom of expression, how can we argue for an egalitarian, pluralistic and liberal understanding of our religion? How can we aspire to a just and democratic society without equality for women?

AL: Yes, we must not forget that interpretations that are injurious to women all stemmed from despotic contexts. They came into being as a result of despotism and the lack of liberty. The discourse about women should take place in a liberal environment, otherwise it's completely worthless.

Musawah had just started our first research project, to critically engage with *qiwamah* and *wilayah*, two concepts rooted in the Qur'an, which, as interpreted and constructed by Muslim jurists, placed women under male authority. I wanted to know about Asma's reading of the Qur'anic verse 4:34 that is used as a justification for male authority, and her approach to the Qur'an more generally.

ZMH: We talked about how the Qur'anic concept of hijab was distorted to justify women's seclusion and keeping them out of the public sphere. Can we now turn to verse 4:34 and the concept of *ta'a* or *tamkin*, which, as defined in *fiqh*, requires a woman to obey and submit to her husband in marriage? Is this a Qur'anic concept?

AL: I am astonished that whenever we want to talk about the exemplary Muslim woman, then the concept of women's duty of obedience, *ta'a*, is invoked. It is not a Qur'anic concept; it comes from some Hadith, but they should be understood within their context. Verse 4:34 is not about women's obedience, but marital conflict and its resolution, and it must be read contextually. It has nothing to do with the kind of obedience prevalent in the orthodox discourse of Islam. That sort of obedience does not exist in the Qur'an. Jurists interpreted the term *qanitat* in the verse as women's obedience, but the *qanit* is the one who is faithful to God and to no one else. In the Qur'an, Mary is depicted as *qanita*, yet there is no evidence that she was married. I challenge anyone to find a verse that enjoins obedience as a marital obligation for women.

Verse 4:34 is particular and peculiar; it needs to be carefully contextualized and approached within the basic structure of the Qur'an. In my analysis of the Qur'an, there are three types of verses that need to be distinguished. The first comprises those with universal aims. These verses, which make up over ninety per cent of the Qur'an, advocate values such as justice, equality, fairness and respect for human dignity. These verses constitute the basis of the Qur'anic message and address both men and women.

The second category are verses that are the product of a special set of circumstances, and their application is confined to the time of the revelation. They are now outdated and no longer accepted; for example, those about slavery and certain corporal punishments (e.g., *hudud* such as the severing of limbs). These verses are linked to a given historical period and context, i.e. seventh-century Arabia.

The third category of verses are specific, but nonetheless contain universal principles. I put verse 4:34 in this category; it deals with a family matter in a manner consistent with the patriarchal expectations and structures of seventh-century Arabia. But it contains a universal principle that is applicable to our time – though it needs reinterpretation in the current context.

ZMH: How should we read verse 4:34 in our context? And how do you understand the concept of *qiwamah* in the verse? Is it universal or specific?

AL: The concept of *qiwamah* is derived from the Qur'anic term *qawwamun* or *qiwwamun* and is not authoritarian. Apart from verse 4:34, this term appears in only two other verses. In verse 4:135 *qawwamin al-bilqisti* (stand firmly for justice), and in verse 5:8 as *qawwamin lillahi shuhada bilqisti* (stand firmly for Allah, as witness to fair dealing). In these two verses the concept of *qiwamah* is general (*'am*) and applies equally to both men and women. They both have to take charge and be honest and just in the handling of their socio-political affairs. But when verse 4:34 says 'men are *qawwamun* of women', *qiwamah* is specific (*khass*) to the family unit. Why? Well the verse explains it – if I can reduce it to the most basic and general terms – because, at a certain stage of their marital life, women go through a period of vulnerability, they bear children, give birth, they breastfeed. It would be unfair to ask or expect women to be a hundred per cent active or productive in other spheres, some take up to two years of maternity leave to perform their new responsibilities. The notion of family does fluctuate depending on societal context, but its core – a man and woman who get together to have offspring – remains the same. And this is the context in which marital *qiwamah* comes into play. It is to be responsible and accountable; *qiwamah* here is to step up and to take care of one's wife while she is in a vulnerable state, and should imperatively be tied to the other verses about marriage. In verse 4:34 God is describing a fact peculiar to the family unit, while in 4:135 and 5:8 He commands men and women alike to engage in the socio-political struggle for equity and fairness.

We can't just pick verses such as verse 4:34 that happen to be specific (*khass*), take them out of their context, and claim that they are in favour or against women. We need to conduct a holistic reading of the Qur'an; other verses are just as important, such as those on *khilafa* (human as vicegerent of God on Earth) and *wilaya* (mutual support), and we must read them with fresh eyes. These verses are central to gender equality, and for me crucial to our understanding of *qiwamah*. God has put us in charge of this wealth of creation and made us responsible for its protection (verse 2:30); this was not only bestowed upon men, it has been given to both sexes, and it cannot be achieved without the involvement of both.

While working on this concept, I realized that it has not been fully developed and studied. We forgot that humans are God's *khilafa* (vicegerent) on Earth – a responsibility shared between men and women to protect and take care of the Earth and of creation – and instead we focused our attention on the hallowed political institution of Caliphate. The verse on *wilaya* (9:71) couldn't be clearer; believing women and men are partners and allies, they mutually protect each other. Protection here is in the sense of the Prophetic Hadith that states that believers are in solidarity like the different organs of the body; if one of them falls ill, the whole body sympathizes actively through fever and sleeplessness. Therefore, both sexes reinforce and support one another. The verse begins with the qualities of these believers: they enjoin what is good and forbid what is wrong. It then goes on to speak about ritual worship. So, socio-political activity is given priority here over devotional practice. Another reading in accordance with our context would be that of egalitarian citizenship.

ZMH: It's amazing how *qiwamah* has been understood in isolation and interpreted in such a patriarchal way that it became the lynchpin of patriarchy in Muslim contexts. In fact, verse 4:34 is the only one known by most Muslims when it comes to marriage, and then in total isolation from other Qur'anic verses.

AL: Yes, this is why it is important to read them with fresh eyes; only then will we be able to appreciate the extent to which the spiritual message of Islam on gender is one in which equality and justice are inseparable. I charted all the verses in the Qur'an that have to do with marriage and I found so many magnificent Qur'anic concepts such as *sakina* (serenity), *mawada wa rahma* (love and compassion), *al-ma'ruf* (that which is commonly known to be right) and *al-fadl* (abundance), meaning the rich moments that you have shared. The Qur'an also states that men are garments (*libas*) for women, and vice versa. It is more than even intimacy, it is like having a second skin.[17]

The patriarchal interpretation of *qiwamah* is built on the claim, by ulema, of the superiority of the man over the woman. Some jurists assert that the man loses this degree once he is no longer capable of economically supporting his family, and the woman may acquire it if she's providing the financial maintenance. Therefore, it is a flexible concept, not a biological predisposition that God has bestowed upon men relative to women. I could cite other verses about gender equality, such that, once they are considered, the much-hyped notion of *qiwamah* becomes trivial and unimportant. It should not be given such importance; it must be given its due place and interpreted in the light of other more important verses.

There is another thing that should be considered, and something that I intend to do, which is to examine all those verses that are addressed to men. People tend to forget that the Qur'an was revealed in an extremely patriarchal Arab context, the remnants of which we are still witnessing and experiencing to this day. Given this particular backdrop, the Qur'an had to address men initially. There is a verse (65:1) addressing men on the issue of divorce, that says, 'Do not drive them out of *their* homes (*buyutuhina*).' It didn't say *your* homes. The Qur'an is referring to the woman's home and recognizes that the post-marital home belongs to the woman. It would be interesting to go over the verses that address men specifically and chastise them, such as when the Qur'an tells men to treat women with compassion

---

17 *Sakina* (al-A'raf. 7:189); *mawada wa rahma* (al-Rum, 30:21); *al-ma'ruf* (al-Baqarah, 2:229); *al-fadl* (al-Baqarah, 2:237); *libas* (al-Baqarah, 2:187).

(*ihsan*), or to remember, in relations between themselves and their wives, to behave according to *ma'ruf* (that which is commonly known to be right) (2:229). *Ma'ruf* is a big concept in the Qur'an that captures the *zeitgeist* and adjusts to what society deems best for a particular society in a particular time and context. For example, a concept like human rights can be said to be part of the *ma'ruf* now, because most people see it as an important issue in our time. The very fact that the revelation was sent down to the specific environment of seventh-century Arabia, predominantly addressing men, telling them to act within the boundaries of *ma'ruf*, on its own constitutes a significant argument for gender equality.

ZMH: But the question is whether the concept of equality as we understand it today is the same as that which you find in the Qur'an.

AL: I see what you mean. Is the equality, as we understand it in the twenty-first century, the same as the one described in the Qur'an? Of course not! Equality is in fact a shifting concept, and this is true of practically all human concepts. But I believe that the Qur'an gives latitude and flexibility. And that is exactly why we say that the Qur'anic values are universal. They are constructed in such a way as to enable and empower individuals like me to use those values. There are verses in the Qur'an that clearly speak of women's equal share in public life. For instance, verse 9:71: 'The believing men and believing women are allies of one another. They enjoin what is right and forbid what is wrong and establish prayer and give *zakat* and obey Allah and His Messenger.' We also have verse 10:14 on humans as God's vicegerent (*khalifa*) on Earth, which is both a male and female prerogative; verse 7:189 and verse 33:35, where God speaks on all aspects of equality. These verses enjoin what is right and forbid what is wrong and establish prayer and giving *zakat* and obedience to Allah and His Messenger; however, they are interpreted as referring only to spiritual equality, not other aspects. Now, for our *fuqaha*, men and women are equal spiritually but not in their rights and responsibilities. This doesn't make sense; how can it be that I, as a woman, am only equal to man spiritually, but not otherwise? How do we gain access to paradise? Surely not only through our observance of ritual obligation; there is also our participation with good deeds in the human society, attained only in the presence of certain rights. Clearly the interpretations deviated and didn't represent the real spirit of the Qur'an.

Of course, equality in the Qur'an is not like the equality proclaimed in international conferences and treaties. But the Qur'an gives us a framework. This is the crucial role that we Muslims must play: to interpret the text and perform *ijtihad* according to the context, otherwise we will not be able to develop this spiritual message of Islam. I do believe that its universal values converge with the principles of those treaties. The more I read the Qur'an, the more I feel that justice rests at its core. The human (*insan*) is honoured throughout the text without any discrimination of gender, race, ethnicity or religion. Over ninety per cent of the Qur'an refers to the human, the *insan*, laying the path for proper actions or behaviour. This is such a central issue that it demands that we reflect upon the notion of the *insan*, because the Qur'an does not consider the idea of the status of man or the status of woman, that is a relatively new concept. Rather, men and women are referred to as *insan*, or as members of a collective.

The Qur'an says: 'The most honoured of you in God's eyes is the one with most *taqwa*' (verse 49:13); the ulema interpret *taqwa* as the fear of God, and confine it to ritual practice. But it is something much deeper: it is knowledge, faith and perseverance. There is an important account of when Omar [the second Caliph] approaches a great scholar and asks, 'What is *taqwa*?' The scholar responds, 'Omar, if you were walking on a road sown with thorns, what would you do?' Omar says that he would lift his garment, be watchful and struggle (*ijtihada*) to avoid its spikes. The scholar says, 'Well, that is *taqwa*.' Therefore, *taqwa* is *ijtihad*, life is perseverance, and struggle (*jihad*). That is how I understand *taqwa*: for me it means moral integrity and honesty in one's behaviour. It is not someone who is praying all the time and spending his day waiting for the call to prayer. That too is good, but it is not enough.

In early December 2010 I went to Rabat for another conference; I stayed a few days more to explore the possibility of holding Musawah's first workshop on *qiwamah* and *wilayah* in Rabat. But we could not find a Moroccan women's group willing to host such a meeting; they were hesitant and above all suspicious of 'Islamic feminism'. I also met with Asma, and invited her to write a background paper for our project.

On the last day of my stay, Doris Gray called me to say that Fatima Mernissi wanted to see me. I had lost touch with her, but I knew she was no longer working on women's issues. I went to see her at home, taking a selection of Musawah's publications with me. She was still full of energy and plans, connecting people, wanting me to do collaborative work in Morocco on Islam and women, telling me that Musawah must come to Morocco. When I told her about the reluctance of women's groups to host a meeting with us, she said, 'Go and talk to Asma Lamrabet – she is incredible, read her books.' I said, 'I know her and her books, and she is going to write a paper for our Musawah project; she is one of your fans!' Mernissi asked me to call her right there, which I did. This is how they first met, which led to a deep friendship.

The next time I was in Rabat, they were working together; they had formed a study group in which writers, researchers and intellectuals with different orientations met on a monthly basis to share their work. It was called *Vivre Ensemble* (Living Together), and in November 2013 Zainah and I were invited to talk about our work in Musawah. By then, Lamrabet had already participated in our meetings, as well as contributing a background paper for our project.

We were in Rabat for a consultative meeting that Musawah and the Rabita Centre for Women's Studies had co-organized. The idea behind this meeting was for us to present our findings on the knowledge-building initiative on *qiwamah* and *wilayah*, and to begin a constructive dialogue with religious scholars. But it did not happen. Only two religious scholars from Rabita joined the meeting. Those we had approached from Al-Azhar in Egypt wanted a five-star hotel and business-class air travel, which we could not afford and was against our principles; we ended up with a Shaykh recommended by Egyptian friends who had heard him on TV and thought he sounded progressive. He came to the opening session in the morning, but after he realized that his presentation was scheduled for the second day he complained and disappeared for the whole day: we learned that he had gone shopping for his wife! He reappeared on the second day to present his paper, which was basically an attack on Musawah; he told us in a loud voice that we were not qualified to talk about Islam, and if we wanted to understand Shari'a concepts we should have come to Al-Azhar ... When he had finished, he walked over to where Zainah and I were sitting, slammed his paper down on the table in front us, and walked out of the room. I said, 'This was *qiwamah* performed!'

Everyone in the room was shocked, and our Egyptian friends felt angry and ashamed. Mr Abbadi said some conciliatory words. This was the first and last meeting that we organized with Rabita's Centre for Women's Studies. But the meeting was fruitful in the sense that it led to the publication of a book in Arabic based on the proceedings,[18] including translations of papers presented by Musawah, as well as to a survey of public attitudes and perceptions of *qiwamah* and *wilayah*.[19]

---

18 Al-Sharqawi and Boucheri, 2014.
19 This project, partially funded by UN Women, was led by Aicha Al-Hajjami and Malika Baradi.

EVOLVING RELATIONSHIP WITH
HIJAB, KHIMAR AND RABITA

I went to Rabat again in mid-November 2014, this time with Zainah, to attend an international symposium convened by Rabita on "Women in Monotheistic Religion". By now Asma Lamrabet had become even more of a public figure; her talks were often controversial, and covered in the Moroccan press – the latest being about hijab and the mixing of genders in mosques. After the conference, I stayed a few days longer to record anther conversation with Asma at her home on 16 November 2014. This time we talked about her changed position on hijab and her difficult relationship with the ulema in Rabita.

ZMH: When we talked in 2010, you wanted to write an article about the difference between 'hijab' and *khimar*. I wonder whether you did that article. I also want to get some clarification on what you mean by *khimar*.

AL: Yes, it's now available in English, on my website, it is called: "How does the Qur'an address the issue of Muslim Women's Veil or 'Hijab'."[20] I have another one in which I criticize the colonial vision of hijab as well as the traditional vision in Islam, and argue for a 'decolonial vision'. There I am equally critical of both sides, of the whole focus on hijab, the focus on control over woman's body that these two visions have in common.[21]

The term *khimar* in the Qur'an means head covering. As I say in the first article, if there is a term referring to this supposed outfit for women, it is *khimar*, and the Qur'an is explicit about it. If you read the *tafasir* (exegesis) you see that men also wear *khimar*, cover their heads; several Hadith mention that men come with this *khimar*. It is not only for women but also for men.

But for me, *khimar* is not important, it is not the point. For me, the point is that the Qur'an's injunction is about inner and outer modesty and decent manner in behaviour. There is a verse that summarizes what God wants: *'wa libas al taqwa khair'* ('the best dress is that of *taqwa*,' God-consciousness, righteousness);[22] this sums up what Allah wants from us on this issue. The

---

20 http://www.asma-lamrabet.com/articles/how-does-the-qur-an-address-the-issue-of-muslim-woman-s-veil-or-hijab

21 http://www.asma-lamrabet.com/articles/muslim-women-s-veil-or-hijab-between-a-colonial-ideology-and-a-traditionalist-islamic-ideology-a-decolonial-vision/

22 Qur'an, *al-A'raf*, 7:26.

debate over hijab and *khimar* is outdated; for me this verse is enough; and it is not an obligation at all – and my criticism is of this political vision of Islam.

I tell you in confidence that I was manipulated as well. Now I take responsibility for wearing it. I cover my hair in solidarity, because of Islamophobia, but not as identity for a Muslim woman. It is not about spirituality or conviction; I no longer have that conviction at all. This has been the case for the past three years; I am now convinced that it was manipulation from the beginning. When you read the books of *tafasir*, hijab is about separation; there are one or two Hadith about women with *khimar*, but not saying that you have to put on *khimar*. There is no discussion, no debate about hijab meaning covering. With colonialization and the discourse of the Muslim Brotherhood, we find that we have to wear 'hijab'; why, because the visibility of women with head covering is the visibility of Islam; so, if women are wearing hijab, Islam is visibly growing. I now think political Islam has taken advantage of our vulnerability as women.

The majority of the ulema also say this so-called 'hijab' for women is an obligation. I was not convinced that it was an obligation, but when I heard it from the ulema – and in the Arab world we accept whatever they say as sacred – I thought, 'they know better than me,' but when I read the verses, I said 'it is not hijab but *khimar*, and perhaps God asked me to wear that, so I do it for God.' This was my argument: 'I am doing it for God, I mean, not doing it for men, so it is not submission, it is spirituality.' But I gradually realized that this argument was weak; inside me there was a voice saying, 'This is absurd. God is not waiting for me to wear *khimar*.'

ZMH: Of course! Why should God care about us covering our hair?

AL: I was horrified when I read the Hadith in which 'Omar ibn Khitab said that slave women are not allowed to wear the *khimar* to cover their head. This is discrimination based not on gender but on status. This is against the justice that makes me love the Qur'an and Allah. So, this is now my discourse about hijab. I said it first in public last year, and it was all over the press in Morocco: Asma Lamrabet says hijab is not an obligation, it is not a pillar of Islam.

I did it because I said to myself 'Asma, you are not a hypocrite.' I have never been a hypocrite, never. When I started wearing hijab I believed this was what God wanted from us women. I was convinced once, but no longer. I openly say that I don't believe in it, but I am wearing it. By doing this I believe I am giving women the choice, by freeing them from the sense of guilt inculcated in all of us. Because if this is said by a woman who doesn't wear it, she can be accused of being 'Westernized', not a real Muslim! But when I say it is not an obligation, not a pillar of Islam, yet I wear it – that has an impact. When I said all this in public in June [2013] in a university conference in Rabat, it caused an uproar. The day after, I was in all the papers, for one month I received daily insults on the web. They are still available on HESPRSS[23] – if you Google my name in Arabic, you can see them all.

This hijab remark, and another one when I said that men and women should not be segregated in mosques, made me famous – not my books! During a panel discussion at a big conference in Rabat I said that there is no gender segregation in Islam, that at the time of the Prophet, men and women prayed together in the same space. This appeared in *Quel Tel*,[24] and was then turned by the Salafis into: 'Asma Lamrabet wants to put a disco in the mosques.' This was put on posters all over Rabat. Rabita was in a big trouble, so Mr Abbadi wrote in my name – the *droit de réponse* – something to the effect that what I said about mixed prayers at time of the Prophet is true, it is in the Hadith. It is good to be part of Rabita – so they protect you as well!

ZMH: By the way, secular feminists have also been critical of your discourse; what is happening on that front?

AL: Since the big explosion over my position on hijab and mixed mosques, the secularists have begun reading my work. For the Islamists I have become enigmatic – they say, we don't know where Asma Lamrabet stands; but with the secularists and civil society activists, you can't imagine how much I am in demand; they all want me in their meetings. But I feel that there is an element of instrumentalization, and they want to use me and my discourse for political purposes against the Islamists, and that is not my aim, I have no interest in it. I just want a good society, justice in society, I don't want to be with either Islamists or secularists.

ZMH: But how can you avoid that? It's not in your hands, you have no control over it.

AL: By being what I am, an independent person; by speaking the truth to all of them. I have the same discourse, Ziba, I have the same discourse when I

23 The most popular online news website in Morocco, launched in 2007.
24 Moroccan French-language weekly magazine, known for liberal views and critique of Islamist ideology.

am with the ulema as when I am with the seculars. I don't change my discourse; of course, I use a different language ... but the meaning, the implications of my discourse, are the same. I do my best to be honest with myself; this is how I am dealing with it, but maybe it is not perfect.

ZMH: But Asma, what you are doing is very political, not in the sense of being part of a political party, but in its impact.

AL: Yes, yes, all we do is political, to struggle for justice in society is political, but it's not from one perspective or ideological position [whether Islamist or secularist].

ZMH: When we talked earlier, you had just started your cooperation with Rabita. And when the office of the Women's Centre was established, it was housed in a different place, but now it has just moved to this beautiful building that is Rabita's headquarters. What is it like working in a religious institution, what is your relationship with the ulema there?

AL: I have been working on a voluntary basis, and that was my condition from the outset. I have no relationship, apart from two or three directors who are open-minded, and came also to the seminar with Musawah [in 2013]. The Centre is separate, I do not see anyone else; I do not go to any of the meetings with the ulema; I go to my office two afternoons in the week and largely to do interviews and meet visitors. My link to Rabita is solely through Mr Abbadi, otherwise I am very much marginalized; they marginalize me. But for me, it is not a problem, I am not interested in getting involved.

The Arabic translation of *Le Coran et les femmes* was published in 2010, as the first output of the newly created Women's Centre in Rabita. But copies of the book never reached the bookshops in Morocco; they stayed at the Centre and were gifted to foreign visitors. Asma had told me that this was because of the fierce opposition of Rabita's ulema, who found that the book did not meet their 'scientific' criteria.

ZMH: By the way, did you ever find out why the Rabita Executive Committee banned distribution of the Arabic translation of *Le Coran et les femmes*? What were their objections?

AL: It was absurd, really nothing to do with the substance of my argument. Dr Abbadi recognized this; he had written a foreword to the book. He had a meeting with them [the Rabita ulema] and asked what the problem with book was; they said, we will send you all our explanations. They provided a list of twenty objections, two of which were valid, relating to historical matters, and the rest were grammatical errors by the translators! Mr Abbadi probed further, as he had read the manuscript for me to check the accuracy of theological terms, Hadith references, etc. Eventually, one of them said: 'This woman is a medical doctor, she is not an *'alimah* [female religious scholar], she is not trained in our courses of study; she is doing her own interpretation, and as ulema we do not want this.'

ZMH: This is the dilemma: if a woman is trained in a religious institution to become an *'alimah*, she won't be allowed to produce something like your book, because the whole structure and culture of learning there don't allow her to ask new questions, to think outside the box. Reformist and feminist scholarship in Islam, their logic and methodology, are not tolerated in centres of religious learning. It is a question of authority, who speaks for and on behalf of Islam.

AL: There is also the question of language. With my books in French, there is no problem, because they know they cannot be accessed by the majority; but when you write in Arabic, and from within the institution, this is really dangerous.

I have a story to tell you. Last June [2014], Abbadi organized an international colloquium on the Qur'an and World Vision – people were invited from the USA and Europe, and as well as the Rabita, ulema came from all over Morocco. He insisted that I present a paper about Qur'an and Women. I reluctantly accepted and prepared a paper in Arabic; I was not as 'subversive' as I am when I speak in academic conferences or secular spaces, not because I am not sure of my arguments but because I do not want to have conflict with the ulema. My paper basically was about the holistic vision of the Qur'an as egalitarian, that we don't have to reject equality between men and women, because the Qur'an is about universal equality; and in support I cited some verses.

I didn't go for the opening day, and I thought that, since it was an international meeting, only a select group of Rabita ulema – the broad-minded ones like those who came to the Musawah workshop – would attend. When I arrived for my panel on the second day, I saw all these traditional Moroccan *jalabah*-wearing Shaykhs. Only six or seven in the audience were 'international', the rest were from Morocco: Shaykhs of Casablanca, Agadir, Marrakech . . . and I was scared, not for myself, but because I thought that they would not understand, and I would put Dr Abbadi in a very bad position. So I called him and said that I didn't know that all these Moroccan ulema would be there, and that my discourse was not for them; it would be shocking for them. He said: 'It's okay' – you know how Abbadi is. 'Just be cautious, and please don't say everything in your paper' [her views on gender equality in the Qur'an]. I said, 'No, I shall do this presentation my way or I quit.' I asked whether he would take responsibility, and, he said, 'Yes, I will.'

We were six in the panel; the chairperson was a Tunisian man, the rest were women, one Egyptian, one from Sudan, two Moroccan *alimat* (female religious scholars) and myself. I was the last to present; I had fifteen minutes, and I read from my text, which was very clear. When the session ended, you know, Ziba, all the questions were for me, and all came from the ulema. Friends in the audience later told me that the atmosphere was quite tense while I was presenting. One of them said that the question and answer was like an inquisition; I also felt this, as if I was on trial accused of heresy.

Their questions were ironic, they wanted to humiliate me. The first who came to the microphone said in very elaborate Arabic, 'I am sensing the presence of *Shaytan* (Satan); this *Shaytan* wants us to be Westerners, wants us to destroy our tradition, our past, our golden age.' He didn't name me, but I knew it was for me, because the other presentations in the panel were classical – two Moroccan *alimat* talked about sky and heaven, that Islam gives honour to women and all is well. The last questioner said, 'Dr Asma Lamrabet, we respect you, but this is not your job; you are a physician. I am an *'alim*, what would you think if tomorrow I wrote a book about cancer? What is your answer for me? When you speak about equality, do we want in our society, Muslims, Moroccans to be homosexual?'

Just like that. You should have been there, Ziba, it was really hilarious! The chair was passing me notes in Arabic, 'Resist, be patient, this is an arrogant mentality, just be strong.' You know, these men don't have the courage to support us openly.

Then another *'alim* said, 'We are going to ask Mrs, no, Dr Lamrabet, who is talking about equality in the Qur'an, have you ever read the verse of *qiwamah* in the Qur'an? Do you know what *qiwamah* means? Maybe she is not aware of this verse in the Qur'an.' You know, the ulema by now were laughing – ha-ha-ha! – and he went on: 'I am sure you don't know what *qiwamah* is; that is why you are talking about equality.'

At that point Dr Abbadi was quite tense and asked for the session to come to an end, but I specifically asked for more time. I told myself, 'Asma, you have two choices. Either keep quiet, but then you are dead, you are not Asma Lamrabet. Or answer them.' He gave me five minutes; I answered and really gave all that I have in my heart. I said, 'Perhaps you respect me but I respect you more, because I recognize your work but you do not want to recognize mine. I will tell you why: because I know the reality of my context, but you are blind to it; you may know the text, but you do not know the context. You are not real ulema as the ulema were in the past; those ulema knew the text and context and they dealt with both. You may know all the verses; you memorize the Qur'an but you don't know the meaning of the Qur'an; you do not want to recognize that our society has changed, evolved. I will respond about *qiwamah*, perhaps we don't have the same interpretation, but listen to what the word means in the Qur'an for me.'

Then I went through the verse, word by word. '"Men are *qawwamun* over women" is not authority, it is responsibility; why? Listen to the rest of the verse, which says, "according to what God favoured some over others (*bima fadad-lahun ba'dahum*)"; there is no man and woman in that phrase. This whole sentence is about economic responsibility; the favour (*fadl*) in this verse goes to those who give from their wealth (*anfaqhu min amwallihim*). Do you think *fadl* here denotes the superiority of men over women? Are there any verses in the Qur'an that say men are superior to women? Okay, I am ignorant of the Qur'an, you are the scholars of the text, so please give me one verse that says that man is superior to woman. Just one. Please answer me.' I said, '*fadl* for me is in three concepts; the first is *taqwa*, God-Consciousness, as in "The best of you is the one with *taqwa*."[25] The second is *'ilm*, knowledge: "Are those who know and those who do not know equal?"[26] The third is good deeds: "Whoever does good, whether male or female."[27] This is action by men and women. Am I wrong? I want to learn from you; maybe I am wrong, just please correct me.'

One stood up and said, 'The Qur'an says *Laysa dhakara kal untha* (the male is not like female), and this verse says a man differs from a woman, so he is superior.'[28] I said, 'No, you are wrong, excuse me; maybe the other ulema can correct you. In this verse, it is the mother of Maryam who is

25 Al-Hujurat, 49:13.
26 Al-Zumar, 39:9.
27 Al-Nahl, 16:97.
28 Al-'Imran, 3:36.

speaking to God, complaining that her baby was a girl but she wanted a boy, because she wanted to give the baby to the temple. She was complaining to God, because the temple did not allow her to fulfill her vow.'

ZMH: That verse simply says man and woman are different. Funny, it is always this verse and verse 4:34 that are summoned in support of men's superiority.

AL: Yes, yes, I told them all this; I said, give me one single verse on male superiority. They did not say anything; they did not applaud me, nobody. When the session was over, the chair said, 'You are amazing.' I wanted to say 'Why didn't you say anything?' I couldn't, but he must have sensed it, because he continued, 'You know these are ulema; we can't talk with them.' The two women on the panel also said, '*Ustadha* (female teacher) ... you have been great.' I said, 'Why don't you speak? you are *alimat*, you have doctorates in *fiqh*, in Shari'a, why were you not with me?' Because they were afraid for their position as *alimat*.

ZMH: Yes, of course, they were working in a religious institution. But there is a lesson here for us. To be able to challenge, we first need to build our credentials, our power base, from outside these religious centres of learning; once you are inside these institutions there is no way you can oppose or have a voice. I learned that lesson during my research in Qom some time ago.

AL: A few in the audience approached me after the event to show their respect or support, but I wish they had been courageous enough to support me while I was being attacked in front of the crowd, rather than hiding and approaching me afterwards, on the sidelines of the event. I wanted to tell you this story, because it was a life-changing experience for me; it removed any fear I had of facing the ulema. I will never forget that day, it was a very good experience for me, but I was quite shaken by the event and I fell sick for two days.

ZMH: Asma, what gave you the courage to stand up to those ulema that day? I know too well that it is not easy!

AL: The strong conviction I have in my heart that God is not unfair; Allah is just. It was easy to do it at the moment, it was hard later. At that moment, I was sure that they were wrong, they were discriminating against women, but Allah gave me this power.

ZMH: They are afraid too, they speak from a place of fear.

AL: Yes, I felt this fear. They are not bad, they are very nice people when you speak to them. After all, most of them are fathers of daughters, they care, and their mutual concern is palpable in their conversations, but so is their sense of pride and ownership over the text. They see it as the only thing they have, it defines their identity, their authority, and it is sacred to them, and therefore they are afraid that my views will dismantle their sacred institution.

But their knowledge of the text is superficial. All their arguments come from weak or misinterpreted Hadith; this 'alim said that, that Shaykh said this, and the Prophet *sala wa salam* [peace be on him] said this in Hadith; they have locked the Qur'an in the closet and are relying on the *tafsir* (exegesis). When you have a holistic vision of the text and fully grasp its textual and contextual meanings, it is impossible to conclude that there is discrimination. I have been studying the Qur'an and *tafsir* for over twenty years, and I have not found anything in the Qur'an that strikes me as discriminatory. This is my deep conviction. I don't write about Islam out of professional or academic impulse but rather because of spirituality. It is what drives me and my work.

ZMH: What is this spirituality; can you describe it?

AL: It is the connection with Allah, with the ethics of life. A commitment to do your best, to be good for all humanity. For me, that is spirituality, and central to it is justice. The more I read the Qur'an, the more I feel that justice rests at the core of the Qur'an. The human (*insan*) is sacred throughout the text, without any discrimination by gender, race and ethnicity, or religion. I am at a phase of my life when, for me, the human is sacred and this is the ethic of spirituality. We all have to go back to this ethic instead of sticking to dogmatic or superficial readings; and return to the basic essential which is the ethic of spirituality.

Ninety per cent of the Qur'an refers to the human being, laying the path for proper actions or behaviour. It gives a great deal of importance to other concepts that are interconnected with the human, such as reason ('aql). The human and reason are treated equally: if you do not have 'aql you are not *insan*. Yet, what is incredible is that when you read the *tafsir* or Hadith literature you have twenty or more chapters about marriage (*nikah*), prayer (*salat*), ablutions (*wadu*), but none whatsoever about reason, nor justice ('adl) nor knowledge ('ilm). What is the human being without justice and reason?

When the ulema study and memorize the Qur'an, they study these kinds of materials, void of any discussion of justice or reason, and I don't know why. Doesn't it seem political? You are being diverted from using your reason, against engaging with justice, and we are simply guided to perform the ulema's orders, something that the political authorities approve.

ZMH: These are the questions that I am asking in my own work. As you say, the problem is not with the text but the context, and the ways in which the text is used to sustain authoritarian and patriarchal structures. But in Muslim countries the political system does not allow us to talk about these issues in an open way and bring them into public space. For now, all those who are willing to do so are either silenced in their own countries or cast aside as irrelevant.

AL: This is my problem. Inside this institution, my limits are political limits; I am gradually hitting a wall; because I ask, Why is there no justice? Why is there discrimination? Why are they not using their reason ('aql)? Why, Why? We are not only working for women.

ZMH: Yes, it all comes down to politics and power; the production of knowledge is closely linked to the exercise of power. This is where, I believe, a feminist approach can be helpful, because we need to question this dynamic; it is impossible to have an egalitarian understanding of the Qur'an without challenging political authority. It is a Catch-22. We need to democratize the production of religious knowledge, which is not possible without a democratic political system and an open society, which is not going to happen in our generation.

AL: Sure, it won't be achieved in our lifetime, but it's our obligation to lay the groundwork for future generations.

AN UPDATE

In September 2015, Musawah held a board meeting in Rabat, where we had applied for permission to register as an international NGO. We were all optimistic, and we began planning to move our small secretariat to Rabat. Asma had organized a dinner for us, and invited Fatima Mernissi to meet us, saying that her health was not good, so she could only stay for an hour. In fact, she stayed much longer, talking with us enthusiastically about Musawah and our plan to move to Morocco.

In late November, Musawah was again in Morocco. This time we were holding one of our capacity-building courses – Islam and Gender Equality and Justice (I-nGEJ) – in Dar Eddiya, only an hour away from Rabat. On the second day of the course (30 November 2015) the news reached us that

Fatima Mernissi had left the world. It was around noon, during amina wadud's session on "Reading for Gender in the Qur'an: Text and Context", with Zainah Anwar as facilitator. This was amina's first visit to Morocco, and she had been keen to meet Fatima for the first time. Asma Lamrabet had arranged to bring them together over lunch, but Fatima was too ill to come; there was no chance to schedule another meeting, as Asma had travel plans, and amina was leaving before the end of the course. So they never met.[29]

On the day Mernissi died, Asma sent us an email, saying:

> Just wanted to share with you the last words on the phone with Fatima when she apologized for not attending the lunch with Amina ... she said 'tell her that she is a pioneer and Musawah is the future.' With a very weak voice. She was suffering but still with hope for the future ... *Rahimaha Allah.*[30]

When the week-long course was over, I stayed behind with two others (Zainah Anwar and Marwa Sharafeldin) to follow up the progress of our application. Asma had returned from her travels, and she took us to visit Fatima Mernissi's grave. We paid our respects and recited the *fatihah* prayer together. It was a moving moment for us all, especially for me who had known her longest – since 1988 when I did fieldwork in Rabat and was mentored by her.[31]

I now saw Asma as her heir, as the one to continue Mernissi's vision, and Morocco as the right place for Musawah to continue its work. But, despite our lobbying, we never heard about the fate of our application, so we had to abandon the plan to move to Morocco.

In 2018 Lamrabet became the centre of another controversy, which led to her resignation. This time the context was a decade-long campaign to reform the discriminatory inheritance laws. In 2015, civil society activism for reform had gained new momentum, when the Moroccan National Council of Human Rights urged the government to end all forms of discrimination against women, including in matters of inheritance.[32] A collected volume of twenty-three studies by Moroccan scholars from different disciplines, including Asma Lamrabet, was published in 2017 in three languages (Arabic, French and

---

29 In March 2016 Musawah published an online tribute to Fatima Mernissi (Musawah. 2016), including contributions from Lamrabet, amina wadud, Zainah Anwar and myself.
30 Mir-Hosseini, 2013b.
31 See my contribution to the Musawah tribute to Mernissi, Mir-Hosseini, 2016.
32 Erwin, 2015.

English).[33] The book was edited by Siham Benchekroun, a well-known psychologist and novelist, who also initiated an online petition to abolish the rule of *ta'sib*, according to which, if a man dies leaving only daughters, half his property goes to his male relatives. This petition was signed by over 100 Moroccan intellectuals, again including Lamrabet.[34]

On 18 March 2018, following a newspaper report in which Lamrabet was quoted as saying that the Qur'an supported women's and men's equal rights to inheritance, she resigned from her position as Director of the Centre for Study and Research on Women's Issues at the Rabita. Her resignation, widely covered in the national press, provoked a range of reactions. Her picture was on the cover of the outspoken liberal magazine *Quel Tel*, with the headline, "Asma Lamrabet: Sacrificed on the Altar of Patriarchy".[35] The conservative press considered Lamrabet's reading of the Qur'an as 'deviant', and welcomed her departure from Rabita.

She declined all press requests to speak, but on 26 March she broke her silence with a ten-point statement on her website; the second point clarified: 'On the occasion of an academic conference presenting the collective work on inheritance, my words, expressed in a strictly personal capacity, and reported by a newspaper, have sparked an outcry and a great controversy during the 20th session of the Academic Council of the Rabita. Faced with such pressure, I was forced to submit my resignation because of the differences relating to the approach to gender equality within the religious framework.'[36]

After her resignation, Asma called me in distress, so I knew how much the whole media controversy over her resignation upset her, not least because it would detract attention from her cause: the demand for reform in inheritance laws. She gave no further public statements. Since March 2019 she has been living in Pretoria, South Africa, where she accompanied her husband to a new diplomatic post. She now works as an independent scholar, as prolific and as much in demand as before.

An-Na'im's warning in 2009 about the perils of working with religious centres of learning came true on this occasion. He correctly predicted that, because of institutional dynamics and vested interests, the ulema would not tolerate us and our reformist vision.

---

33 Benchekroun, 2017.
34 Kasraoui, 2018b.
35 Mende, 2018.
36 The original French is to be found in Filali, 2018. For samples of press coverage in Morocco, see Kasraoui 2018a; for international coverage, see Lindsey, 2018.

While editing the transcript of our conversations, I realized that it was incomplete without some discussion of Lamrabet's resignation from Rabita. I sent her the edited draft for comment, and asked if we could have a further talk, in which she could give her own account of the resignation, and I could also ask her whether she still thought it was feasible to work with the ulema. She wrote back saying, 'I cried reading it [my draft] because it reminded me of all those things . . . you know it is our history . . . it is not academic . . . it is very sincere and honest.' So we arranged a third conversation, which took place online, on 13 February 2020.

ZMH: You never talked publicly about how your cooperation with Rabita ended; what happened? And what has been its impact for you?

AL: Everything started with the publication of our collective study on inheritance in Morocco; the coordinator was a woman writer, with twenty-three contributions ranging from theology to sociology and psychology. Later, there was a seminar to launch the book, held at the University of Rabat, and I was one of the panellists. I said what I always say: the need for reinterpretation, and then suggested that, as happened with the reform of family laws, perhaps there is a need for a consultative committee to revise the inheritance laws. This was reported in an online Arabic news website – HESPRESS – with a heading like "The Director of Women's Studies Centre at Rabita says inheritance laws should be reformed." It appeared on the same day that Rabita was holding their annual meeting in Marrakech; and the ulema protested. I was in Spain teaching when I received a call from Mr Abbadi's assistant, asking me to write a statement to HESPRESS that the report was not true. I said. 'No, I'm not going to lie, the headline is problematic, but not the content of the report. It was an academic seminar and I talked in my capacity as an individual, not on behalf of Rabita.' These exchanges were with his assistant, Mr Abbadi was not talking to me. Then I texted him, 'Sorry about this hassle, am happy to resign if it is causing you problems.' He responded, 'I am sorry, I have to accept your resignation.' Three days later, Abbadi issued a press statement that 'The Institute of Women's Studies at Rabita has a new director, the Qur'anic scholar Farida Zomorod, who respects Shari'a and our tradition.'

That's how it happened – so suddenly. Then it all started: telephone calls, texts, requests for interviews. I rejected it all and have never talked about it to the press. Yusuf, my husband, took me away to a place with no internet or telephone for a week, but he said that I must clarify my position, and so I did put a statement on my website to explain the reasons for my resignation.[37]

I was tired of the work, I told you that. Several times I had told Abbadi that I wanted to resign, but he always said, 'No, we have work to do, etc.' I wasn't expecting it to happen in that way. [Working at Rabita] was important in my life – it feels like a rupture. I am now invited as an independent intellectual, which is fine. Before, I was seen as part of a religious institution; the Islamists respected me; they knew I was a reformist. I feel that there has been a break in relations; some of them sent me messages, saying 'We do not agree with you, but we respect you.' When I removed the veil, some said 'Oh my God, we respected you and you should have kept your veil, because for us it was like you were reformist but with your veil we trusted you . . .' It seems it was all about the veil.

ZMH: So, why did you decide to remove your veil, which you called *khimar*?

AL: Yes, I called it *khimar*, for a long time, as you write very well in your draft. As I told you, later I just wore it for solidarity, to oppose Islamophobia. Eventually I arrived at a point where I just felt like a hypocrite with myself and with the creator, God. So, I said, 'I must accept that my ideas and solidarity should be in other forms, I must be what I am and accept what I am.' One day, I just said, 'it's over, I can't handle this any more. For me it was like I reached a point, how can I say . . . in a certain way, it was like agreeing to play the game of the Islamists, because they do play games.' You know, the majority of women wear their veil with a deep and spiritual conviction – I was one of them – but [the Islamists] have used and instrumentalized the veil for political purposes. I felt like I was manipulated by political Islam and their slogans; they want us to be visible; for them this visibility is important, to have women with the veil, it comforts them and confirms that they are politically very strong. As I said, the majority of women are really vulnerable, there is a real vulnerability in this matter. I wore it because I wanted to be spiritual, I wanted to do it for myself and for God, but then I became aware of this manipulation and struggled with it for years. I used to remove the veil when I went in Europe, and only wore it for the conference; you know, it had become just like a habit. For the past two years, I just put it on at work in the hospital.

One day last year [2019], I had to go out and I went to my car without my scarf; and I felt so free, so relieved . . . it had been like a responsibility, a

---

37 The statement is no longer on the website, but see earlier note for where the French text can be found.

lie, something on my shoulder; I said, 'Oh my God, I am now Asma, I am what I am.' Spiritually, I was free. When I went to South Africa in September, I decided to put my statement on Facebook. Why? Because I have a lot of followers, and people were talking about my action. Some were saying, 'She's done it because she moved to South Africa.' Others were saying, 'Asma Lamrabet is now liberated, she is now a modern, emancipated woman.' They were using it against each other, so I had to make the statement to say that 'to veil or not to veil' is not the point, it is about tolerance, diversity, the right to choose, and many other things, please free woman's body of all these. I didn't want to enter in this polemic because some modernists are as dangerous as Islamists in manipulating this. I officially put up my picture without it and said, 'I have the right to choose; in the past I chose *khimar* and now I choose not to wear it.'[38]

ZMH: Asma, when we talked in 2010 and 2014, both of us were keen on working with religious institutions and within religious institutions; I was optimistic then, but no longer. What about you? Do you think it is still possible to cooperate with ulema?

AL: I don't think so really . . . but you know I don't want to say it officially, because I don't want to make young researchers despair about religious institutions; there are many good researchers, theologians who want to work for reform, but they are under pressure to avoid it; we have to break the dam. I am sceptical, but I hope we can do it one day.

I share Lamrabet's conviction concerning the need to keep the conversation with the ulema going, while also sharing An-Na'im's scepticism about their willingness to change, which he expressed to me in 2009. The writings of Muslim feminist and reformist scholars still have no place within the centres of religious learning; they are either excluded from the curriculum or heavily censored and selectively invoked and cited to show students the 'errors' in their approach and their lack of knowledge of the Islamic scholarly heritage.[39] But I believe that this is bound to change, as the old ways of thinking no longer satisfy the younger generations; reformist and feminist writings provide answers to their questions and are gradually making headway. Time is indeed on their side.

---

38 Her latest piece of writing on the issue appeared on her website, Lamrabet, 2019.
39 See the article by Farida Zomorrod (2019), the Qur'anic scholar chosen to replace Lamrabet in Rabita, and my response: Mir-Hosseini, 2019.

5

Khaled Abou El Fadl

Any normative system loses legitimacy if it is no longer persuasive and unable to ensure the consent and deference of those who are supposed to be loyal to that system. But if a system does not rest on a consensual foundation, its very character becomes coercive and not normative – a normative system that depends only on the power of coercion is a contradiction in terms.[1]

Khaled Abou El Fadl is a prominent scholar of Islam and Islamic law, and the Omar and Azmeralda Alfi Distinguished Professor of Law at the UCLA School of Law. Born in Kuwait in 1963 into an Egyptian scholarly family, he began his religious studies at an early age. After thirteen years of formal training in Islamic jurisprudence in Egypt and Kuwait, he became a qualified Islamic jurist. Meanwhile, in 1986 he obtained a BA in Political Science from Yale University, followed by a JD from the University of Pennsylvania Law School, and an MA and Ph.D. in Islamic law from Princeton University in 1999. A prominent public intellectual, Abou El Fadl is a strong advocate of a scholarly approach to Islam from a moral point of view and one of the foremost critics of puritan and Wahhabi Islam.

Abou El Fadl has written prolifically on the universal themes of humanity, morality, human rights, justice and mercy, and is well known for his writings on beauty as a core moral value of Islam.[2] As both a qualified Islamic jurist and an American lawyer, he is a strong proponent of human rights, and the 2007 recipient of the University of Oslo Human Rights Award, the Lisl and Leo Eitinger Prize. He was also named a Carnegie Scholar in Islam for 2005, and received the Martin E. Marty award for his contribution to public

---

1 Abou El Fadl, 2014, pp. 50–51.
2 For an analysis of his work, see Duderija, 2018, pp. 123–146.

understanding of religion in 2020. Abou El Fadl maintains an active presence on social media; two websites are dedicated to his work: *Scholar of the House*,[3] which is run by his students and supporters, and *The Search for Beauty*, which is run by his wife Grace Song.[4] In 2005, 2017 and 2018, he was also listed as one of Lawdragon's Top 500 Lawyers in the Nation. In 2013, he was recognized among "The 50 Smartest People of Faith" by TheBestSchools.org, and was awarded the "American Muslim Achievement Award" in 2014. He has been ranked among "The Power 500 List of the World's Most Influential Arabs" and "The World's 500 Most Influential Muslims".

I first encountered Khaled Abou El Fadl and his work in 1999 in Washington, at a seminar where I was speaking in a panel with him and Zainah Anwar.[5] I found his presentation refreshing and powerful; his voice was that of a jurist, an insider to the tradition, who was bringing the basic values of the faith into conversation with modern norms and ways of knowing and living. After the meeting was over, the three of us continued the conversation, all of us enthusiastic and optimistic about the future. We exchanged books; I gave him a copy of *Islam and Gender*; he gave me what he called his short book, *The Authoritative and the Authoritarian in Islamic Discourses*. I immediately noticed the dedication: 'This work is dedicated to two majestic women in my life: My mother Afaf, and my wife Grace. How can I ever satisfy the debt?' It was only many years later – during our conversation for this book – that I came realize the importance of these two women in shaping his ethical understanding of Islam and his search for justice and beauty, constant themes and concerns in his writing.

Published in 1997, the book originated in an essay in which Abou El Fadl expresses alarm with the ways in which Muslims in the United States understand and relate to textual authority. He analyses in detail a fatwa issued by the US-based 'Society for Adherence to the Sunnah.' The context was the 1996 controversy resulting from a Muslim professional football player's refusal to stand up while the national anthem was being played. The fatwa provided religious-based arguments for the football player's action, based on two Hadith. Taking this fatwa as representative, in both style and method, of what he saw as the dismal state of contemporary Muslim discourses, Abou El Fadl

---

3 http://www.scholarofthehouse.org/info.html
4 https://www.searchforbeauty.org/about-us/welcome-from-the-director
5 Marnia Lazreg, then at the World Bank, invited us to speak about our research to a group of Bank experts.

embarks on a series of fascinating legal reasonings that dismantle the basis of this fatwa from within Islamic legal theory (*usul al-fiqh*). He takes the reader step by step through the process by which the sacred text (in this case, two Hadith) has been used to give religious legitimacy to a particular ideological or political standpoint. He writes: 'the speaker presents himself or herself as embodiment of the text – the speaker and the text become inseparably attached as one. Ultimately, the speaker by the employment of the text becomes the voice of the authoritarian and the voice of Divine judgment.'[6]

Abou El Fadl expands the argument in *And God Knows the Soldiers*;[7] in *Speaking in God's Name: Islamic Law, Authority and Women* he is concerned with the same problem – the rise of authoritarianism among contemporary religious scholars, and how it is subverting the richness and diversity of Islamic tradition – but this time on a much larger scale.[8]

In *Speaking in God's Name*, he develops a conceptual framework to address the problem of textual authority and authoritarianism, shedding light on the complex relationship between text, reader and context. He takes the reader through the nitty-gritty of Islamic legal epistemology, enabling us to see the extent to which moral, social and philosophical assumptions can be masked in the process of deriving laws from textual sources. When issuing a fatwa, the jurists often do not reveal the process of their legal reasoning, so a lay person cannot see the working of socially and morally contingent assumptions and how textual sources are co-opted to portray them as objective, immutable and divine. When presented with any ruling, we can also ask: Is it is fair? Is it just?

Abou El Fadl critically engages with the methodological problems that beset fatwas on women issued by one of the most powerful religious institutions: the Saudi Permanent Council for Scientific Research and Legal Opinions (CRLO). In an Appendix to *Speaking in God's Name*, he provides a full translation of these fatwas, addressing issues ranging from the 'unlawful' deception of women wearing brassieres in order to appear younger; the prohibition against women driving (issued shortly after the women's driving demonstration in Saudi Arabia in 1991); the invalidation of a Muslim man's prayers if a woman passes in front of him; the prohibition on women who continue their education instead of marrying; the beliefs that women constitute the majority of those in Hell and that women should tolerate a husband's

---

6 Abou El Fadl, 1997, p. 44.
7 Abou El Fadl, 2001a.
8 Abou El Fadl, 2001b.

mistreatment and obey a husband's orders; and some other misogynist opinions, including one on "The Dangers of Women in the Workplaces of Men". Supported by Saudi money, these fatwas have played a role in shaping the discourse of mosques, communities and individuals in the Gulf states and many other Muslim countries, as well as Muslim communities in the West.

He also provides the reader with a set of theological/normative arguments and conceptual tools to distinguish between that which is 'authoritative' in Islam and that which is 'authoritarian'. He starts from the premise that in Islam 'there is no authoritative centre other than God and the Prophet, but both God and the Prophet are represented by text.' In other words, 'it is the Qur'an and Sunna that stand as the authoritative centre of Islam.'[9] The role of the Muslim jurist is to provide information about God's instructions embedded in texts, and what gives him the authority is his knowledge of the texts and his supposed ability to apply textual interpretations to concrete cases. In doing so, he must endeavour to keep the text and its teachings open, dynamic and relevant. Since it is impossible for a human being to represent God's truth, a jurist can only represent his or her own efforts in search of this truth, and this he must do in accordance with five key criteria: honesty, self-restraint, diligence, comprehensiveness and reasonableness.

For me, *Speaking in God's Name* came at a critical juncture in my own journey; Abou El Fadl demystified the whole process of juridical construction, and enabled me to see how what is claimed to be a religious law (*hukm shar'i*) is constructed as such, and how to approach textual sources from an ethical perspective in line with contemporary notions of justice, to which gender equality has become inherent in the course of the twentieth century. This book was an important contribution to women's struggle for an egalitarian gender perspective in Islam, in that it offered a concrete methodology for approaching the Hadith literature which is used to support gender discrimination. Muslim feminists have mostly focused on challenging patriarchal readings of the Qur'an, whereas discriminatory laws have been largely supported and legitimated through the Hadith literature. In *Speaking in God's Name*, Abou El Fadl shifted the focus from the hermeneutic to the legal – a shift that I regarded as essential in any attempt to challenge unfair and unjust laws regarding women's place in family and in society.

In the years after our first meeting in 1999, I read Abou El Fadl's work and we coincided in a number of other meetings. Then in 2008, when Musawah

---

9 Ibid., p. 11.

sought an authoritative background paper on Islam and Human Rights, we asked Abou El Fadl for permission to abridge his article "The Human Rights Commitment in Modern Islam", to which he agreed. Even in its abridged version, it is the longest chapter in the resulting Musawah book, *Wanted: Equality and Justice in Muslim Family Laws*. We met again in June 2011, when he spoke at the first conference of Inspire, an organization founded in 2008 to challenge gender inequality and Islamist extremism.[10] Then, once I knew that I would be in Los Angeles in January 2014, I emailed Abou El Fadl, told him about my book project, and asked if he would agree to a recorded conversation. He agreed, inviting me to visit him.

Our conversation took place on 10 January 2014 at his home, where his personal library of over 100,000 books was housed – along with a number of large rescue dogs. His wife Grace Song joined in occasionally, whenever she was in the room. I told him about Musawah, about the final stages of our research on *fiqh* notions of male guardianship over women, and about my own Conversations project. He had just submitted the manuscript of *Reasoning with God: Reclaiming Shari'ah in the Modern Age*, and spoke of it as his magnum opus and an intellectual autobiography that he dedicated to his mother. It had taken him over ten years to finish the book, and though he knew it was too long he wouldn't have cut out any part of it because 'it is an interconnected theory of epistemology and justice.'

We chatted for about an hour before embarking on the recorded conversation, which lasted over three hours. I have arranged the following abridged transcript both chronologically and thematically to enable the reader to follow the development of his thought while appreciating Abou El Fadl as both a person and a reformist Muslim scholar.

MAJOR INFLUENCES: MOTHER, TEACHERS AND GRACE

I began the conversation by asking him about his intellectual and spiritual journey; the major influences that formed him as a person and a scholar of Islam.

---

10 In 2021, Inspire is no longer active. For the conference papers, including those by Abou El Fadl and myself, see Fazal, 2011.

KAF: I grew up in a family with a strong religious anchoring and respect for tradition. My father was a reader, he had books in the house and was always reading; he was a lawyer as well as an Islamic jurist (*faqih*) and knew most of the religious scholars with whom I later studied – he introduced me to them. I began my religious studies around the age of seven by first memorizing the Qur'an and Hadith, which ended around the age of twelve, all patiently guided by my mother alongside my normal schooling. She was the one who would read us the very first stories about the life of the Prophet, would drive us after school to the religious scholars for us to learn and memorize the Qur'an; it was always the same: after school, we go home and rest, and then to religious classes. It is interesting that my brother and sister, after a certain age, were not attracted to this type of activity and did not want to continue.

What really made an enormous difference in my life was the character and nature of my mother. She was an educated woman and her father was a *qadi shar'i* (religious judge); her own mother was illiterate, but she too was an amazing and beautiful woman. It was my mother who instilled in me the love of knowledge, and formed my initial attitude and stance toward women and gender relations. For instance, my mother never allowed us brothers to boss my sister around over what she was wearing; she removed the so-called proposition that 'because you are the brother, you can boss her around'. Even in my fanatical phase, if I tried to boss my sister around, my mother would punish me by having me perform extra chores at home. I grew up in an environment where, from a very young age, I had to learn to treat women as equals; it is something that you have to be raised with, it has to be instilled in you as a matter of *adab* (proper behaviour).

I vividly remember what my mother told me the night after the *hafl*, the ceremony that celebrates those who have memorized the Qur'an. She said: 'Now that you have finished memorizing it, you can begin the difficult process of understanding it; you are now the carrier of the Qur'an, your morality and conduct must be illustrative; if you are not acting in a respectful or respectable way, then that is insulting God's book.' After that, whenever I did something wrong, she would say 'Shaykh Khaled! Shaykh Khaled!' That would embarrass me; it is remarkable that for the rest of my life I would hear her voice. She passed away in 2011. Grace can tell you about her saying 'Shaykh Khaled!'

GS: She was trying to shame him into better behaviour. She was really a beautiful and calm person, she would sit for the whole conversation and say nothing, always with a smile. She was an amazing woman, who would leave such an impression on all who met her.

KAF: As soon as Grace met my mother, she loved her. My mother had a very peaceful and tranquilizing demeanour. Among things that I remember about her ... I must have been fourteen, in seventh grade, there was an incident in the newspaper that four guys abducted a girl and raped her. I was at school and the boys were talking about it as though it was exciting – arousing. I was bothered and surprised that they would talk like this; when I said 'no, I don't find it exciting,' I was made to feel weird, that something was wrong with me; I went home and I told my mother. Just the way she talked to me about it: she gave me another story that involved a boy who had been abducted and raped, and in this case murdered. She said, 'See, this happens to boys and girls, you have to put yourself in the place of someone who is suffering, and think how would they feel' – as simple as that. Whenever I complained about somebody, she would not say I was right or wrong, but would tell me to put myself in that person's place before judging whether they were acting justly. A day does not pass without my hearing her voice inside me. On my challenges with health: the first time I was hospitalized, she would ask about other patients in the ward. She would say, 'Think about this woman whose colon was removed, or that man who didn't recover after a cardiac arrest,' and so on. 'How would you have felt if you were in their place ... shift your gaze toward the other so that you can see it differently.'

She was a constant source of safety and comfort for us. My father had political problems at the time of Gamal Abdel Nasser, and he publicly criticized Nasser's military rule and the 'cleansing' of the legal profession, so he was often away travelling and or in meetings. One day he told us that we had to leave Egypt, and I remember my mother was hurriedly burning documents on the balcony, concerned about disturbing the neighbours; at the same time that we had to leave the country, our citizenship was taken away.

ZMH: Can you say some more about your religious schooling? Who were your main teachers there?

KAF: We had to live outside Egypt for many years; my first Qur'an instructor – we were living in Kuwait – was Shaykh Wadi, an Azhari exile from Egypt. In fact, my teachers were always Egyptian, with the exception of Shaykh Khalifa, a Palestinian, when we lived in Jordan. Others that I can note are Shaykh Wadi, Shaykh 'Adil al-Radi in Egypt, Shaykh Hassan 'Abd al-Ghani in Kuwait. I am indebted to many other instructors, all of whom

I have listed and thanked in *The Search for Beauty in Islam*.[11] I owe them a lot.

I knew that Abou El Fadl was also a student of the revered scholar Mohammad Ghazali (1917–96), who had many followers. His work is characterized by a reformist approach with continuity of tradition; his book, *The Prophetic Sunnah: Between the Jurists and Traditionalists*,[12] became a bestseller but also faced fierce denunciation. Many rebuttals appeared in the Saudi-sponsored newspaper *Al-Sharq Al-Awsat*, and conferences were held in rejection of Ghazali and his work.[13]

ZMH: You also studied with Mohammad Ghazali; when was that? And what did you study with him?

KAF: I was seventeen when I started attending his *halaqa* (learning circles) in Abbasiyah [a neighbourhood in Cairo]. Al-Ghazali and my mother came from Nikla al-'Inab, a small village in Egypt, and our families were connected; that greatly facilitated meeting him and was particularly helpful when I studied with him. He would always address me as *baldiyati*, meaning 'homeboy; from my hometown', and that granted me a kind of special access. Together we read Hanafi Usuli texts; he influenced my thinking and I would ask questions to get a rise out of him. I remember one embarrassing incident. A couple of friends and I had read a Hadith that said that whoever dies and has not given the *bay'at al-imam* [oath of allegiance to a religious leader], dies a *jahili* [pre-Islamic] death. I was the ringleader of my group of friends and we went to al-Ghazali's house, and woke him up – it was about 10 p.m. – and said, 'Shaykh, we want to give you *bay'at*.' He was so disappointed that he threw us out of his home and said, 'You understood nothing of *usul al-fiqh*!'

I studied *usul al-fiqh* with Shaykh Ghazali. I loved the man; his view that God is just had an enormous impact on me. We would be reading all these thick Usuli texts and he would always digress to talk with a great passion about the theme of one's moral conduct and his utter dismay at Muslims who were backward and Muslims who did not observe *akhlaq* (ethics/morality). I remember that during one entire *halaqa* he went on for two

---

11 Abou El Fadl, 2006, pp. 130–131.
12 Ghazali, 1989.
13 See Foer, 2002.

hours, citing all the various theologians in Islamic history that talked about God's attribute of justice, that God is justice and that He would give the upper hand to just people, whether they were Muslims or non-Muslims. This was before the controversy over his book, *The Prophetic Sunnah*, which was a direct criticism of Wahhabi scholars for their manipulation of Hadith to justify fanaticism and undermine jurisprudence, and of how this was defiling Islam's reputation.[14] I remember him saying that what they are doing is attempting to control the tools of the trade, that their claimed objectivity in Hadith authentication is wrong, that they are trying to invent a religion basically to control *fiqh* by using only those Hadith that suit their aims.

By the mid-1980s Saudi money had fully infiltrated Al-Azhar. Some Shaykhs would go for a sabbatical to Saudi Arabia and come back much better off; we called them *Saudia Shaykh*. Gulf countries invited Shaykhs to be on the boards of Islamic investment companies – they were paid handsomely. Gulf money changed the lifestyles of some Shaykhs, but not those with whom I was studying. Throughout his life, Shaykh Ghazali lived in a humble apartment.

I still remember, when I was in Kuwait, I bought a fan as a gift for Shaykh 'Adil. His wife had told us he wanted one. Of course, the Saudi-connected ones lived in air-conditioned offices. This had a huge impact on me. I found it extremely upsetting to see the complete lack of proportionality between the level of knowledge and the level of material success. Another teacher, Shaykh Wadi, was now rather old and couldn't afford medicine. We, his students, were effectively collecting money so that his wife could buy medicine. The state hospitals were useless. To see that, at the same time, one of these Saudi-connected Shaykhs could afford to go for treatment to London!

I lived through that transformation. The case of Yusuf Qaradawi is very telling.[15] In the late 1970s and early 1980s, we used to attend his classes. Then, he was this brave young scholar who lived a humble life. During my life, at least, Qaradawi has gone from Egypt to Algeria, to Saudi Arabia, to Qatar and become one of the wealthiest people around. The Qaradawi I

14 He writes about Ghazali and this controversy in Abou El Fadl, 2014, pp. 261–265.
15 Yusuf al-Qaradawi (b. 1926) is one of the best-known Muslim scholars; he lives in Qatar and his TV programme *Shariah and Life* attracts an audience of over 50 million worldwide.

knew, when he wrote *Halal and Haram in Islam*,[16] one of his first books, was a very different type of person. He was friends with Shaykh Ghazali. But when the Saudis funded this whole campaign against Ghazali because of his book *The Prophetic Sunnah*, in which he criticized those who were using Hadith to undermine jurisprudence, Qaradawi did not defend him. That hurt Ghazali enormously. He felt betrayed because he knew that Qaradawi knew he was right. They had given a couple of *halaqas* (learning circles) jointly demolishing the arguments of the trend of using Hadith to establish the validity of interpretations. But now he kept silent. It was so disheartening to all those who knew both of them. It broke our hearts. When Saudi Arabia dedicated full pages in *Al-Sharq Al-Awsat* to attacking al-Ghazali and so on, I would go, especially in summer, to see him. He would comment about how this Shaykh had sold out and that Shaykh had sold out.

ZMH: You were passionate for Islamic Studies and knew these eminent scholars, yet you opted to go to the US, where you studied in the most prestigious universities: your BA at Yale, a JD at Pennsylvania, and then a Ph.D. in Islamic studies at Princeton. May I ask why you didn't continue your studies in Egypt?

KAF: I had wanted to study in Egypt and in fact I enrolled in law school there but, because of the political situation, I had to leave in 1983. At that time, the government had started to arrest people. They chased Shaykh Ghazali, who went to Algeria, and Shaykh Qaradawi as well. A friend of my father, who had studied at Yale, told him that I would end up a political prisoner because, among other things, I wrote a lot of poetry and short stories that were published in the newspapers. I published in *Sharq al-Awsat* and Kuwaiti newspapers and I published in Egypt in *Al-Shab*. Much of what I wrote was critical of *istibdad* (despotism) and I was also constantly among the *halaqa* circles. The same friend helped me get to Yale.

I was nineteen, approaching twenty. It was very hard because this was the first time I had been to the States and I had to work harder than ever before. Those undergraduates who came to Yale from prep schools could all read 100 pages per hour; I was reading five pages. That was very hard. I began studying law at the University of Pennsylvania. But I would go back to Cairo in summer to attend *halaqas* and do the oral defences for the *ijazah* (certificate). Then in 1985, what my father's friend had feared happened. I

---

16 Al-Qaradawi, 1967; 1980.

was detained in Cairo in Lazoughly.[17] It was just horrendous. After three weeks, without being convicted of anything, I was released. It was just brutal. I didn't go back to Egypt for many years.

This was a new phase in my life. If you look at my library, you'll see different sources from the different stages of my life. You'll find, for instance, a huge Marxist section from my time at Yale; political and legal theory and Marxist thought. Then you'll find a lot of liberal political theory; lots of books by Robert Dahl,[18] Ronald Dworkin,[19] Rogers Smith.[20] This was after the Marxist phase. Then, as we get closer to my graduate work at Princeton, you'll see all the works on Jewish theology and law, Christian theology and Buddhism.

In my first year at Princeton – it was 1991 – I mentioned to Shaykh Ghazali that I was reading Jewish law. He was very proud of me. He was proud that I was learning, and did not consider that I was learning the thought of the 'enemy'. It was the idea of seeking knowledge; that a Muslim should pursue wisdom (*hikma*) wherever you can; that God distributes *hikma* among humanity with an equal hand. I used to get a lot of obnoxious comments – why do you read about the enemy's faith and so on – and at times like this my mother always said, 'Since when did you listen to ignorance? What do you have to fear, your faith of God is strong.'

Another incident that had a great impact on me was in either 1991 or 1992, my first or second year at Princeton. Back then, Saudi Arabia had created an organization for giving money and property to mosques and other religious institutions as a form of *awqaf* (endowment).[21] The son of a very well-known leader in the American Muslim community, one of the big names in that context, got an Egyptian woman pregnant. She wanted the man to admit that they were married. His parents completely refused to acknowledge the marriage and said, 'Yes this was our son's doing, but it was out of wedlock, she is a whore,' and things like this. This was largely because

---

17 An infamous detention centre in a Cairo Square with the same name.
18 Robert Dahl (1915–2014) was an American political scientist, best known for his pluralist theory of democracy.
19 Ronald Dworkin (1931–2013) was an American jurist and philosopher best known for his theory of law as integrity.
20 Rogers Smith (1953–) is an American political scientist, best known for his writings on political development.
21 *Awqaf* (endowments), under Islamic law, are typically inalienable charitable donations of a building, a plot of land or some other asset for religious or charitable purposes, with no intention of reclaiming ownership.

she was a dark-skinned woman, which was unacceptable to them. Her father contacted me, then came and met me, and we brought the case to two people: Shaykh 'Adil and Shaykh Ghazali. 'Adil refused to get involved. Everyone in her family had gone to the Muslim community, but nobody wanted to get involved. Shaykh Ghazali was the only one who wrote a fatwa – I must have a copy of it in my papers – that there was enough evidence that they were indeed married.

Shaykh Ghazali told me, 'I know now why the Islamic movement failed in the US.' It was because they did not have the moral character to stand by this woman. He said, 'I have no hope for the Islamic movement in the US.' I remember that so well and what was so disheartening for me was that this was before the controversy exploded over his book. It was very disheartening to see that Shaykh Qaradawi refused to back her, because he travelled to America a lot to lecture and he wanted to keep his relations with everyone. And the so-called leadership in the Islamic community completely turned their backs on this woman.

ZMH: Was she a student in the US?

KAF: No, her father was the Imam of a mosque in the Connecticut area, and had US citizenship. So did she, but because of this event she ended up leaving the US. She finally got remarried to someone else and now has children. It was so devastating. And my helping her and going to Shaykh Ghazali to get the fatwa had embarrassed the Muslim leadership. It was something that put me on their blacklist for a long time. I got a lot of garbage for it. I was not invited to ISNA [Islamic Society of North America] conferences. I will tell you: the one who told me that I was not her son if I did not help this woman, was my mother. This was before Grace and I met.

I could now see how all these experiences shaped Abou El Fadl's deep commitment to revive a tradition of learning which he was exposed to as a youth, and which he now saw as having been in gradual decline since the 1970s. In an op-ed in the Los Angeles Times, 14 September 2001, he criticized the Saudi-sponsored and exported 'puritanical and ethically oblivious Islam' – which led to death threats.[22] There he reflected on how the expansion of an intolerant Wahhabi brand of Islam resulted in a crisis at the core of the faith by eroding the Islamic intellectual tradition. I could also see something of the importance

---

22 See Foer, 2002.

of two women in his life: his mother Afaf Ahmed El-Nimr and his wife Grace Song. He went on:

KAF: Grace reads everything I write.

ZMH: She also responds to emails on your behalf; and she was a great help to Musawah when we were abridging your article for our launch in 2009 . . .

KAF: The only way I can sustain a semi-normal existence is thanks to her, and some help from the students. Grace is in every sense my right hand. As I am talking to you, I am waiting for a phone call from the hospital as to when a bed is available so that I can admit myself. This is a constant interruption but, as I told you, I firmly believe that my health ailments are very much a part of the process of moral growth and moral understanding. The insights I have gained through all the pain of these ailments and medication; the empathy I constantly feel for the vulnerability of the weak, their suffering and helplessness, is invaluable. I would be lying to say I would have been capable of this growth without these experiences, because our nature is like this. As odd as it sounds, I am liberated by my physical ailments. I am liberated spiritually. But it also gives me a sense of seriousness: I don't have time to play intellectual games. You know the politics of academia. I have zero tolerance for these games and I don't play them. I am constantly asking where my input is most needed and directing it toward that. I wouldn't be able to function without Grace.

ZMH: There must be a reason that you two got together. When was that, Grace?

GS: We met in 1995. It's an interesting story, because we were a most unlikely pair to have met. He was just getting his Ph.D. at Princeton and I had graduated with an MBA from Cornell and was working at Johnson and Johnson outside Princeton. I had converted to Islam before we met. A friend sent me a tape of a lecture that the professor had given on women jurists in Islamic history, as a gift. I was so blown away. By that time, I had been Muslim for about a year and I had been exposed to the Wahhabi conservative approach. When I converted I had not really met many Muslims; I came to Islam primarily through reading and I was attracted to just the ideas and the faith. It was such a weird dichotomy: I came to the faith for something and I got completely different experiences when I entered the Muslim community. So, when I listened to his lectures, it was like a breath of fresh air to a dying person. It was like: 'Oh my God, this was why I came to this religion.' I said I want to find out who this person is, where he is teaching, and I want to learn from him. As it turned out, he was literally living ten minutes from me. So when you look at the circumstances of how we met and how things fell together, it was really amazing.

KAF: My mother liked Grace right away as well.

GS: For me it is the greatest blessing because I am so passionate about his writing, his work, his thought. I really believe the hope for Islam and the future lies with his thought, though we might not see it in this lifetime. It's so depressing to see how Muslims have become. But I know that, for me personally, reading his work and learning so much, it's been just transformative, so empowering. It's such a beautiful thing. I feel the Islam I've seen is very different from what most Muslims see. It's through the vantage point of knowledge, the importance of knowledge in and of the tradition, and an awareness of the liberating Islam of the past that Muslims really seem not to know about.

KAF: I often get into trouble with Grace because it's very hard for me to agree with her about the hope for the future and the hope of Islam, and all what she says about me.

GS: He's very humble. He gets very uncomfortable when I say these things.

KAF: The other thing is getting into arguments online; she is far more hot-blooded and fiery than I am, so she will go off fighting online over subjects like hijab and dogs.

GS: A friend of mine invited me to join this Facebook page for Muslim convert women. She knew that we have lots of dogs, and there was some discussion about people with heart-breaking stories about dogs, who, once they converted, had to give up their dogs. So she said, 'Can you join and chime in?' I joined the page and began reading to get a sense of what it was like. I hate to get into discussions about hijab because I think it's a waste of time. It's a stupid topic, just so ridiculous and overblown. But I had to jump in when someone asserted that it's a major sin not to wear hijab. Of course, they say this as though it's just the truth. I jumped in and said, 'No, you can't say that; and be aware that God will hold you accountable for anything that you pass on as truth. I want people to know that, so just don't shoot off your mouth, because if anyone takes what you say as truth and then you are wrong, that's your sin.' So I started writing these things, and the very authoritarian owner of the page removed my comments. That made me even more upset.

My friend then started a discussion about dogs. She said, 'It's very simple: outside is okay, inside is not.' So I wrote, 'There is so much more to say than this summary statement,' and I respectfully asked, 'If anyone is seriously interested in this conversation, let's start by reading these two articles' – and I put the links for two articles that Khaled had written on this subject: one is in the *Encyclopaedia of Religion and Nature* as an entry about dogs and Islamic tradition,[23] and the other was a chapter of his book, *The Search for Beauty*, called "A Fatwa on Dogs", where he talks about this wonderful exchange where he is sitting in a *halaqa* with a Shaykh and the Shaykh is grilling students about this fatwa and dogs. The Shaykh goes through all the evidence you hear about – why dogs are impure, not allowed – and disputes and refutes all these so-called arguments in an entertaining and engaging way.[24] So, of course, no one was willing to read it. They continued to send out these soundbites of Hadith: 'This Hadith says that ... of course dogs are impure; when you allow dogs, then you have to do XYZ.' It was really frustrating. When people can't read even two short articles so that we can have an informed dialogue, what do you do? I mean, people jumped in saying, 'The Maliki position is this and Hanafi position is that.' These are converts: they don't know what that means. But they get the idea that 'I need to know what school I belong to; there must be something really big here; I'm doing something wrong; I'm doing something *haram*.' I know the mindset, because I've been through that. You feel really inadequate. You feel you're supposed to know about these different schools. We were having this discussion that is so irrelevant. Everything has changed: that whole epistemology is not there any more.

REASONING WITH GOD

Khaled Abou El Fadl is prolific; he has written ten books, over fifty articles on Islamic law, as well as numerous opinion pieces, commentaries and public talks. I asked him which of his books he thought best defined his intellectual development.

KAF: The book that is closest to my heart, the one I love the most, is *The Search for Beauty in Islam*. In various chapters, I actually describe my

---

23 Abou El Fadl, 2005.
24 Abou El Fadl, 2006, pp. 316–330.

encounters and interactions with the Shaykhs, the love and respect, and the kind of relationships that I have had with them. Intellectually, *Speaking in God's Name* is the one that best describes the idea of rejecting authoritarian constructions of knowledge and the dangers of constructing an authoritarian, despotic text; and my belief that divinity is *too* serious, *too* important, *too* immutable for human beings to try to claim, to represent and package.

The one that describes my latest thought is the new book: *Reasoning with God: Reclaiming Shari'ah in the Modern Age*. It took me ten years to complete it. What I argue there is that it is not sufficient to search the text comprehensively and systematically. One must also take an ethical stance as a reader. In *Speaking in God's Name*, I imply that we should search all the indicators, all the *adilla*, to know God's will, including *dalil al-'aqli* (indicators/proofs/arguments from reason) and *dalil al-khalqi* (indicators from creation/nature) and so on. But it is in *Reasoning with God* that I develop the notion of the *ultra-text dalil* – indicators of the divine will beyond the textual – that entails reasoning outside the text.

I am sceptical of approaches taken by Muslim reformist thinkers who have complete faith in reason. I don't have that faith. I think that reason could very easily become a hedonistic God and that reason does not resolve a lot of ethical problems or issues of virtue and ethics. All the philosophical constructs that have tried to create simply reason-based ethics or notions of virtue are ultimately not thoroughly compelling to me. But at the same time, the idea that we remain locked within a text that is frozen in an epistemological picture is thoroughly irrational and thoroughly limiting to the Divine. I think reform in the Muslim world will really begin when we stop approaching complicated intellectual issues with an ideological pre-set paradigm, where everything we want already existed in this ideological and preconceived construct. You are not going to find the story of liberation in the tradition and you are not going to find a constant narrative of just oppression. We end up throwing away the very tools that would allow us to chisel a solution.

In *Reasoning with God*, I argue for an epistemological shift in our approach to the Shari'a. I argue that it must be understood and approached as a moral dialogue through parables. The Qur'an is not an instruction book. It is a book of wisdom and an infinite engagement in layers of reflective thinking about our moral being, our existential situation, where we are coming from and where we are going. Take the whole story of creation, when God tells the angels and jinns[25] to prostrate themselves before Adam. The angels, according to the Qur'an, say to God: 'You created someone who will cause corruption and shed blood on Earth.'[26] This is before the whole parable of *jannah* (paradise), Adam and Eve eating the forbidden fruit, and their fall. So the angels already know that humans are going to end up on Earth. Therefore, the Qur'an itself presumes that the reader is reading the text quite intelligently as a moral parable. And then God tells the angels:'I know what you do not know: I taught Adam the names.'[27] We have to ask, what do 'the names' mean? Muslim theologians all had a hard time with this. Of course, it opened up enormous epistemological possibilities for Muslim philosophers. Muslims of more mystical orientation understood names as holding the true nature of things, and more esoteric things. I talk about the implications of this. Among them is the creation of many human beings capable of going against God and how the major failure of this human being is corruption and shedding blood. That is in itself a moral burden that we must reflect on; what does 'corrupting the Earth' mean? I go through every instance in the Qur'an where it talks of *fasad fi-l-ard* (corruption on Earth). I look at the way the Qur'an uses *ihsan* (kindness, goodness, compassion, that which is commonly known to be good and moral), or uses *ma'ruf* (that which is commonly known to be right, commonly acknowledged as good law), or uses these various indicators of goodness. If you don't engage in such a dynamic, then you are not giving the Qur'an its true weight.

I don't say that there is no Islamic law. Part of my whole argument is that there is Shari'a as moral order. I go through the discussion of the Qur'an's usage of *hudud*. One of the things that I notice is that, as far as we know, the initial usage of the term *hudud* in the Qur'an concerns disputes about women's share or something that involves women. The Qur'an comes and settles the dispute in one way or another and then emphasizes, 'Do not offend them, do not transgress upon them and be mindful of *hudud Allah* (God's boundaries).'[28] Look at the moral dynamic here: there was an interactive process in which there was a problem and you realize that it's as though the Qur'an every time knows that humans resist doing what is just,

---

25 An intelligent spirit of lower rank than the angels, able to appear in human and animal forms and to possess humans. See El-Zein, 2017.
26 Qur'an, 2:30.
27 Qur'an, 2:31.
28 Qur'an, 2:229.

resist the trajectory of justice. The Qur'an emphasizes it by telling you that these are the boundaries of God.

The challenge is that Muslim tradition is not attuned to the notion that God speaks through parables. There have been Muslim theologians such as Ibn Arabi and Mulla Sadra who understood this challenge and believed that, while God conveyed His message through parables, if legal matters were to be read literally they would be locked up epistemologically. That is precisely the problem behind the types of challenges that we face today, and this process leads to the types of laws we struggle with today; for instance, when Tariq Ramadan proposed the suspension of *hudud* punishments and received a public backlash in the Middle East and so on.[29] In the book, I use that incident to demonstrate just one instance of the remarkable epistemological paradoxes facing us Muslims. On the one hand, we cannot stomach the application of *hudud*. On the other hand, we do not want to let go of it normatively.

In *Reasoning with God* I approach the question of *hudud* in this way.[30] I go through all the reformist arguments about the *hudud*; that the *hudud* were constructed subjectively through this interpretation and that interpretation. We can do all of that – and that's fine. I do this too. I go on to say, 'Let's assume that something is as objective as it can be in a Qur'anic text such as 'you shall cut off the hand of the thief', or that 'you shall lash this person a hundred times if he does this or that.' So the questions to ask are: Did God pick this punishment because God understands that this punishment for this crime is the best punishment forever? Is there something about this punishment itself that is beyond our rational abilities? I engage in this discussion. You know how my inclination is to resist simplification and summarizing. I ultimately reach the conclusion that there is an epistemological evolution in our understanding of the idea of punishment and the idea of crime or offences. It would be a form of *kufr na'ma* (ingratitude) to assume that God, in revealing this text, had no clue or no idea that these epistemological developments would occur, or that God was incapable of dealing with them.[31]

The argument that, somehow, we are not being devout by not reading the text literally but reading it as parables of knowledge is in fact completely

---

29 Ramadan, 2005.
30 Abou El Fadl, 2014, pp. 291–308.
31 Ibid., pp. 300–303.

flawed. You honour the divine by being constantly engaged with it, by constantly asking the wonder question: What moral trajectory is God helping me toward? It is utterly dangerous to freeze God in a historical moment or in an epistemological paradigm. If we study the nature of criminal laws and the pattern of Qur'anic treatment of criminal laws in the context of Near Eastern law at the time, we cannot lock the text epistemologically. The notion of *qatl* (murder) evolves. The very notion of *sariqa* (theft) evolves. And the very notion of what is appropriate punishment evolves. I therefore chase and respond to various theological and philosophical refutations to this argument. That is why the manuscript is 800 pages and I don't want it to be cut.[32] At the same time, I know that it is not going to be read by activists, because it takes patience.

Earlier in our conversation Abou El Fadl had said that he knew that his books, with the exception of *The Great Theft*,[33] were not easily accessible to activists. I agreed with him that his writings need to be mediated; I said that I see that as my role, that is, linking scholarship with activism, and that I found working with activists instructive because, at the end of the day, we need action on the ground, and they are the ones to translate these ideas into practice.

KAF: One thing that you might get a kick out of in the book is my refutation of the myth of the Wahhabis as a reform movement, according to which they arose in Mecca because Islam had become completely corrupted; in Medina and the Hijaz, *kufr* (unbelief) had spread everywhere and Mohammad Abdul Wahhab restored the faith. I show that, on the contrary, it was not *kufr* that had spread; it was the various ways that Islam was epistemologically negotiated. The Hijaz was actually like a little tapestry or microcosm of how Islam was practised. Many movements like the Sufis had their representatives in the Hijaz. Every orientation, any Muslim who was anyone, was there. What in fact Wahhabism did was to come in and say, 'We know the correct Islam and all these negotiated forms must disappear,' which resulted in the famous clashes with Indian Muslims, Egyptian hajj pilgrims and caravans from the Levant. I hope that I show convincingly that people who saw Wahhabis to be true Islam had it wrong. We find the first articulation of this among Orientalist scholars who compare the Islam

---

32 The published version is 499 pages long.
33 Abou El Fadl, 2007.

of the Wahhabis with the Islam of the Ottomans, or some other form of Islam. They say, 'This is the true spirit of Islam because it is the Bedouin Islam; this is the true Islam that the Prophet Mohammad wanted.' And Muslim authors who repeated that same argument were people who had a Western education, like Ameen Rihani,[34] who later became a close friend to Ibn Saud but then eventually felt betrayed by him, or the Egyptian advisor Hafiz Wahba. They assumed that Wahhabism is something it is not. What they were basically saying is that it was good enough for religious people, or they thought it was good enough in Saudi Arabia. But when they came into contact with its actual practices, they could not stomach it. I show the controversy when the Wahhabis took over. The first to recognize the Wahhabi takeover as Najd taking over sovereignty from the Hijaz were European powers. The Muslim world remained in shock. For a period of time, Iran refused to recognize them, India refused, Egypt refused.[35]

My point in saying all this in the book is to show that the Shari'a as a moral order is a historical reality that we have lived through. This is how Islam was practised and thrived throughout the ages with such rich diversity: the Islam of Indonesia, the Islam of the Philippines, the Chinese, the Uyghurs. The Wahhabis saw all this richness and diversity as corruption and called it *fasad fi al-ard* (corruption on Earth). I say this is *not* the corruption that the Qur'an is talking about at all. If the Wahhabis see this rich diversity as corruption, that is a fundamental rejection of sociology. And religion without sociology is itself a corruption because it tries to hammer human beings into statues, sorts of idols.

IMPLICATIONS FOR GENDER JUSTICE

Khaled Abou El Fadl is one of the few male reformist thinkers who has directly engaged with the issue of women's rights from the outset. In *The Search for Beauty in Islam*, there are essays with telling headings, such as "Women as an 'Awra", "On Obedience", "Colonizing Women", "On the Beating of Wives" and "Women as a Colony".[36] In these essays, Abou El Fadl offers insightful reflections on women's rights, drawing on the wisdom of past scholars and the

---

34 Lebanese American writer (1876–1940).
35 Abou El Fadl, 2014, pp. 215–251, especially p. 241.
36 Abou El Fadl, 2006.

ethics of gender justice in Islam. And, as already mentioned, *Speaking in God's Name* was groundbreaking and much appreciated by women struggling for gender equality, as it gave them both the confidence and a methodology to question Hadith-based arguments. I told him about Musawah's research project on rethinking male authority and how useful we have found his work, and then I asked him about the implications of *Reasoning with God* for gender rights and family law reform.

ZMH: I want to take this on to the question of law reforms; how are we to read the Qur'an when it speaks about the family, women and gender rights? I mean those verses on which current conceptions of gender relations and the unequal rights of women are based. Are they parables?

KAF: Part of what we desperately need to understand is the historical context and epistemological issues at the time of revelation. I am more and more convinced that there are many layers and angles to this issue, which we tend to miss or overlook. For example, let's take the logic that the Qur'an sought to empower women through the granting of property rights, and so it gave them a half share in inheritance. So why not an equal share? We are told that at the time of revelation there was an incident in which men protested that women, because they do not take part in battles, should not inherit at all. The Qur'an then comes and resolves the issue by saying, 'No, women will inherit'. Therefore, we see clearly that the idea that inheritance should be completely proportional with taking part in battle is rejected. Yet our apologetic argument usually goes on to say that Islam wanted to empower women, so it gave them half a share of their male siblings. What is missed in this argument is that the empowerment of women is thoroughly grounded in sociological and epistemological realities. We cannot really say that what was empowering a thousand years ago is empowering today. We must understand what empowerment for women entails today; what the moral lesson of the Qur'an is on the issue of women's inheritance.

The most important thing about engagement with the moral lesson of the Qur'an is to understand where these lessons are taking us, where they want us to go. I argued – knowing that there would be a backlash – that there is no reason today for women not to inherit equally.[37] We cannot take a component of positive commandments in the Qur'an and apply the letter of the law without destroying the *maqasid* (the objectives of the law). In the

---

37 Abou El Fadl, 2014, pp. 377–382.

past, there were cases in which a non-married woman could sue her brother or uncle for their failure to provide for her wellbeing and sustenance, whereas these are causes of action that would not be allowed in any legal system today. So we either reinvent the historical world where they would be allowed, or we give them a full share in today's world. Part of my argument is that modern Muslims keep talking about *maqasid al-shari'a* (objectives of Shari'a) – so many projects and research groups are sponsored by Muslim states – but none of them apply it to change any of the positive commandments, because they are afraid. Their approach is to say, 'Look at all the purposes that Shari'a served in the past, isn't that wonderful!' I see that as truly a betrayal of the *maqasid al-shari'a*. A true service of the *maqasid* is to take the Qur'an's moral trajectories as far as our ethical beings, we as human beings, are able to serve justice.

You know well from my writings on Islam and democracy that I have an issue with the idea of a state that embodies the Divine.[38] But if that is the case, let's look at the sociological reality of our lived life. For example, when a woman is divorced after thirty years of marriage and is given one year of alimony, she will cry out that it's unfair or unjust. I say, 'Okay, if you want to apply Islamic law, then look at the Qur'an – when God heard a woman arguing with the Prophet about her husband, God responded with relief.' I use that parable to say that today we are so high and mighty and arrogant. We do not respond with any form of relief, saying, 'Women can scream all they want, we just want to talk about the glorious past.' I see this as a form of idolatry, as turning the Shari'a into the antithesis of justice, replacing beauty, *hasn*, with ugliness, *qubh*.

He was referring to the opening verses of the Qur'anic chapter *Al-Mujadallah* [*She Who Disputes*].[39] The occasion for its revelation is reported to have been an incident in Medina when a Muslim woman came to the Prophet with a complaint and did not leave until she got justice. Her husband had told her, after years of marriage and childbearing: 'You are to me as my mother's back.' This was a pagan oath that, once uttered by the husband, made sexual relations with his wife unlawful, and resulted in a form of separation called *zihar*. The husband would be released from all his conjugal duties, but the wife was kept in a state of limbo for the rest of her life, unable to leave her husband or

38 Abou El Fadl, 2004, pp. 3–46.
39 Qur'an, 58:1–5.

remarry. Having no way to sustain herself and her children, the woman who came to the Prophet wanted the marital bonds renewed. As reported in one account, the Prophet at first could see no way out and told her: 'You are [now] forbidden to him,' implying that the marriage could not be renewed. But she did not accept this and kept arguing her case with the Prophet – 'they went back and forth in this manner' until God intervened. It was then that the opening verses of chapter 58 were revealed: 'God has indeed heard the words of she who disputes with thee concerning her husband and complains to God. And God hears your conversation. Truly God is Hearing, Seeing.' The following verses (58:2–5) abolished this form of separation.[40]

KAF: To take the technical positive commandment literally – in a sort of superficial way as the traditionalists do – is to make a mockery of general or moral terms like *ma'ruf* and *ihsan* and so on. To give full measure to moral commandments like *ma'ruf* and *ihsan*, we have to negotiate the positive details of the law. We can't have it both ways. Our attempts at consistently trying to do this through the years has put us in a thoroughly apologetic and laughable situation. While the world continues to discuss theories of justice, we continue to take a rather primitive approach to justice. Here is when I hear the voice of Mohammed Ghazali; that the very notion of a Muslim being marred by backwardness and retardation is inconsistent with divinity. I am not talking about societies, I am talking about individuals: whether we strive to be godly or we allow ourselves to drift into ungodliness or godlessness. Striving to be godly is far more difficult, because no specific laws provide such guidance.

ZMH: That is a different realm. If we all had the capacity to live godly lives, then we wouldn't need laws in the first place! Now, let us talk about verse 4:34, from which the concept of *qiwamah* that places women under male authority is derived. I have carefully read what you wrote about this verse in *The Search for Beauty in Islam*, your focus being on the second part of the verse, i.e. men disciplining women.[41] However, I want to turn your attention to the first part of the verse: *al-rijal al-qawwamun 'ala al-nisa*, men are *qawwamun* of women.[42] I see this part as the core, because the whole edifice of family law in Islamic legal tradition, which assumes that men are in

---

40 See Nasr, 2015, p. 1343.
41 Abou El Fadl, 2006, pp. 107–113, 200.
42 See Chapter Four for Asma Lamrabet's discussion of the verse.

charge of women, is justified with reference to this part of the verse. So the questions that we ask in the Musawah project are: What is *qawwamun*? Why do we have this verse? Does the Qur'an have a certain notion of family or gender rights? I wonder if you have reflected on such questions in the *Reasoning with God*.

KAF: We have to take the discourse of the Qur'an as a whole. We need to ask whether the verse wants to lock the word *qawwamun* into a specific sociological context and sort of say, 'khalas, we are done!' When I look at the text itself, I see that the idea of moral or ethical superiority does not exist where it says that men have a degree (*fadl*) over women. And when I look at the historical narratives, I see how women, for instance Aisha, the Prophet's wife, or Sukayna (the Prophet's great-granddaughter),[43] interacted with men at the time. So the interpretation that this verse stands for the notion that the men are *forever* placed in a position to be in charge of women, regardless of the context, is challenged by the historical record and, more importantly, the verse itself, as it is recognizing a financial structure, a socio-logical reality.

We come back to the same problem: When the Qur'an acknowledges sociological reality, is it doing it normatively, is it prescribing it? Or is it recognizing it and then giving us the tools to achieve ethical purposes that might transcend the sociological reality? In *Reasoning with God* I address this issue, the first sentence of verse 4:34. I say that when we reach a point at which epistemologically we see our experiences and our observations as part of indicators of divinity through creation (*adilla khalqiyya*); when we see that there are some women leading countries who are far wiser and far more competent than some men; when we witness that women are outper-forming men in school and academia, it is then that we come to realize that creation itself defies our desire to lock sociological reality and say that the text freezes that sociological fiction. If we follow this line of logic, we cannot accept the notion that God would want us to believe in something that is refuted or denied by all indicators of human experience; that, for example, God is telling me, 'Don't bother, I don't care what evidence lies out there, I don't care about women's IQ, their genes, their educational levels or anything of that matter and I want you to firmly believe in the sociological reality that existed at a certain time.' God is in fact *not* telling me this.

---

43 Sukayna bint Hussain was renowned for her beauty and intelligence. For her life, see Khan, 2007, pp. 233–236.

Instead, He is acknowledging a historical moment which should be recognized as a phase in the process of a larger moral project. God also is giving us a variety of tools to navigate the path ahead.[44]

ZMH: What tools does God give us in verse 4:34?

KAF: One tool is the term 'qawwamun' itself. If God wanted to choose a word that could be flexible enough to be negotiated from different angles, I couldn't think of a better word than qawwamun, which is fascinating in its own right and open to multiple interpretations and various legitimate uses. Some state that it can mean 'servant' and they are correct, as are those who note that it can mean 'supervisor' or 'administrator of.' Qa'im-maqam means a 'representative of' in Arabic, which is a perfectly legitimate use of the term.

Another tool is how the text conditions the term with bi ma anfaqu (because of what they spend). The fact is that in comparison to other religious texts or texts of authority, the Qur'an is remarkably open in terms of its epistemological possibilities when it comes to these types of gender interactions. The question that Muslims must decide is what to do with this open-endedness? It is not a matter of happenstance.

I was interested to know how the concept of qiwamah translated into early historical processes; especially in legal procedures, to what extent it was translated into definable legal concepts. I found one usage that I thought was really interesting. It was in a case that involved a slave boy whose master had left him in charge of a certain property; in that legal usage, qiwamah meant 'responsible for'. Another case was in a dispute about orphans, where the guardian of the orphans was said to be 'responsible for' something about inheritance, an instance of stealing from a trust. Does this usage suggest any hint of superiority? Not in law. In legal practice, qiwamah then did not imply superiority. It is about who brings the charges, who is responsible.

When I look at some earlier tafsir (exegesis), the ones that we have from 120 hijra [eighth century CE], it is quite remarkable that we find very little said about this verse. There are some references that teasingly refer to a legal procedure. But from the fourth century onwards, we see the term become far more regimented. It starts to take the form of 'having authority over'; for example, who the wife can visit, who can enter the house and who can't.[45]

---

44 Abou El Fadl, 2014, pp. 379–382.
45 Omaima Abou Bakr reaches similar conclusions; see Abou Bakr, 2015, pp. 44–65.

The question is: Do I have the right to go back and try to renegotiate that term epistemologically, before it became so regimented within a patriarchal structure? Can I project backwards the patriarchal structure that developed within the legal system upon this term? I think that, methodologically, this would not be correct either. I don't think either would be correct or appropriate. If we take our tradition seriously, we should attempt to engage with the text and its application critically instead of locking God into a situation that we may view to be ethically unjust.

ZMH: That requires rethinking many core concepts in Islamic jurisprudence; *qiwamah* is only one of them.

KAF: You know . . . that is the case with all jurisprudential issues. I feel that the Islamic legal system, like all legal systems, evolves. The maxims and basic, fundamental principles remain the same, but the language is renegotiated in response to actual social demands that arise. It is true that law is very slow to change . . . I try to imagine a legal system in which there has been development and, suddenly, all the words are frozen within a sociological and historical moment and that legal system now refuses to renegotiate any of its core concepts any more – that legal system becomes a museum piece.

ZMH: Yes, and when sanctity is claimed for that legal system, then it becomes even more difficult to renegotiate core concepts, such as *qiwamah*, so we have to start from the premise that no law is sacred, all laws are human made and mundane.

KAF: This is really an interesting point, because one of the basic divisions in legal systems that can be traced back to the Greek philosophers is the difference between duties owed to God and duties owed to human beings. This comes to the fore in the difference between *'ibadat* and *mu'amalat* and the distinction between *huquq Allah* and *huquq al-'ibad*. Much of the argument in *Reasoning with God* goes back to this particular framework, which is deeply influenced by Greek philosophy.[46] Muslim jurists started with this idea of the bilateral division. When we look at dealing with adjudication and settling disputes in courts, I would say that up to the sixth century *hijri*, even sometimes up to the ninth century, you see Islamic law was a vibrant, living legal system and was sociologically alive.

What I say in *Reasoning with God* is that this was a legal system that was functioning within the rationale and logic of law. When looking at adjudication, you see that the law didn't refer to this Hadith or that Hadith or to

---

46 Abou El Fadl, 2014, pp. xlvii–xlix.

the Qur'anic verses. It is perfectly normal within such a legal system. You know that you are selecting precedents, and some precedents you do not want to overrule explicitly; you just want to ignore them. You want just to marginalize them by consistently ignoring them. But as Islamic law began to develop into a *fossilized* being, the *mu'amalat/ibadat* distinction in turn was ignored in practice, so was the *huquq Allah/huquq al-'ibad* distinction. I see clear evidence, even from a book like Waki''s *Akhbar al-Qudah*,[47] that family law was earlier seen as part of the *mu'amalat*, of human relations. But now family law is in this weird twilight zone between *mu'amalat* and *'ibadat*. This is what happens when theologians speak about law as if it is theology and they are no longer thinking within the paradigm of lawyers. What happens is that you fossilize a legal system, you freeze it, and force it to face its own inconsistencies. And then it breaks down.

ZMH: This is where we are now, in the middle of an epistemological crisis.

KAF: Exactly. In *Reasoning with God*, I give an example by analogizing it to the US legal system.[48] In the US we say, 'I sentence you to three life terms to be served consecutively.' Logically, no one can serve three consecutive life terms. However, we don't want to confront or disturb the legal system with this inconsistency, for a variety of technical reasons. For example, if we did address this issue, we might not be able to lock people up for life and they might get early release. One hundred years from now, if someone looks at the American legal system, they may claim that we either did not understand that individuals only live once, or they may even claim that we had a conception of reincarnation. I put a lot of what is said about Islamic law within the same paradigm. This fact is reflected in reality as well.

The issue of *qiwamah* is one example among the many comparisons I make in the book; it's stated in the Qur'an and it's negotiated and negotiable. People who live within the Muslim culture – individuals like you and I – know that the notion that the man just orders and the woman obeys is often an exception. Even in villages, we witness the complexities of various power-plays and dynamics within families, which paint a much more complicated picture. It is rare for a judge to adjudicate a case on the basis of a raw conception of *qiwamah* without taking the context into consideration, unless it is politicized and becomes an ideological concept, which would then be extremely corrupting of the legal system.

---

47 Waki' ibn Hayyan, 1947.
48 Abou El Fadl, 2014, pp. 347–348

ZMH: This is what we are now witnessing with the so-called 'Islamization' of legal systems.

KAF: That's why it is so disastrous. If we wish for Islam to function as a legal system again, we must revisit our epistemological concepts. We can't have it both ways. We must either forgo the idea of applying Islamic law – whether 'ibadat or mu'amalat – or, if we want any type of application, in any form, it must be reinvented and rethought because the reality is that there has been a period of non-development and suspension.

ZMH: Do you think it's feasible? Is it even a desirable vision, or are we just better off forgetting about the idea of 'Islamic law'?

KAF: In order for such a vision to come to fruition – and before considering any sort of involvement of the state – Islamic law must renegotiate its authority with the *people*. The state must completely stay out of the process and Islamic law must work on completely rational terms. It was an incredibly transformative experience for me to study law in the US because, for the first time, I understood *why* we have legal constructs in Islamic law and I could see that there are imperatives and linguistic practices in the law which enforce and imply certain outcomes. To ignore them is to ignore certain truths and, frankly, that approach doesn't work. Unfortunately, the current reality is that jurists are no longer intellectually compelling. That is why they resort to power. In my view, a competent legal sociologist is more of a jurist today than our Mullahs and Shaykhs. Therefore, to answer your question: in the perfect world and scenario, the jurists will have to discuss God's will and earn the respect of the people. If they are unable to do so, they are better off forgetting about it.

AN UPDATE

In December 2017, in an online event, Khaled Abou El Fadl opened the Institute for Advanced Usuli Studies ('The Usuli Institute', www.usuli.org). This is a non-profit Islamic educational institute that is 'dedicated to reclaiming what it means to respond to the divine call for mercy, beauty, ethics and justice, for the benefit of all of humanity', established as a venue for dissemination of 'the teachings of the school of thought that arises from Abou El Fadl's voluminous and expansive scholarship.'[49] Grace Song acts as its executive

---

49 1 August 2020 email from Grace Song.

director. All its educational events are free and available online at the Institute's website and on its YouTube channel. She regularly speaks at these events, to share her own experience of life as a convert, as someone who has been empowered and enlightened by Abou El Fadl's work.[50]

The Institute began its activities with monthly *halaqas* (learning sessions) and conversations revolving around Abou El Fadl's lifetime study of the Qur'an and his approach to the text. One of its activities is an ambitious project called "Illumine: The light of Qur'an" – a 'comprehensive chapter-by-chapter intensive study of the Qur'an with Khaled Abou El Fadl,' aiming 'to recapture the ethical message that sparked the passion of early Muslims and apply those lessons to our modern-day challenges.'[51] In January 2021 the Usuli Institute moved from Los Angeles to an undisclosed location in Ohio. The move took months, involving the transfer of Abou El Fadl's library: this is a major collection of Islamic and Usuli books, and includes his father's library as well as his own. In this way, with the help of Grace, Abou El Fadl has now recreated the learning environment, the richness and openness of traditional *halaqas* intended to contribute to recovering the ethical message of the goodness and beauty of the Islamic tradition.

---

50 http://www.youtube.com/c/TheUsuliInstitute
51 https://www.usuli.org/new-quran-project/

6

Mohsen Kadivar

Legal justice reflects the perfection of human societies, and legal discrimination the imperfection of them. Reason perceives such perfection and imperfection in a general way: Perfection is in the interest of humankind and imperfection leads to injury. People of reason, as they are reasonable, make this judgment to obtain beneficial consequences and to reject harmful consequences for humanity. The Lawgiver necessarily concurs with reasonable people, because it is a basic principle of the 'People of Justice' that the Lawgiver is reasonable and, in fact, is the head of all reasonable people.[1]

Mohsen Kadivar is one of the leading figures in the trend of Iranian reformist thought known as 'New Religious Thinking'. Currently he is Research Professor in Islamic Studies at Duke University. Born in 1959 into a politically active family in Fasa, near Shiraz, he was a student of electronic engineering at the time of the revolution. In 1981 he moved to Qom to pursue Islamic studies at the traditional seminary. In 1997 he attained his *ijtihad* certificate (the highest seminary level),[2] and in 1999 his Ph.D. in Islamic philosophy and theology from Tarbiat Modares University in Tehran. He taught Islamic jurisprudence, methodology and philosophy in the Qom seminary for fourteen years, and afterwards philosophy, theology and political thought in universities in Iran, but in 2009, when he was a tenured associate professor at Tarbiat Modares, he was dismissed because of his critical political and theological views.

---

1 Kadivar, 2013, p. 217.
2 *Ijazat al-ijtihad* is a certificate, in written form, granted by a Shi'i seminary teacher in *fiqh* to a student who has reached the required level of knowledge; it indicates the capacity to deduce religious rulings from Islamic sources. The recipient becomes a *mujtahid*.

A versatile and original thinker, Kadivar has pursued his reformist project by opening a constructive conversation between Islamic jurisprudence and contemporary notions such as human rights and gender equality. He has published books on Islamic philosophy, Shi'i critical theology, Shi'i political thought, human rights and Islam, and foundational reforms in Shari'a. Kadivar has been a vocal critic of Ayatollah Khomeini's doctrine of the absolute guardianship of the jurist (velayat-e motlaqeh-ye faqih) in Iran, and an advocate of democratic and liberal reforms, which led to his imprisonment in 1999. He was a visiting scholar at Harvard Law School (2002), and visiting associate professor at the University of Virginia (2008–9), after which he stayed in the US, pursuing a vigorous project of reform and making some of his considerable corpus available on his website in Persian, Arabic and English.[3]

I have been following the evolution of Kadivar's thought and writings since the late 1990s, when he came to prominence in Iran. I first met him in 2005 at a conference organized by the Irish Centre for Human Rights at the National University of Ireland in Galway, where we were both among the speakers, and I managed to engage him informally on his views on hijab. In 2011 we collaborated in the context of the Oslo Coalition's project "New Directions in Islamic Thought". [4] I translated into English his first publication on gender rights – "Revisiting Women's Rights in Islam" – for the Oslo project book Gender and Equality in Muslim Family Law.[5] As I was doing so, we had a number of Skype calls in which we exchanged ideas. This gave me an insight into both his reformist methodology and his gender perspective, and I was delighted to find him open to the feminist arguments and literature that I recommended to him.

I have found two of Kadivar's reformist ideas of particular importance and relevance for rethinking fiqh rulings on gender rights. The first is his notion of a human rights-based understanding of fiqh, which he first aired in summer 2001 as a lecture to the annual gathering of the largest student organization in Iran (Daftar-e Tahkim-e Vahdat). This lecture – "From Historical Islam to Spiritual/end-oriented Islam" – was published in a book that contains the edited texts of his lectures, interviews and journal articles between 2001 and 2005. Published in Iran in 2008, the book became a bestseller, but reprints

---

3 https://english.kadivar.com/biography-mohsen-kadivar/. For a recent discussion of some of Kadivar's work, see Ridgeon, 2021.
4 See below, and https://www.jus.uio.no/smr/english/about/id/oslocoalition/islam/
5 Kadivar, 2013.

were banned in 2009.[6] An English translation of the book, with a new introduction by Kadivar, situating his reformist approach as a contribution to the
study of Islam and human rights, has been published as *Human Rights and
Reformist Islam*.[7]

The second idea, which is of particular relevance to gender rights, is what
Kadivar calls 'ijtihad in principles and foundations' (*al-ijtihād fi al-usūl wa
al-mabānī*), that is, 'structural *ijtihad*', in which he argues for holistic reform
in Islamic jurisprudence. Instead of piecemeal reforms of *fiqhi* rulings
through juridical devices and legal maxims, such as *maslaḥah* (public
welfare), *zamān* (time), *makān* (place), *zarūrah* (necessity), *darar* (harm) or
ḥārjah (hardship), structural *ijtihad* 'focuses on the fundamentals and principles of Islamic legal theory and attempts to reconstruct the Islamic tradition's indigenous type of thought and cosmology, a system that encompassed
philosophy, ontology, theology, linguistics, anthropology, sociology, morality,
and *fiqh*.'[8]

Kadivar's first articulation of structural *ijtihad* in English is in his 2013
essay, "Revisiting Women's Rights in Islam", in which he defines himself as an
'Usuli Shi'i jurist', and his approach as '*ijtihad* in foundations' (*al-ijtihad fi
al-usul*), that is, *ijtihad* in the theoretical and philosophical foundations of
Islamic law.[9] He begins by setting out three key premises: first, the Qur'an
and the Prophetic tradition uphold the principle of justice in the area of
women's rights, for which there is both textual and rational evidence; secondly,
justice is exterior to religion, which means that its conception and justification
belong to the realm of human reason, not divine knowledge; thirdly, both
reason and Shari'a require that women be treated with justice and according to
what is commonly accepted as good or right (*ma 'rūf*). He goes on to show that
traditional *fiqh* rulings on women's rights are informed by a version of the
Aristotelian notion of justice, which entitles women to lesser rights, as they are
seen to be 'inherently inferior to men'. Such a notion of justice, which Kadivar
calls 'deserts-based' (*al-'adalat al-istihqaqiya*), can no longer be defended or
justified on rational grounds. It needs to be replaced by 'egalitarian justice'

---

6 Kadivar, 2008, pp. 15–34. An English translation of the lecture appeared as Kadivar, 2011.
7 Kadivar, 2021a.
8 Mavani, 2020, p. 54.
9 Kadivar, 2013, p. 213. The Usuli ('People of Principle') school advocates rational judgments
in deriving laws from textual sources, in contrast to the Akhbari ('People of Hadith') school that
emphasizes adherence to texts, especially the Hadith. In the eighteenth century the Usuli
became dominant, and it now forms the majority in Shi'i *fiqh*.

(al-ʿadalat al-musawati) because, in contemporary human rationality, women are:

> entitled to equal rights because they are human, and it is humanity – not gender, colour, race, class, religion, political ideology – that carries rights, duties, dignity, and trust and divine vicegerency. This position is more consistent with the Qur'anic spirit and Islamic standards; evidence for legal inequality, because of its temporariness, cannot be counted an obstacle to the realization of legal equality.[10]

In October 2017, I engaged Kadivar in a conversation with a view to including it in the present book. At the time I was teaching a semester at NYU Law School, and was hoping to be able to arrange a meeting with him while there, but eventually we decided to talk on Skype. Our conversation was conducted in Persian, and necessarily included much taʿarof,[11] which sounds odd if translated literally into English. An abridged translation follows, punctuated by some background and contextual comments. There are three parts: the first is about Kadivar's intellectual journey, which has been closely linked to post-revolutionary developments in Iran; the second introduces his reformist ideas and his proposed methodology for reform; and the third focuses on their implications for rethinking aspects of marriage and gender rights in fiqh.

BECOMING A REFORMIST MUJTAHID

I began with a brief account of my own intellectual journey since the early 1980s (as described in the introduction) as I wanted to set the tone and direction from the outset. In our earlier conversations in 2011, I was merely the translator of his text; here I wanted us to exchange ideas as scholars from different disciplines, talking on equal terms about subjects that we came to with different expertise and standpoints.

ZMH: My first question is about your own intellectual trajectory. I am curious to know why, after the 1979 Revolution, you abandoned your studies at

---

10 Ibid., p. 232.
11 The Iranian 'code of politeness'.

Shiraz University, one of the most prestigious in Iranian, and went to the Qom seminary to become a cleric.

MK: In 1978 I received my high school diploma in mathematics and phys-ics, and I passed the national entrance exam (*konkur*) for university the same year. I ranked among the top 100 students, which meant that I could choose any subject for university study. Meanwhile, Iran was experiencing a revolution and it was becoming increasingly evident that it would be successful. My parents wanted me to study medicine. They even had my transcripts translated and sent to my uncle, who was a medical doctor in the USA. I received an offer to study medicine at the University of California at Berkeley. But I did not want to leave my country when there was a chance to change society, so I tore up my offer letter. I was uncertain what subject I should study and went for advice to my high-school maths teacher, who had strongly influenced my thinking. After listening to me, he said: 'It's clear that you don't know what you want. If you choose a subject like engineering, it would be easy to switch to social sciences and humanities later on, but not the other way around.' I accepted his advice and enrolled in the electrical engineering programme. That was how my story started.

Now, as for why I did not continue in engineering. In February 1979 the revolution succeeded; a year later the universities were closed down for two years because of the 'Cultural Revolution'.[12] When they reopened, I changed topic and decided to study law. But the quality of the classes was far from what I had expected. Meanwhile, under the influence of what was happen-ing in Iran at the time, I began to study religion in the Shiraz seminary, and in June 1981 I transferred to the Qom seminary (*Howzeh-ye 'Elmiyyeh-ye Qom*). Of course, my parents were not happy with my decision to abandon my university studies.

You asked me about my decision to become a cleric. I wasn't thinking of a clerical career; I was interested in becoming an expert in religion, a very different thing – the former is a job like any other jobs; I wasn't look-ing for that. I was passionate about both religion and the humanities. Before the universities were closed, my friends and I would invite ulema to come and talk there. I was impressed by the depth of their knowledge

---

12 Between 1980 and 1983 the universities were closed in order to 'cleanse' them of 'Western, leftist and non-Islamic elements'. Widespread purges took place, and many teachers lost their jobs or left the country.

of religious studies. I remember that at the time I much admired Morteza Motahhari.[13] This was the image of experts in religious studies that I had in mind then. But if I had known then what I know now, I would have continued my university education for sure. I was looking for something that I felt we had lost; for an ideal. Inspired by Motahhari, I thought I would find it in 'Islamic' humanities. But after ten years of study I came to realize that social sciences are social sciences, and that there was no such a thing as 'Islamic' or 'non-Islamic' humanities. For this reason, while I was still in the seminary, I enrolled in university courses in theology and philosophy.[14]

ZMH: It is fascinating to see how the 1979 Revolution and its aftermath shaped the fates of individuals like us; you ended up in the seminary and I in England!

I told Kadivar briefly about my own university education and my failure to get employment as a university teacher after the Cultural Revolution, as I have described in the introduction. I did not mention that my interest in studying Islamic law began in 1983 when my marriage broke down – by then many of the reforms introduced in pre-revolutionary family law had been dismantled, and I needed to find an 'Islamic' way to free myself from my marriage. Instead, I asked about his time in the Qom seminary and the subjects taught there.

MK: Frankly speaking, when we say 'Islamic sciences', we mean *fiqh*, which constitutes the largest portion of what a student studies – the term 'religious scholar' ('*alim-e dini*) generally refers to a *faqih*, an expert in *fiqh*. Other subjects like philosophy (*falsafeh*), mysticism (*irfan*) and *tafsir* (Qur'anic exegesis) exist on the margins. So, if I wanted to learn the religious sciences, I had no other option than to devote most of my studies to *fiqh*. Because of my background in mathematics and physics, I advanced much faster in these subjects than other seminary students; I was more inclined toward rational subjects, and really liked – and still like – logic and philosophy, which were the easiest subjects for me. When I began studying

---

13 Morteza Motahhari (1919–79) was a celebrated clerical intellectual in pre-revolutionary Iran, whose ideas and books played an important role in the ideological discourse of the 1979 Revolution. He was assassinated soon after the revolution.

14 MA in Islamic studies and theology at Qom University (1993); Ph.D. in Islamic Philosophy and Theology from Tarbiat Modarres University in Tehran (1999).

fiqh, I became infatuated with *'ilm ul-usul*[15] (knowledge of principles), which is the basis of *fiqh*. Of the two Shi'i schools of law, I was attracted to the Usuli, which could be called Rationalist, since reason – like the Qur'an and the Sunna – is among the sources. This is not the case in the other school, the *Akhbari*, which takes a literalist approach to textual sources.

I studied and taught *'ilm ul-usul* in Qom for seventeen years. I tried to choose the best teacher in any subject, irrespective of his political orientation. I also taught it to students at different levels, and I can say that I came to know and feel this topic and to realize which parts include valuable concepts, and which parts of it need rethinking and revision. During my years of study in the *Howzeh* I endeavoured to understand, not to criticize. This is an important point; I had gone there to understand, and I spent nearly two decades working within the traditionalist framework of my teachers. All my teachers operated within that framework, including Mr Montazeri, the most important mentor in my *dars-e kharej* [highest level of studies]. I left the Qom seminary in 1997, and a year later went to prison.

Grand Ayatollah Hossein-Ali Montazeri (1922–2009) was a close ally of Ayatollah Khomeini, who designated him his successor as *Vali-ye Faqih* (Guardian Jurist) in November 1985. He had impeccable revolutionary credentials: he had spent years in the previous regime's prisons, played an instrumental role in inserting the *velayat-e faqih* (guardianship of the jurist) into the Constitution, and had published discussions on the subject from both theoretical and theological angles. But he was also a vocal critic of state policies, unwilling to compromise his religious standing and beliefs for the sake of power, and in 1989 he was dismissed. Under Khomeini's successor Ali Khamene'i, Montazeri became one of the Islamic Republic's most outspoken dissidents.[16]

In the June 1997 presidential election, the reform-minded Mohammad Khatami won a landslide victory, which inaugurated a brief period of press freedom and a vibrant civil society. But his policies soon met with resistance, sometimes violent, from the conservative establishment, notably the judiciary and sections of the Revolutionary Guards. In late 1998 a series of

---

15 Also called *usul al-fiqh*: it teaches the basic principles for deriving legal rules or laws from the sacred sources (*'adaleh-i shar'i*), which in Shi'i law are: Qur'an; the authentic Sunna of the Prophet and the twelve Shi'a Imams (infallible guides); consensus (*ijmā'*); and reason (*'aql*).
16 For an engaging account of his life and thought, see Siavoshi, 2017.

assassinations of political dissidents and intellectuals was uncovered in Tehran, termed by reformist journalists the 'chain murders', and President Khatami revealed that they were planned and carried out by 'rogue elements' in the Ministry of Intelligence.[17]

Meanwhile, on 14 November 1997, a few months after Khatami's election, Ayatollah Montazeri, in a sermon to his students in Qom, launched a critical appraisal of the institution of *velayat-e faqih*, for which he had been one of the main theoreticians. He now openly advocated the separation of the clerical establishment from government. He questioned the religious credentials of Ayatollah Khomeini's successor, Ali Khamene'i, and encouraged the new president, Khatami, to use the mandate given him by 22 million voters to reform the system.[18] The reaction to the sermon was swift and harsh. Montazeri's house was attacked, his classes were closed and he was put under house arrest. The press was banned from even mentioning his name. But some of his students began to speak. The most outspoken was Mohsen Kadivar, who almost overnight became a household name. His talks and interviews, in which he offered a cogent critique of what was being carried out in the name of Islam, angered the clerical establishment.[19] At that time, I went to Iran regularly and closely followed these developments, including Kadivar's arrest and trial, widely covered in the press. There was a lively public debate, which raised some taboo subjects, though not without consequences for those involved.

Kadivar and I now reminisced about those years, when there had been so much hope for change. I asked him to talk about the reasons for his imprisonment, and his time in prison.

MK: You know, I was the first [political] prisoner during the presidency of my friend Mr Khatami. He was completely against it; but he couldn't do much, it was the work of the judiciary and the regime's hardliners.[20] The charges given in indictment during my trials were two. One was a talk in which I condemned the recent assassinations that were rumoured to have

---

17 For a concise account of these developments and the reformist phase of the Islamic Republic, see Mir-Hosseini and Tapper 2006, pp. 29–36.

18 For this sermon see Mir-Hosseini and Tapper 2006, pp. 103–108; Siavoshi, 2017, pp. 171–172.

19 Mir-Hosseini and Tapper, 2006, pp. 108–110.

20 See Roodi, 1999. The book, compiled by Kadivar's wife, documents the process of his arrest, trial and defence, and letters written to the authorities. A letter by Kadivar's seven-year-old daughter to President Khatami, and his response to her, appear in lieu of an 'introduction', pp. 13–17.

been sanctioned by religious fatwas. In Ramadan that year, on the night of Qadr[21] [12 January 1999], I gave a talk in Isfahan's Hosseinabad grand mosque, on the invitation of the *Imam-Jom'eh* [Friday prayer leader], Mr Taheri.[22] I spoke for over two hours, and produced religious arguments as to why assassination of dissidents is forbidden (*haram*) in Islam, and according to Shi'i *fiqh* no jurist may give permission to assassinate anyone for whatever reason. The title of my talk was "Shari'a Condemns Assassination".[23]

The other [reason for my arrest] was my interview with the newspaper *Khordad*.[24] I had said that the doctrine of guardianship of the jurist, *velayat-e faqih*, is in effect a religious version of Iranian despotic monarchical rule; that the revolution changed the name, but not the nature of the rule; it is still one-man rule.

But the real reason was two books that I had published. One was on the theory of governance in Shi'i *fiqh*, the other was a *fiqh*-based critique of Khomeini's theory of *velayat-e faqih*.[25] In both books, I tried to be descriptive and analytical, and avoided current political issues. But they [the conservative clerics] understood what I was saying and obviously did not like my argument. Meanwhile, I applied to run in the elections for the Assembly of Experts (*Majles-e Khobregan-e Rahbari*) in Tehran which were due to be held in October 1998.[26] But I was disqualified; then in February 1999 I was arrested.[27]

I was in prison when I learned that one of my friends, Saeed Hajjarian, had survived an assassination attempt. The assassin was a member of the *Basij* [a militia of the Revolutionary Guards] and it was obvious that it could not have been done without the sanction of the authorities; everyone

---

21 The night when the Qur'an was believed to have been first revealed to the Prophet.

22 Ayatollah Taheri had been appointed by Khomeini as Imam-Jom'eh of Isfahan, the stronghold of Ayatollah Montazeri. He was one of the high-ranking clerical supporters of the reformists.

23 The full text of this lecture was published in Roodi, 1999, pp. 169–207.

24 One of the earliest and most daring reformist newspapers.

25 Kadivar, 1994; 1999a. For discussion and analysis, see Matsunaga, 2007, p. 318; for concise outlines, see Siavoshi, 2017, pp. 206–207; for analysis, see Sadri, 2001.

26 Only clerics can run for election to this assembly, whose task is oversight of the ruling jurist; https://www.brookings.edu/blog/markaz/2016/02/09/everything-you-need-to-know-about -irans-assembly-of-experts-election/

27 Kadivar was arrested on 28 February 1999, and spent eight weeks in solitary confinement; after his trial on 31 April 1999, he was transferred to Evin prison to serve his sentence.

knew his name. He was later pardoned. By now it became clear to me that the Islamic Republic had been using violence in the name of Islam to silence the opposition, and to physically eliminate those defined as opponents. I could not remain silent in my trial in the Special Clergy Court.[28] I told [the judges]: 'Aren't you ashamed of yourselves? You are convicting someone [Kadivar] who says that "assassination of a dissident is forbidden in Islam", which means that you are saying assassination in the name of Islam is permitted!'

I was in prison for eighteen months. After the trial was over I was allowed to receive books, of course after inspection by the prison authorities. I would ask my family to bring me books, and I used my remaining year of imprisonment to embark on a 'microscopic' study of violence in *fiqh*. I began to reread *fiqh* texts, from Shaykh Saduq[29] to modern times, and I took copious notes. It was then that I realized that there are matters in our *fiqh* books that could lend themselves to interpretations that, in today's idiom, are incorrect and unacceptable – and contrary to human rights.

ZMH: That must have been unsettling; after years of study in Qom, mastering the religious sciences, achieving mujtahid status, to come to such realization.

MK: Yes, I can say that around 2000/2001 I went through a huge transformation in my intellectual orientation. In effect, I experienced a kind of paradigm shift. I'll tell you something interesting. Before my imprisonment, I took part in a debate that the journal *Kian* organized on "Islam and violence". One of the participants was Mohammad Mojtahed-Shabestari, one of our pioneers of new religious thinking, and my senior in age.[30] He was arguing that *fiqh* is not reconcilable with human rights, as many of its rulings constitute violence by the standards of human rights. At the time, I was arguing that we could have a non-violent reading of these rulings from within the existing *fiqh* framework. You can find our debate and reasonings in the journal.[31] When I began my in-depth study

---

28 This court, directly accountable to the Leader, functions outside the Iranian judicial system; it was established after the 1979 Revolution to prosecute clerics and scholars for offences, improper conduct and activity unbecoming of a clerical class.

29 Shi'i scholar (923–991), and author of a Hadith collection, one of the Four Books of Twelver Shi'ism.

30 For a succinct account of his ideas and work, see Amirpur, 2015.

31 Kadivar, 1999b.

in prison, I realized that, working within the existing *fiqh* framework, we can be neither compliant with modern human rights principles nor capable of preventing violence in the name of religion. Much later, I wrote to Mr Shabestari and told him that he was right then, and after further studies I came to agree with him.

In other words, I knocked on every door and learned whatever was there, to find any opening in support of reforms within a *fiqh* framework. For example, take the question of Islam and democracy, which was a hot topic early in Khatami's presidency. I then supported the concept of 'Islamic democracy' that Khatami advocated, and even tried to explicate its basis in Islam; I wrote articles on the topic. However, in the new phase of my intellectual journey, I have made it clear in my writings that I no longer defend 'Islamic democracy'; what I defend is that we can have a democratic interpretation of Islam. These are two different positions. In the first, modern concepts such as democracy are confused with concepts from the Qur'an and Sunna such as *shura* (consultation) and *bay'at* (allegiance). In the second position, which I currently adhere to, the idea of democracy is a modern concept, like human rights and the nation state . . .

ZMH: Or gender equality and feminism . . .

MK: Yes, these are all modern concepts. We should not try to derive them from pre-modern texts. But we could say that [religious] texts have the potential to be understood, by those who believe in them, from a justice- and freedom-orientated perspective, and in an egalitarian way. It is possible to be a religious believer and also to believe in such modern ideas and principles, which happened to me when the new phase of my intellectual journey began.

I'll tell you something to show how much my views by then differed from those of my teachers. When I embarked on analysing relations between *fiqh* and human rights, I concluded that, realistically speaking, there are six areas of conflict between *fiqh* and human rights laws – I am not saying 'Islam' or *fiqh* as it ought to be, but *fiqh* as it is. These are: (1) inequality between Muslims and non-Muslims; (2) inequality between men and women; (3) inequality between slaves and free human beings; (4) inequality between commoners and jurists in public affairs; (5) freedom of conscience and religion versus punishments for apostasy; and (6) extra-judicial punishments, violent punishments and torture.

In summer 2001, I decided to consult Mr Montazeri, who was under house arrest at the time. I wrote him a letter and sent an outline of my findings above, asking for his views on how to address these areas of conflict. I ended the letter,

> Given these large areas of conflict between *religious* rulings (*ahkam-e shar'i*) and international documents of human rights, and given that the basic natural laws and the rights of human beings are essential to the principle of justice, we must rethink our *fiqhi* inferences. Otherwise, we must provide arguments and proofs that rulings inferred are in line with the natural and in-born rights of human beings, which is what is endorsed by sound reason. This is a vital problem for the Muslims in our time, and any hesitation in addressing it will jeopardize *shari'at*, *fiqahat*, and even religiosity. A solution to this problem is not possible without your knowledge and your juristic insight, as the benevolent *faqih*.[32]

He wrote back, encouraging me to do it myself; he said he would comment on my work.[33] When I completed my research on relations between Islam and human rights, I went to see him. It was summer 2003, and he was allowed to receive visitors. I said, 'Do you remember what you promised? Please tell me your opinion.' After reading my *ijtihad* and arguments, he said: 'If I endorse these, it would mean negating my own *ijtihad* in the last seventy years; what you have written is very different from the standards of traditional *fiqh*.[34] This is of course your *ijtihad*, and I respect your opinions and support you so that you can express them; meanwhile, these are your judgements, not mine.'

You see the extent to which my views came to differ from those of my teachers, especially my most important mentor, Ayatollah Montazeri. You can find the account of this meeting in the book that I wrote about his life and thought, soon after he passed away. It is around four hundred pages and includes all my correspondence with him. The title is *In the Presence of a Noble Theologian: My Mentor Ayatollah Montazeri*.[35]

---

32 See Kadivar, 2015, pp. 37–38.

33 Writing notes or comments on a text (*hashiye-nevisi*) is a common style of scholarship in seminaries.

34 Ayatollah Montazeri made his views on human rights public in the form of a *Resaleh-ye Huquq* (Treatise of Rights); for a discussion see Siavoshi, 2017, pp. 243–263.

35 Kadivar, 2015. The first edition was published in March 2010, three months after the Ayatollah's death; the expanded second and third editions were published online, February 2013 and August 2015: https://kadivar.com/14618/.

ZMH: This is fascinating and important. Your teacher, the Grand Ayatollah, didn't agree with your findings, but he respected your *ijtihad* and supported you.

MK: That is how he was. His magnanimity and his mentorship were such that he could say to a student, 'If your studies brought you here, this must be respected. This is your finding, which is different from that of your teacher. I will defend you if you are attacked.' His support and his mentorship meant a lot to me.

Ayatollah Montazeri died in December 2009 at the peak of the protests that followed the presidential elections in June. This election, like that of 1997, became a stage for confrontation between the contending forces of the Islamic Republic, between the unelected *velayat-e faqih* and the presidency chosen by direct popular vote, but this time the dividing line was drawn even more sharply. Although Khatami's two terms as president (1997–2005) had failed to bring the promised reforms, they had raised future expectations. The demand for political reform and personal freedom had gone deep into society. The election of Mahmoud Ahmadinejad as president in 2005, with the backing of Khamene'i, conservative clerics and the Revolutionary Guards, polarized society. When his first term ended in 2009, he was opposed by popular reformist candidates Mir-Hossein Mousavi and Mehdi Karroubi; but the conservative forces were not prepared to tolerate another reformist president, so they took no chances in June, and declared Ahmadinejad the winner in an election many believed had been stolen. Mousavi and Karroubi proclaimed that the election was rigged and mass protests against corruption followed. Ayatollah Montazeri denounced the regime as neither Islamic nor a republic but a religious dictatorship. He became the spiritual leader of the protestors, now known as the Green Movement.

The security forces, using considerable violence and brutality, drove the protestors off the streets. Ayatollah Montazeri's death in December brought huge crowds from all over the country to Qom for his funeral, and his seventh-day memorial – coinciding with Ashura, the 10th of Moharram (high point of the Shi'i calendar) – became the stage for another violent confrontation. Untold numbers were killed and imprisoned during the year following the election; the Green Movement was reduced to inactivity, except for a show of solidarity with the democracy movements in Tunisia and Egypt called for on 14 February 2011 by Mousavi and Karroubi; the result was the house arrest of the two leaders, which continued ten years later.[36]

---

36 Mir-Hosseini, 2017.

Kadivar was abroad on a visiting professorship during the 2009 election, but his support for the Green Movement was heard. He has not been able to return to Iran since then. Meanwhile he developed his reform approach, which he expounded in 2015 in an article in English: "Ijtihad in Usul al-Fiqh: Reforming Islamic Thought Through Structural Ijtihad."[37]

REFORM METHODOLOGY: STRUCTURAL *IJTIHAD*

ZMH: Let us now go back to your 'paradigm shift' and the development of your own thinking. As someone who has been following your work, I consider one key moment in your reformist trajectory to be your lecture in summer 2001, published later as "*Az Islam-e tarikhi ta Islam-e ma'navi*" ("From historical Islam to end-oriented Islam").[38] What did you intend by this?

MK: By *Islam-e ma'navi*, I had in mind an understanding of Islam that does not confine itself to the time and place of revelation. I used the term *ma'na* in the sense of purpose, end or objective. I mean the understanding of Islam that is *ghayat-madar*, i.e. end/purpose-oriented. When my article was published in English, I suggested that the best translation for this concept is 'Islam as an End in itself'.[39]

ZMH: Can you be a bit more specific? I mean, what is its impact on the legal sphere?

MK: When we study *ahkam-e shar'i* (religious rulings), we see that each has a shell, a form (*shekl*), but we should not stop there because behind each legal form there is a purpose, a desired end (*ghayat*). For instance, take the punishment for the crime of theft at the time of revelation: the 'form' was 'cutting off the hand'. But that is not all. Behind that form, if we carefully examine, we see that the 'purpose', 'the intention', was to warn people not to commit a crime. The legal form of a religious ruling, *hukm-e shar'i*, can change over time but its purpose can remain the same.

ZMH: How do we distinguish the 'legal form' from the 'purpose'? In practice we see that the two are not separated in traditional *fiqh*.

MK: Yes, because these jurists believe that we [humans] cannot know the 'purpose'. Only God knows. I disagree. This is a rational act. In my writings,

---

37 Kadivar, 2015b, pp. xx–xxvii.
38 Kadivar, 2008, pp. 15–34.
39 Kadivar, 2011.

I have argued that this might be the case [that only God knows the purpose] in matters relating to *'ibadat* (devotional acts) or *muharramat* (prohibitions). However, in acts that fall in the area of social interactions (*mu'amalat*), the purpose behind a ruling is not hidden from us. It is open to rational scrutiny and verification; we can carry out empirical and sociological studies of a particular form of punishment that we uphold as a religious ruling, in order to ascertain its impact on the rate of incidence of a crime. Socio-historical studies show that in pre-modern times punishment took a physical form, but that began to be eliminated when humans realized that physical punishment is the least effective. We can investigate whether, in countries like Iran and Saudi Arabia, which do apply such laws [classical *fiqh* rulings], we are witnessing a more ethical society than in others that do not.

ZMH: Of course not; we witness the opposite: a great deal of hypocrisy and injustice, as the majority of victims of these laws are the poor and women.

MK: This is what happens when the purpose and the legal form are not separated. When we see that a law does not produce the intended results, then clearly something is not working. We can explore and find another legal form that works. In my writings, I have demonstrated that, at the time of the revelation, *ahkam-e shar'i* were all, according to the standards of the time, more just, rational, moral and effective than the other existing laws. Among these four criteria, the most important is justice, which acquires a particular significance in the area of women's rights. And it is where the Qur'an puts the emphasis. The traditionalists claim that [by adhering to classical rulings] they can establish justice. I disagree; we need to establish justice according to the standards of our time, not according to seventh-century Hijaz.

ZMH: If we take these four criteria [justice, rationality, morality, effectiveness] as conditions, then a large portion of current *fiqh* rulings are indefensible, I mean they no longer qualify as 'Islamic' or can be defined as *ahkam-e shar'i*.

MK: That is my conclusion. We should be willing to accept the transformation. I believe that if we consider these four conditions as principles, our penal law should be entirely changed. In family law, most but not all rulings will be transformed – I can talk in more detail on women's rights. This is what I call *'Islam-e ma'navi'*. I also call it *'Islam-e rahmani'* (merciful Islam) by contrast with the violent and brutal conceptions of Islam that some groups are advocating. They believe that people's religiosity can only be safeguarded by force, and that people would not practice religion if they were left free.

It is clear that since the nineteenth century we have reached a point where most of the rulings in the category of *mu'amalat* cannot be regarded as just, reasonable or moral, and are less effective than other laws. We must ask ourselves: Are these rulings Islamic? I say they *were* Islamic because they *were* reasonable, just, moral and more functional than other existing laws at one time; they were in line with the values and standards of the people at the time of revelation, and that is why people accepted them. I contend that many of these rulings no longer meet the four criteria of justice, reasonability, morality and effectiveness according to the standards and values of our time.

These four requirements are, of course, interconnected; I have separated them to underscore the significance of each. We can defend each of them on rational grounds, but first the pre-modern worldview of the jurists needs to be adjusted. For example, the jurists of the old world would place women in the same category as children and slaves, even animals, that is to say, [they thought that] women have less capacity for rational thinking. We [jurists of today] say, fine, we accept that this was their [pre-modern] understanding, which they imposed on the Qur'an and Sunna; but we say that this understanding is wrong, and so we disregard its imposition. We enter this via our faculty of reason (*'aql*). We say that physical difference does not justify legal discrimination; there should be no discrimination between men and women when it comes to social, political and economic rights. This is very simple. An example that I often use in my classes [in the USA], and is well understood, is racial discrimination in the eighteenth and nineteenth centuries. At the time, there was a belief that white, Germanic and Aryan people were superior to others, even a scientific cloak was woven for it. Now, we laugh at such an idea and say it was erroneous. If someone now argues that women are inferior to men, we ask how this argument is different from saying a black person is inferior to a white person – the logic is the same. Differences of colour, race, gender or religion do not justify legal discrimination. What I say is that these are matters that are exterior to religion. If there is a Hadith [to the contrary], we 'throw it to the wall' [discard]. If we are referring to the text of the Qur'an, we should prioritize the verses – and there are so many of them – that are egalitarian.

ZMH: To do so, we need a wholesale transformation in Islamic sciences! This is a tall order!

MK: Yes, it is a tall order, but we have over a century of reformist thought. I am building on the work of many thinkers, notably Mohammad Iqbal's ideas in *Reconstruction of Religious Thought in Islam*[40] and Fazlur Rahman, as well as Mohammad Arkoun, Nasr Abu Zayd, 'Abid al-Jaberi, Abdulkarim Soroush (his former approach, not his recent one), Mohammad Mojtahed-Shabestari, and many others. I may have my disagreements with some of their ideas, but their work and ideas – as well as those of Jewish and Christian theologians – have been critical in my thinking that eventually guided me to a comprehensive reform methodology, which I call *ijtihad dar usul va mabani* (*ijtihad* in principles and foundations) – in other words, 'structural *ijtihad*'.

By the term *usul*, I have in mind the juristic methodology (*usul al-fiqh*) and contend that we need to go beyond traditional *ijtihad*, which is in effect derivative *ijtihad* (*al-ijtihād fi al-furū'*). By *mabani*, I have other areas of Islamic sciences in mind, notably theology (*kalam*), ethics (*akhlaq*), Qur'anic exegesis (*tafsir*), and compilation of and commentary on the Hadith ('*ilm al-hadith*), as well other sciences, linguistics, anthropology, sociology and so on. Here again I argue for the need to revisit some of their underlying assumptions and the worldview on which they are built. In other words, to reconsider certain epistemological, ontological, philosophical and anthropological premises that underlie the jurists' worldview and their approach to scriptural sources.

ZMH: Can you elaborate further – in what ways does the structural *ijtihad* approach differ from traditional *ijtihad*?

MK: In traditional *ijtihad*, one primary principle (*asl awwali*) is that all textual injunctions are timeless unless proved by definite evidence to be time-bound. Accordingly, the main function of religion is defined as delineation of the duties of humankind by 'the law' as found in Islam's textual sources (Qur'an and Sunna). The original Lawmaker is God or His Prophet. Deriving legal rulings from Islam's textual sources is the job of jurists, and their products are religious rulings (*ahkam shar'i*), which cover all areas of human action without distinction. All are parts of *fiqh* and the jurist does not need any special knowledge or expertise for discussing each of them. One can derive rulings on each area from scripture as long as one is an expert in *fiqh*. This means that parliaments in Muslim-majority countries would not be allowed to make any laws that are inconsistent with the so-called Shari'a rulings. In other words, maximal *fiqh* – a *fiqh* that covers every aspect of life.

---

40 Iqbal, 1934.

By contrast, structural *ijtihad* holds that all legal rulings derived from the Qur'an, Sunna and *fiqh* are time-bound, unless we can find valid evidence that they are timeless and permanent. The Qur'an never called itself a 'book of law' but a 'book of light', and light is guidance, which can be found in divine ethical virtues or moral values. It is meaningless to seek light or guidance in verses relating to penal codes or polygamy or slavery. How could the Qur'an be a book of law, when its legal verses are less than one per cent of the whole (and less than three per cent if matters of *'ibadat* are included)? There are about fifty legal verses in the Qur'an.[41] The content of these verses can be divided into two: permanent Islamic values and criteria, and temporary rulings fitted to the time of revelation and to Arabia. For example, the verse: 'Cut off the hands of thieves, whether they are man or woman, as punishment for what they have done – a deterrent from God: God is almighty and wise' (Q. 5:38) expresses a permanent precept that theft is a sin and crime that should be punished by governments. But cutting off the hands of a thief is, without any doubt, a temporary ruling.

Likewise, the prophet Muhammad did not identify his mission to be the completion of a legal system. Instead, he said, 'I was sent to complete the noble morality.' In the spiritual legacy of his prophetic tradition the terms that are legal in nature can be divided into two. First are his administrative rulings, which are due to his role as ruler, not as prophet. There is no evidence that such rulings are permanent and timeless. Second are rulings that are due to his prophethood, which undoubtedly are our respected Sunna, Tradition. But there is no Shari'a indication that his teachings on human interaction (*mu'amalat*) are intended as permanent and timeless rulings.

ZMH: Then what is the basis for determining which rulings, which norms, are timeless and which are time-bound?

MK: This is a big question. In Islamic tradition, we find two main approaches to ethics and virtues (*akhlaq*). One is an absolutely rational approach, holding that morality and ethics are universal disciplines and common ground in all religious and non-religious traditions. The role of religion is to support morality and ethics with the guarantee of rewards and punishments in the next world. In other words, ethical and moral principles are not among

---

41 Jurists have differed on the number; some have said that as many as 500 verses (out of 6,035) are 'legal'.

al-ahkam al-ta'sisi, the positive rulings that Islam created or founded, but are classified as *al-ahkam al-imda'i*, meaning existing rulings that were ratified by Islam. In ratified rulings, human reason – which is God's gift – creates the ruling, and religion plays only a confirmatory role. This approach is shared by the Mu'tazilites, who once constituted the majority, and in contemporary times by Usuli Shi'ites.[42]

In the other approach [Ash'ari], moral values are defined by divine revelation: ethical values and moral norms as well as Shari'a rulings were determined by the Lawgiver and Muslims should consult scripture to discover them. The methodology for deriving ethical principles is not rational, but textual. This is the mainstream of all major theological schools of Sunni Islam.

Structural *ijtihad* operates within the framework of the first approach, i.e. rational ethics. Of course, Muslim scholars may highlight some moral values and ethical rulings, and prefer others at a time of probable conflict between them. But do we have any moral and ethical principles that are exclusive to Islam and have no parallels in other traditions? If the response is *no*, then we must admit that the Qur'an and the Sunna are not the primary sources for morality and ethics. When we examine the injunctions in the Qur'an and Sunna, we see that they were directly relevant to the economic, political, social and cultural situation of early Islam, i.e. in line with *'urf* (custom) and notions of justice and ethics in seventh-century Arabia. In short, the Qur'an and the Sunna are not the primary sources for morality and ethics; they are the secondary and necessary sources for any Islamic discussion, and have a great role in clarification of these principles.

ZMH: The question becomes then, how can we differentiate between a ruling that is Shar'i, i.e. sacred, and a ruling that is *fiqh*, i.e. juristic? It seems to me that ultimately it is the jurist who decides.

MK: In the language of traditionalists, Shari'a is the same as *fiqh*. But I say that once we dig deeper, we find that Shari'a is the eternal, universal values that are deliberated within an Islamic perspective – values like human dignity, decency, justice and fairness, and others, which I listed in my discussion of *Islam-e rahmani* (Merciful Islam). These values are highly significant and inseparable from the religion of Islam.

---

42 The Mu'tazilites were a rationalist school of Islamic theology, dominant in the eighth to tenth centuries, which emphasized the role of human reason, and a belief in the absolute necessity of God's justice and human free will. For an illuminating discussion on reason as independent source of law, see Bhojani, 2017, pp. 25–51.

From the first century after the Prophet's death his companions came to see Shari'a as a set of practical laws, a conception similar to *halakha*, which is the practical/legal side of the religion of Moses. They came to understand Shari'a more as a set of legal rulings, and its moral values were marginalized. The question that now faces us as Muslims is: Does Shari'a consist of moral values, or legal rules and law? In other words, if there are two notions of Shari'a, will it be Shari'a as a body of moral values, or will it be as a body of rules and laws? The historical inclination of Muslims has been the latter, like the Jews. That is to say, Shari'a became law-centred. Whereas, originally, Shari'a was certainly not law-centred but value-centred. The difference is that values can be universal and eternal (timeless), while laws are essentially time- and context-bound. It is hard to say that any law is eternal. For example, take criminal laws, which, as I mentioned, have acquired different forms at different times and places. That is in the nature of law.

The very term 'Islamic law' needs to be problematized. Law in its essence is time-bound. There is a direct relationship between law and the situation of time and place. Values and virtues can be timeless and permanent, but it is difficult to accept timeless rulings and laws. Of course, we can merge a human-made law with our Islamic values and virtues and call it 'Islamic' regarding those values and virtues, but we cannot preserve rulings made several centuries ago in the context of Arabia, especially in their traditional forms and patterns, imagining that these forms and patterns are sacred because they were revealed by God to His Prophet, or made by the Prophet, according to the *ijtihad* of the jurists.

Today Islam is presented as Shari'a-based, and what they mean by Shari'a is a body of rulings and laws. But this is not what the Prophet said. If the Qur'an were meant to be a book of law, then why are only three per cent of its verses of a legal nature? If we reduce religion to law, then we have no choice than to be always looking back, and we cannot move in accordance with the requirement of time and place. Here, Muslims have to make a historical decision. For me, Shari'a is ethical values.

IMPLICATIONS FOR GENDER RIGHTS

Kadivar has addressed the question of women's rights in Islam in a number of his articles, lectures and interviews, all available in Persian on his website. In the introduction to this chapter, I outlined the argument in "Revisiting Women's Rights in Islam", his first publication in English on the theme.[43] In 2011, while translating that paper for publication, I drew his attention to Fazlur Rahman's only writing on the topic of gender rights – "The Status of Women in Islam: A Modernist Interpretation" – as an instance of the application of Rahman's interpretative process for revival of the Qur'anic ethics for our time.[44]

I now told Kadivar that I thought his article was as important as Fazlur Rahman's, and followed up by asking his opinion as a jurist on aspects of discriminatory *fiqh*-based family laws.

MK: This is like a door that leads to other doors – I build on Fazlur Rahman's arguments and methodology. If we want the transformation in *fiqh* rulings then we must start in *usul al-fiqh*; that is what I have in mind when I say *ijtihad* in principles. We should revise the method, not the after-effect! The theory of structural *ijtihad* is based on the premise that we attribute our own perceptions and predispositions to the Qur'an and Sunna. Yes, we have verses in the Qur'an that affirm equality between the sexes. At the same time, we have verses that could be interpreted as indicating male dominance. The authenticity of neither group of verses can be disputed. What the Traditional jurists have done is to derive rulings from the second group of verses and to interpret the first group as mandating equal rights in ways to justify men's superiority.

ZMH: That is to say, deriving laws from the textual sources always rests on a set of presuppositions. For instance, we come up with totally different rulings if we take as our basic postulate the opening verse of Surah al-Nisa, which speaks of ontological equality between men and women, rather than verse 4:34, from which the concept of male authority over women (*qiwamah*) was derived.

MK: Yes! In that article ["Revisiting Women's Rights"], I quoted the opening verse of Surah al-Nisa and other verses that denote equality between men and women. I said we can also read the Qur'an in this way. I also quoted those other verses [understood as denoting inequality] and interpreted them on the basis of egalitarian principles. I showed that interpretation is contingent on presuppositions. A jurist should first clarify and state

---

43 Kadivar, 2013.
44 Rahman, 1982b.

his methodology and foundational assumptions, and only then start interpreting the verses. This is the same mistake that ISIS and similar groups make: they interpret a text outside its context. In other words, what is the primary principle (asl al-awwal)? What is derived from it (fara')? What is our principle or 'rule of application' (qa'ida) [for doing this]? I call all these, which are exterior to the Qur'an and Sunna, underlying foundations (mabna). For a traditionalist jurist, [the foundation] is men's superiority over women. By contrast, reformist thinkers like me, for whom equality between men and women is a given, interpret the Qur'an from an egalitarian standpoint. They [traditionalists] have no right to tell me that this is not 'Islamic' and that only what they believe in is 'Islamic'. I would respond, 'Your fiqh is based on that of the Prophet's companions (sahabah) and past jurists.'

Gender ideology and the position of women in the modern era are different from those of the premodern era. The rulings for these two eras could not be the same. Those who want to impose the rulings of the premodern era onto the modern era, without any meaningful change or with just a few minor revisions, and think that this is the implementation of sacred Shari'a or divine law, are completely mistaken. What they preserve is only the early customs of the Arabs of Hijaz, or abrogated Islamic rulings. What should be preserved are the divine permanent values and timeless criteria and standards.

ZMH: Let me ask you about something that I have found so baffling. In classical fiqh, marriage (nikah) is defined as a bilateral act, a contract ('aqd) that requires the consent of both parties; but divorce (talaq) is defined as a unilateral act (iqa'), which can take effect through the will of only one person – the husband. Why shouldn't the wife have the same right?

MK: In my book Haqq al-Nass, I discussed the question of divorce in the chapter on "Reformist Islam and Women's Rights".[45] In our traditional fiqh, we have three mechanisms for ending a marriage: talaq, which is a man's right; khul', which is a woman's right; and mubarat, which is both parties' right. Another mechanism, annulment (faskh), can be initiated by either spouse upon specific grounds. In talaq, the right rests only with the man – so this is clear. In mubarat the right rests with both spouses, this is also

---

45 Kadivar, 2008, pp. 287–313. This is the text of two lectures that Kadivar gave at gatherings organized by Mosharekat, one of the main reformist parties, in September 2003 (1 & 15 Shahrivar 1382), and first published as an article in the party's journal later the same year.

clear. The only mechanism that is legally problematic is *khul'*. As it has been interpreted, no divorce can take effect without the husband's consent. You see how it has been interpreted in such a way as to give men the final say here too.

They [the *fuqaha*] say that *talaq* is for men, and *khul'* is for women. Then why aren't women allowed unilaterally to end the marriage by *khul'*, as men do by *talaq*? The jurists' argument is that this is because women are emotional. My answer is: if this alleged emotionality is the reason, then it is much more likely to be present at the time of marriage, as wives are most often younger and less experienced than their husbands. We know that the woman's consent is one of the essential conditions for the validity of a marriage, to the extent that if there is slightest doubt in this regard, the contract is rendered void. In *fiqh*, the woman is the only person in charge of consenting to her marriage. Her father does not have the right to speak for her.

I say openly that, if marriage is defined as a bilateral contract, divorce should also be defined as bilateral. If we believe that one or both of the spouses lack the capacity to end the marriage, we should disqualify both and only allow a third party, like a judge, to decide it. Both the husband and the wife should be required to go to court, and the court to decide if divorce should be granted. Neither spouse should have the right to divorce unilaterally. This, in my view, respects the rights of both spouses. It is also more effective in safeguarding the family unit. The current law in Iran is not defensible. It does not meet the four criteria, that is, of being rational, moral, just and more effective than other existing laws. Unequal rights to divorce might have been suitable at some point in history, in the specific circumstances of that time and place. For today, I defend equality in divorce just like equality when entering marriage. Many contemporary legal systems have more advanced family laws than what we have in Islamic laws.

ZMH: What about Muslim women being barred from marrying non-Muslims, while there is no such ban for Muslim men?

MK: I wrote a separate article about this, in which I say that jurists, being all male, were more tolerant with respect to Muslim men marrying non-Muslim women.[46] There is a verse in the Qur'an that says that marrying a non-Muslim from among the People of the Book (*Ahl al-Kitab*) – Jews, Christians and Zoroastrians – is permitted (Q. 2:221). It is a Qur'anic

---

46 Kadivar, 2011b – in response to a question.

verse, not a Hadith. The injunction in this verse, I argue, applies equally to men and women. The traditional *fiqh* ruling [banning Muslim women from marrying non-Muslims] rests on a set of assumptions: (1) men and women are not equal; (2) men have authority (*qiwamah*) over women; (3) therefore, children of such a marriage will be non-Muslims. Since the children of a Muslim must remain Muslim, it is deduced that a Muslim man may marry a non-Muslim but a Muslim woman may not marry even an *Ahl al-Kitab* man.

In that article, I challenged these assumptions and argued otherwise. I showed that young children tend to be more inclined to their mother than to their father, so the child of a Muslim woman is more likely to become a Muslim than the child of a Muslim man. They [the *fuqaha*] ignore this fact. Also, the arguments that they produce are weak. My argument is that the marriage of Muslims with non-Muslims should be either forbidden altogether or allowed for both women and men. Only allowing the marriage of Muslim men with women from the People of the Book (*Ahl al-Kitab*) is discrimination against women. This is unacceptable. I defend the equality of men and women and believe that both can marry someone from *Ahl al-Kitab*. I also provided my arguments and cited those of previous jurists who held the same view. I covered all schools of law, both *Shi'i* and *Sunni*.

ZMH: Custody rights are another area in which women are disadvantaged in Muslim contexts. As defined in *fiqh*, custody has two elements: *hizanat* (care) that can be seen as physical custody, which can go to the mother; the other element, guardianship (*wilayat*), always rests with the father. This in practice creates many problems for mothers, as the guardian's permission is needed in all matters, such as registering the child for school needs, or even if the child needs emergency surgery.

MK: These laws have no solid basis. They are all based on the patriarchal mindset of pre-modern jurists, which I do not regard as Islamic. They belonged to a specific time and place. As we discussed, men and women have equal rights, and in addition, we believe that women are entitled to receive preferential treatment in some instances, like when they are pregnant or for raising children until the age of puberty. The law must guarantee these rights. Besides, we can find ample evidence supporting this in our juristic sources. That is why I believe that traditional *fiqh* is fundamentally different from 'reformist' *fiqh* in the area of women's rights: equal rights in divorce, and protective rights for women in some cases, such as the area of custody. All these can be defended on a rational basis. Before a child reaches the age of puberty, who takes more care of it, the mother or the father? In practice, in most communities, a mother plays a more significant role than a father. Why should we ignore these facts?

I have no problem if legal forms in the realm of *mu'amalat* are altered; there are no restrictions and we must be up-to-date and respect the purposes. In the area of women's rights and the family, the stability of the family must be taken into consideration, as well as equality between spouses. But I am committed to respecting the forms as much as possible in the realm of *'ibadat* (devotional acts) and *muharramat* (prohibitions); rulings in these two realms cover acts that are religious in nature, as we come to know about them only through revelation.

ZMH: Could you elaborate a bit further, and be more specific?

MK: In the realm of *'ibadat* we definitely have 'Islamic' and 'non-Islamic'. The devotional acts of Muslims and non-Muslims are distinctive, i.e. prayer, fasting, pilgrimage (*hajj*) and alms-giving (*zakat*); there is no question about this, they are religious acts, and are not governed by human reason or rationality. On the other hand, actions in the category of *mu'amalat* are about social relationships, so they can be regulated by law and they are governed by human reason. But I believe that there is a third category that covers certain matters in the realm of *mu'amalat* that resemble those in the realm of *'ibadat*. This was said before me, I think, by Mohammad Mahdi Shams al-Din, the progressive Lebanese jurist, who has written on women's rights, not one book but several books in Arabic. One of his books is on women's right to be leaders and their qualification to be judges, which he argues on *fiqh* grounds; and there are no problems.[47]

Shams al-Din uses three Arabic terms to refer to those areas of human action that fall in this category. These are: *mashrubat* (drinking); *ma'kulat* (eating); and *mankuhat* (sexual relations). This category can be called *shibh-i manasik* (quasi-rituals) – I'm not certain whether the term is his or mine. He says that we should be more nuanced in deciding whether an action falls in any of these three areas. For example, even if it is scientifically proven that drinking alcohol without getting drunk is not harmful to your health, we are forbidden to drink alcohol on religious grounds. The same goes for eating pork. Abstaining from pork is one of the practical indicators of being a Muslim. Muslims are also forbidden to eat the meat of an animal found

---

47 Shams al-Din, 2009. Shams al-Din (1936–2001) was a Lebanese Twelver Shi'i scholar; see el-Husseini, 2008.

dead. These are examples of prohibitions related to food and drink that are 'quasi-rituals'. This is also true about matters related to *mankuhat* that involve sexual activity and relationships. For instance, marriage is necessary for any type of sex, divorce is necessary for its termination, sex outside marriage is prohibited and so on. These all define the boundaries of sexual relations.

The category of 'quasi-rituals' (*shibh-i manasik*) was totally new to me, and I tried to probe further and explore its implications for family law. As we shall see, it became clear that we had different views when it came to matters of sexuality. For Kadivar the limits of sexual relations are fixed by divine revelation, thus non-negotiable; whereas for me they are subject to human reason and social norms, hence open to negotiation and change.

ZMH: Is *shibh-i manasik* a new category in *fiqh*? It's new to me; I wonder how rulings in this category differ from those in the realm of *'ibadat*.

MK: It's a new approach that distinguishes two aspects of some actions: what is governed by human reason and what is governed by divine revelation. *Shibh-i-manasik* covers those rulings that we in *fiqh* refer to as *tawqufi*; that is to say, we know them because they are dictated by revelation. The rulings that come under *'ibadat* are referred to as *ta'abbudi*, that is to say, they are devotional acts that require the *qasd-e qurbat* (intention of closeness to God).

ZMH: In my view it would be legally problematic to place marriage in the in-between category of *shibh-i manasik*, which would give *fiqh* the ultimate say. Marriage is a contract between two individuals as well as a social institution, so its rulings should come in the category of *mu'amalat*.

MK: *Fiqh* is a noble science. I stress this. Marriage, its consequences and correlations have always comprised a large chapter of any book of *fiqh* or Islamic jurisprudence. We should not put *fiqh* completely aside from all areas of *mu'amalat*: the limits [of sexual relations] must be defined. The problems are created when *fiqh* is used in realms such as politics, economics and governance. We should not mix rulings relating to each with the other. Marriage has several aspects: the quasi-ritual, the human interactional, the institutional, and so on. These aspects do not exclude each other, they are complementary. The *shibh-i manasik* defines the limits of sexual relations. *Mu'amalat* clarify its legal boundaries. True that marriage is more than sex, but there are certain areas in sexual activity that are not permitted for

Muslims. Marriage as a contract is governed by the general principles of human contracts, but sexual relations are a different matter. These are not problematic in my view. These are details.

ZMH: Details matter! I am concerned because it seems to me that what you are proposing is hardly different from classical *fiqh*, where marriage straddles the boundary between *'ibadat* and *mu'amalat*. As I have argued in my own work, this hazy boundary not only helped to sanctify patriarchy; jurists speak of marriage as a religious duty, an act of worship, but when it comes to its legal structure, they define it as a contract of exchange, patterned after the contract of sale, through which the husband acquires the right to control the wife's sexuality.

MK: Your concern is not warranted. Those aspects of marriage that come under *shibh-i manasik* relate to the limits of sexual relations as specified clearly several times in the Qur'an.[48] This is a religious matter – a matter of *halal* and *haram* for the faithful – an aspect of marriage that I consider to be among the *tawqufi* rulings, and I defend it, which has nothing to do with the legal dimension of marriage as a contract, in which, as I already clarified, men and women are entitled to equal rights. Unlike the traditionalists and their maximal *fiqh*, what I am advocating, i.e. structural *ijtihad*, leads to a *fiqh* that is minimal, a *fiqh* that is restricted to *'ibadat, shibh-i-manasik* and certain elements in *mu'amalat* like usury (*riba*).

I therefore see no reason for concern. There is always the possibility of abusing or misusing an ethical mandate; this does not mean doing away with that mandate; it is the job of the law to close as many loopholes as possible. I must say here that there is a kind of '*fiqh*-phobia', a Shari'a-phobia, that is not the right approach. In the Shari'a as I define it, as Khaled Abou El Fadl defines it, as Fazlur Rahman defines it, these [*halal* and *haram*] are ethical standards, those parts of Shari'a that I believe are not time-bound.

ZMH: I understand your rationale and how rulings in the category of *shibh-i manasik* differ from those of *'ibadat* as well your conception of Shari'a as ethics not laws – a conception that I share. The question that arises is whether defining the limits of sexual relations is a matter that falls in the domain of ethics or that of law.

MK: Stating the limits of sexual relations is a matter of both ethics and law. The question to be asked is: What is our expectation of religion in the real world? What are the areas of human action governed by divine revelation? In

---

48 Qur'an, 23:4–7; 70:29–31; 24:30–31.

other words, what makes a law Islamic? In the era of nation-states, all this goes back to matters of *'urf*, which I elaborated in detail in an article available on my website.[49] In another discussion, on "The Relationship of Religion and Politics" (*Nesbat-e Din va Siyasat*),[50] I say that we can have political ethics but not political *fiqh*, economic ethics but not a *fiqh* of economy and trade, but we can and do have both ethics and *fiqh* relating to marriage and sexual relations. Why? Because the institution of marriage has different dimensions: the social, the legal and the sexual. And, as explained earlier, it is only the sexual dimension of marriage that is subject to rulings that *fiqh* refers to as *tawqufi* – that is to say, we know them because they are dictated by revelation.

ZMH: There is a problem here, because the social and legal dimensions of marriage can and do change in time, as do sexual ethics – we know this through sociological studies. You too consider ethics like justice to be extra-religious matters, that is to say, they exist independent of religion but are contingent on time and place.

MK: Yes, the social side of the institution of marriage of course changes with time and space; I also consider laws governing marriage to be *'urfi* [not religious/secular], subject to time and place. But as to its sexual parameters I consider them to be among the timeless values; in the past, sexual relations outside marriage were considered wrong and they still are. It seems to me that our views are getting closer . . .

ZMH: The sexual dimension of marriage cannot be so neatly separated from its social and legal aspects, and I still fear going back to the classical *fiqh* construct, that any sexual relation that is outside marriage (*nikah*) is *zina* and subject to punishment as a crime.

MK: Sexual relations outside marriage are not allowed, and this is an Islamic value. This is ethical, and, in societies where Muslims live, it is translated into law. You say that you fear that we may go back to classical *fiqh* [*zina* rulings], I say that no, we will not. It is the *urfi* (secular) lawmaker that defines the penalty. Therefore, no aspect of marriage goes back to *fiqhi* rulings. But I defend Shari'a, and have always said so; you too; we agree that Shari'a and *fiqh* are not the same . . . Look, the problem is, as I said, there is a kind of *fiqh*-phobia that leads to fearing Shari'a and Islam . . .

ZMH: Yes, the fear is new and real; it is one of the after-effects of political Islam and the unjust laws that have been advocated in the name of Shari'a

---

49 Kadivar, 2017.
50 Kadivar, 2020.

and Islam! Yes, there is a great deal of orchestrated Islamophobia, but at the same time we cannot deny that wherever *fiqh* has become the law of land, religious despotism has ensued – just look at our own country, Iran!

MK: I agree with what you said; we are facing a terrible polarization with extreme reactions, which is equally dangerous – especially in Iran, where one side is imposing 'Islam' on every area of social and political life and the other side wants to obliterate Islam. You and I are in between! We want to bring change from within the Islamic tradition, and for the sake of reform we cannot put aside everything in our tradition. We are separating those parts of *fiqh* that have become frozen in time, and you and I are advocating justice, equality and fairness – these are the eternal values of Islam and its Shari'a.

* * * * *

Following our 2017 conversation, I invited Kadivar to join a new research project in Musawah that began in 2019, entitled "Reclaiming 'Adl and Ihsan in Muslim Marriages: Between Ethics and Law".[51] Our aim is to build on the findings of our earlier project on "Rethinking the juristic concepts of *qiwamah* and *wilayah*", in order to advocate an understanding of marriage as a partnership of equals. Our conversation has continued, and now includes my colleagues in Musawah. His voice and arguments now reach a different and wider public beyond Iran, where he has had the greatest impact. Most recently, English translations of two of his books have been published by Edinburgh University Press.[52]

Kadivar speaks and writes very clearly, but I have found it difficult translating the *fiqh* concepts and language that run through his argument. When I hear and read his work in Persian, it comes across with more force than I have been able to convey in English – something seems to get lost. However, throughout preparing this chapter for publication, I have been in contact with Kadivar, to check the translation of technical terms, and to make sure that I have reflected his views and arguments accurately.

As is clear toward the end of our conversation, I had trouble accepting his placing of sexual relations in the new *fiqhi* category of quasi-rituals; we had long discussions over this, and when I sent him a final draft of this chapter, he was dissatisfied with how the conversation went at this point. He wrote: 'You

---

51 https://www.musawah.org/knowledge-building/reclaiming-adl-and-ihsan/
52 Kadivar 2021a and 2021b; https://edinburghuniversitypress.com/series-in-translation-modern-muslim-thinkers.

have edited it in a way that highlighted what you think is correct. It is your book and I tolerate it.' But there is so much more that we agree on, and, as he said, 'You and I are in between! We want to bring change from within the Islamic tradition, and for the sake of reform we cannot put aside everything in our tradition.'

But for reform to flourish, we need to have these conversations, to build an overlapping consensus about what aspects of our tradition require rethinking and, perhaps, what must be left behind.

7

Sedigheh Vasmaghi

. . . much of what has been called Shari'a rulings, especially with regard to civil, penal, domestic laws and those concerning women rights, are actually no more than jurisprudential [fiqhi] interpretations, and that it is far from certain that they belong to Shari'a at all.[1]

Sedigheh Vasmaghi is among the few women scholars in Iran who have taught and published extensively on Islamic law. Born in 1961 into a religious family, she began her studies in Islamic sciences in a women's seminary in 1980. In 1983, she enrolled for a BA degree at the Faculty of Theology in Tehran University. She began teaching while doing her MA degree at Al-Zahra University, before joining the faculty. After completing her Ph.D. in 1998 specializing in *fiqh* and principles of Islamic law, she became a tenured professor. She took early retirement in 2009, sensing the political ambience in universities moving toward more restrictions; moreover, for some years she had found it difficult to teach *fiqh* as 'Shari'a rulings', an equation she did not agree with, as she had told her colleagues many times.

Vasmaghi is also a renowned literary figure – her poetry collection, *Praying for Rain*, won the 1989 Best Book Award from Al-Zahra University in Tehran – as well as a major voice of the reform movement in Iran. In 1999 she was elected to the first Islamic City Council of Tehran, and served as its spokesperson (*sokhan-gu*) until 2003. Following the disputed presidential elections of June 2009, the brutal suppression of protesters and allegations of torture and rape of detainees, Vasmaghi joined the voices of protest that came to be known as the Green Movement (see the previous chapter), writing articles, poems and open letters that appeared on reformist websites. Her office became the

---

1 Vasmaghi, 2014a, p. 12.

headquarters for the team appointed by the two main reformist leaders – Mir-Hossein Mousavi and Mehdi Karroubi – to investigate these allegations. In February 2011, Mousavi and Karroubi called for a gathering in support of the uprisings in Tunisia and Egypt, which led to another round of crackdowns and arrests. Vasmaghi, along with some other prominent reformists, chose to go abroad for a while. She first went to Germany as a visiting professor at Göttingen University, and later to Sweden, where she served as an International Cities of Refuge resident research fellow at Uppsala University. At Uppsala, she taught and engaged in some research on a comparative study of Iranian and Swedish family law.

On 17 October 2017, along with her husband, she decided to return to Iran, despite knowing that in 2014 the Tehran Revolutionary Court had convicted her in absentia on charges of propaganda against the state and sentenced her to five years in prison. Upon arrival, she was detained for a few hours at the airport, and was released only after giving a commitment to present herself at court the following morning.[2] She appeared at the Tehran Revolutionary Court on 22 October, and in a hearing that lasted for twelve minutes, the judges upheld the 2014 verdict. She was detained in the women's section of Evin prison until she was released on bail on 4 November, pending her appeal against the sentence.[3]

I first encountered Sedigheh Vasmaghi's work as a scholar of Islam in 2010, during the Fourth International Congress on Islamic Feminism in Madrid,[4] when Dr Nahid Tavassoli (one of the few Iranian women identifying with Islamic feminism) presented me with a copy of Vasmaghi's book: *Beza'at-e Feqh va Gostareh-e Nofuz-e Foqaha* (*The Capacity of Fiqh and the Extent of the Influence of the Fuqaha*), privately published in Iran in 2009. I found the book extraordinary: it was the first time I had come across the writing of an Iranian woman so well versed in the tradition, who critically engaged with the epistemological claims of Islamic jurisprudence (*fiqh*) and its construction of Shari'a rulings (*ahkam-e shar'i*). I knew of Vasmaghi's writings and reformist ideas,

---

2 See https://www.zeitoons.com/36805

3 See https://persian.iranhumanrights.org/1396/08/release-on-bail-sedigheh-vasmaghi/; also "Iran: writer and poet released on bail," *Pen International*, 15 November 2017, https://pen-international.org/news/iran-writer-and-poet-released-on-bail

4 For an account, see Muslim Media Watch https://www.patheos.com/blogs/mmw/2010/11/the-fourth-annual-international-congress-on-islamic-feminism/; there was also an account of it on Iranian news websites, e.g. https://www.jamaran.news/Section-news-9/15784-islam-th-congress-of-islamic-feminism-in-madrid

and read her articles, interviews and poems; had I known that she was also a scholar of Islam, I would have reached out to her years earlier. In the 1990s, during my fieldwork in Qom, I tried hard to meet women scholars teaching there, but none responded to my request for an interview, despite lobbying through my male cleric friends. Interestingly, in the Madrid Congress programme, I was down on the last day to debate with Fariba Alasvand,[5] one of the women scholars I had failed to meet in Qom in 1995. But she did not attend the Congress, and instead her paper was read by an Iranian embassy official.

In early 2012, I met Vasmaghi at a small brain-storming meeting in Paris that brought women's rights activists who had just left Iran together with those living in Europe to discuss ways of integrating women's demands with the Green Movement, which was now active online and in the diaspora. Nothing came of that meeting, but Vasmaghi and I kept in touch; she gave me a copy of her book, *Zan, Fiqh, Islam*, also published in Iran in 2009, and told me that it was being translated into English; it came out in 2014 as *Women, Jurisprudence, Islam*.[6] She had written the book at the height of a heated debate over a controversial family bill that the hardliner government of Ahmadinejad presented to parliament in early 2007. Once the draft of the bill was made public, it became a major focus for women's rights activists, who considered the bill a regressive attempt to undo what remained of the pre-revolutionary Family Protection Law and to render toothless the reforms that had been gradually reintroduced since the early 1990s. They condemned several articles in the bill as a further infringement of their rights: one put a ceiling on the value of the *mahr* or marriage gift (women's only negotiating card in divorce), and another made polygamy easier for men by allowing the registration of temporary marriages. The bill was passed in 2011, but only after those disputed articles had been substantially modified: the ceiling on *mahr* was removed, and registration of a second marriage was once again made subject to the first wife's consent.[7]

In *Women, Jurisprudence, Islam*, Vasmaghi critically engages with *fiqh*, whose discriminatory rulings she holds responsible for the 'negative image of Muslim women'. Not only are they unjust and unacceptable to women, they

---

5 In fact in 2011, Karen Bauer interviewed Alasvand during her research in Qom. For an account of this interview and Alasvand's gender perspective and arguments, see Bauer, 2015, pp. 73–79, 224–246.

6 I reviewed it in the *Journal of the American Oriental Society*, 2016, 136.3, pp. 667–669.

7 For the context of this law and debates around it, see Mir-Hosseini, 2012b; Osanloo, 2014.

are harmful to society; they are so out of touch with the realities of contemporary life that, instead of creating order and justice, they have become a source of disorder and of injustice. Yet those who criticize and attempt to modify these discriminatory laws are accused of opposing Islam and its laws. Vasmaghi locates the root problem in methodology and politics. Her prime argument is that what has come to be known as Islamic Shari'a was blended with the Arab culture and tradition ('urf) of seventh-century Arabia. This blending has been so pervasive that in the process of inferring 'Shari'a rulings' from the sacred texts (the Qur'an and the Prophetic Tradition), the early Muslim jurists came to equate them with the familial, tribal and social relations that prevailed among the early Arab Muslims. This was particularly the case in gender rights and family law, where men did not want to lose their privileges. So she asks: Do these discriminatory laws represent Islam and are they the same as Shari'a rulings (ahkam-e shar'i)?

In *The Capacity of Fiqh*, Vasmaghi asks further questions: What is a Shari'a ruling? What is its scope? Does it relate to every aspect of law? How do jurists come to know it? She seeks the answer to these questions in the intersection of power and legal theory (usul al-fiqh), which not only resulted in an all-encompassing definition of Shari'a but allowed the *fuqaha* to arrogate to themselves the power of law-making. Reflecting the views of reformist jurists, she argues that almost all these rulings are early Arab traditions and laws that the Prophet either endorsed (ahkam-e emza'i) or reformed (ahkam-e eslahi) at the time of revelation, and thus reflect the culture and social conditions of the time. Even those few rulings that Islam established (ahkam-e ta'sisi) are not beyond time and place, so they too are open to rethinking and rational argument. An 'unchanging Shari'a ruling,' she contends, is 'one for which the reasons are evident and which does not depend on conditions, time, place or custom.' But this can apply only to those rulings whose subject matter is beyond the constraints of time and space and human reason; that is, those rulings that relate to creed and acts of worship. By definition, family and criminal laws are not part of the Shari'a; humans make these laws, which must be subject to change and evolution. So a large part of *fiqh* rulings, which relate to social, political and economic issues, cannot come under the Shari'a.

In *Bazkhani-ye Shari'at* (Rethinking Shari'a), her third book on the same theme, Vasmaghi takes her arguments to a new level by asking: Are what we have come to know as 'Shari'a laws' (qawanin-e shari'at), the direct word of God – the Lawgiver (shar') – as transmitted by Prophet Muhammad? This time, she approaches these questions through Usuli methodology, that is, the very tools of the jurists themselves. She began research on this book in 2009 and completed it during her stay in Uppsala, in April 2017. The book was launched in a panel discussion in Paris on 30 September 2017 in which Vasmaghi participated (a week before her return to Iran).[8] By then her work was attracting attention, and there were a number of articles and interviews with her in English.[9]

I recorded two conversations with Sedigheh Vasmaghi; the first was on 27 November 2017 when she was already back in Iran and I was teaching a semester at New York University. I had just finishing reading *Rethinking Shari'a* and was intrigued by her radical thesis. By then we had developed a friendship, and would exchange ideas and sources via WhatsApp or Skype. I knew about her severe eye condition (retinitis pigmentosa) for which she had a special lens for reading things on the computer. We had also coincided in several conferences, where she was always accompanied by her husband, her attentive guide and aide. The conversation was through Skype, but the connection was poor. After working on the transcript, I realized that there had been too many interruptions and gaps. Also, having followed developments since her return to Iran, I had new questions to ask, so we arranged a second conversation, which took place on 20 July 2020.

CHOOSING TO STUDY *FIQH*

I began our conversation by asking what had led her to Islamic sciences and becoming one of the few women with a specialization in *fiqh*.

SV: I was drawn to all things religious as a child, and, as far as I can remember, I have always paid a great deal of attention in religious discussions. When I was thirteen, still in middle school, I bought, with my own pocket money, copies of the Qur'an and *Nahj al-Balagha* (*The Way of Eloquence*).[10] I remember reading them voraciously, alongside their Persian translations, over that summer break. At the high school level, I majored in mathematics

---

8 The launch, reported in the online reformist press (https://www.zeitoons.com/35935), was organized by the Rahman Society.

9 See for example, Alipour, 2013; Rampoldi, 2016.

10 Collection of sermons, letters, *tafsir* and Hadith attributed to Imam Ali, the Prophet's cousin and son-in-law, considered the first Shi'i Imam.

and physics, and I ranked high in my class, but I remained committed to doing religious studies at university. I was the only one in my class who wanted to do theology; the others all wanted to pursue subjects such as architecture or engineering. When asked why I wanted to do theology when I had so many options with my high school major, the answer for me was obvious. At the time, two universities offered degrees in theology: University of Tehran and Ferdowsi University of Mashhad. As you know, candidates for the *konkur* [national university entrance exam] are allowed to write down several majors in their applications; but I decided to write only one, i.e. theology at the University of Tehran. I was that clear about my choice.

ZMH: So it wasn't the 1979 Revolution that influenced your choice?

SV: Not at all! I had already started reading *Nahj al-Balagha* and other religious books. That was before the revolution. I really don't remember when I became eager to do a university degree in theology. I was drawn to religion from childhood, and I always had questions: I encountered certain obscurities and I wanted to find spiritual and rational answers for them. That was what motivated me to look for answers myself. I was hoping to find them by studying theology. The answers that I received from others or read in books did not convince me. But 1980, the year I finished high school, coincided with the Cultural Revolution and the closure of the universities, so I could not take the entrance exam that year. Instead, I began working as a journalist at the *Ettela'at* newspaper.[11] I had been sending them poems and essays since I was a teenager; they had already told me to come and work with them when I finished high school, so I did. Three months later [September 1980], the Iran–Iraq war started. I was the first woman to go to the front as a reporter, in December 1980. At first my father was against my going to the war front because of the dangers involved, but I told him that as a writer I needed to go to the front and see the situation for myself. I was close to my father and he knew how important it was for me, so he said, 'Okay, then I'll come with you,' and he did. Three months on, I went back to the front, but this time with two women friends who were also writing for the papers.

But I was still very keen to study religion, and I was looking for alternative ways to indulge my interest. At the time, there weren't that many

---

11 *Ettela'at* is the oldest Iranian daily newspaper; it has several associated weekly and monthly journals, including one for woman (*Ettela'at-e Banovan*).

options available. I went to Qom to find about Dar al-Zahra.[12] I talked to the principal, and she gave me a tour of the school and told me their rules, which rather discouraged me. There and then I told myself, 'I can't study here.' I came back to Tehran and continued my search. I learned that the Madraseh-ye Shahid Motahhari – before the revolution it was called the Madraseh-ye Sepahsalar[13] – was holding an entrance exam with an interview solely for women. I took the examination and after passing the interview and admissions process I was enrolled. We followed the same curriculum as the Qom seminaries; our instructors came from there – some of them were women. I studied there for less than three years, but I did not like the environment at all. I enjoyed the lessons and was an eager student – I wanted to learn and I believed that they would guide me to find my ultimate calling; but I found the ambience stifling and quite intolerable.

ZMH: In what ways?

SV: There was a pervasive culture that ultimately limited women's sphere of action; simply put, it was not an 'open' environment, but rather an exemplar of the Islamic Republic's treatment of women and its limitations on their choice of proper attire and how to interact with the opposite sex. For instance, they would scold girls for laughing, teaching them that they should behave in a certain way in order to be considered 'pious' (ba taqwa); that they should wear certain clothes and speak in a certain way; and they warned us never to look men in the eye. These things were annoying for a young and energetic person like me. I reluctantly wore the mandatory chador that served as our school uniform, seeing it as an inconvenience but ultimately unimportant compared to my desire to learn. I myself come from a religious family, traditional but not strict; we children were not forced to do things. I don't remember ever being told by my parents that I couldn't do something because I was a girl. My mother treated her sons and daughters the same, and used to tell me and my sisters: 'You girls have the same rights as your brothers' – you know that in the past this was not very common in religious families. When I started writing poetry I would

12 One of three women's seminaries founded in the 1970s. In 1984 they were merged and expanded into *Jami'at al-Zahra*, see http://archive.ical.ir/files/english/pl-05-08.pdf.
13 Founded by Mirza Hossein Khan Qazvini Sepahsalar (1828–1881), a distinguished Qajar reformist, it is the oldest and largest seminary in Tehran, attached to the famous Sepahsalar Mosque. After the revolution, the seminary was renamed after Ayatollah Morteza Motahhari, a close associate of Ayatollah Khomeini; assassinated in 1980, he is known as *shahid* (martyr).

participate in poetry reading sessions and sometimes I would travel to other towns with the group.

In 1983, as soon as the Cultural Revolution ended and national entrance exams were restarted, I jumped at the opportunity to enrol in the University of Tehran, and I was admitted to study theology. The university too imposed annoying restrictions on us students, such as hijab, something I fought against from the day of admission until the day of graduation. It proved a lonely struggle, with no one joining me in my protest.

But again, my aims and interests in studying, researching and teaching in this field were more important to me and couldn't prevent me from following this path. So I went to university and continued my education there, made a definite choice to focus on *fiqh* for my postgraduate and doctoral studies, because I thought that the answers to my questions must lie there. People equate Islam with *fiqh*; something that has caused us Muslims many difficulties in our lives is this notion of *fiqh* as Shari'a rulings (*ahkam-e shar'i*). Conventional understandings of Shari'a and Shari'a rulings always, for me, gave rise to questions and uncertainties. My questions did not really involve issues of morality, philosophy, the interpretation of the Qur'an and so on. Instead, I always thought that these Shari'a laws and rulings played the greatest role in the lives of Muslims, and that's why, to find answers to my questions, I chose this field of study [*fiqh*].

ZMH: You also taught this topic for over twenty years during your tenure at the Faculty of Theology at Tehran University; at the same time, you were involved in politics during the reformist era and in 1999 you were elected to the Tehran Council, becoming a public figure as its spokesperson. It was then that I first heard your name, as it was all over the papers. You are also a well-known poet. Can I ask about these aspects of your life?

SV: I began writing poetry in my teens; the subject matter of my poems has always been social and political. I remember when I was at Kharazmi High School, my teacher asked me to prepare a selection of my poems for the headteacher to send it to the regional office. Two weeks later, the school *Nazem* [a senior administrator] talked to me and tried to convince me to stop writing poetry, telling me that I was a talented student, at the top of my class, and should focus on getting to university, etc. I didn't understand at the time, but I later realized that she was concerned because my poems were too political! After I got my high school diploma [in 1980], I joined *Ettela'at* as a journalist; my essays and reports were on social and political matters; I was also invited by the journal *Soroush*[14] to write for the page "Political Observers", and I had articles published there almost weekly. I stopped being a professional journalist when I finished my MA and focused on my teaching at the university and research in the field of Islamic sciences. But I never gave up writing poetry and I have contributed regularly to journals as well as doing interviews on current affairs.

My involvement in politics began with my election to Tehran City Council and becoming its spokesperson. It was during the reformist presidency of Mohammad Khatami, when we were all full of hope for a democratic turn in politics. I stood for election because the Council (*shura*) is a civil rather than a state body, and I wrote a book, *Hatman rahi hast* (*Surely, There is a Way*) about this, the only period when I was involved in formal politics. I wrote it as a 'historical document' of the experience of the first ever Tehran City Council, and the kind of challenges, interferences that we faced on a daily basis in carrying our responsibilities. If it weren't for this book, I would have wasted four years of my life.

Surely, There is a Way is based on the diary Vasmaghi kept at the time. She began writing the book before she left Iran in 2011. In over five hundred pages she describes the inner workings of the Council at a time when, although reformists were in government and had a majority in parliament, many of their attempts to bring about reform were offset by their conservative opponents in the judiciary and by the Supreme Leader's office. The book was launched in Paris in January 2015 in a gathering that brought secular and religious intellectuals together.[15] At the time, I was in regular contact with her via Skype, to help her to find a publisher for the Arabic translation of *Women, Fiqh, Islam*.[16] She told me about her intention to return to Iran, as well as the risk she would be detained, as she was. I reminded her of this, and asked what motivated her to return to Iran knowing that she would be arrested.

---

14 A cultural and intellectual monthly, sponsored by the Iranian national broadcasting organization.
15 *Hatman, Rahi Hast* was published in December 2014 by Khavaran Press, an Iranian exile publishing house. For the launch, see http://asre-nou.net/php/view.php?objnr=33521
16 The translation had already been done by a young Arab seminary student in Iran. My colleague Dr Mulki Al-Sharmani facilitated the publication and distribution (Vasmaghi, 2018), after Vasmaghi had returned to Iran.

SV: As for what motivated me, well, I don't think one ever needs a reason to justify returning home, in fact it is the opposite: you need reasons to justify staying away. I hadn't left Iran for good; I always wanted to return, but I was forced to extend my stay after receiving threats from individuals [in the security forces] in Iran. I had many reasons for wanting to return. First, Iran is my home and my country. Second, I did not want to live my life in fear of imprisonment. I have never lived a life of fear and did not want to live under the shadows of the what-ifs, and I thought to myself that even if something were to occur and if I were to be imprisoned, at least I would be imprisoned in my own homeland. Anything was possible and is still possible, but I did not want the hypotheticals to scare me, and so my husband Mohammad and I decided to return right after completing the two book projects that I was working on, something we had agreed to do from the start. I wrote them while in the midst of hardships and difficulties, and I am happy that publishing them ended up having very positive results.

One thing that I want you to know about me is that I have always loved travelling, and it has been one of my life projects to go all over the world, to study other cultures, different ways of being in this world; and to some extent I was able to travel. But never for such a long period; I was forced this time to stay in Europe for six and a half years. It was indeed a valuable experience for me, enabled me to learn more about life in Europe, especially good governance, and the welfare system that states provide for their citizens; and gave me an insight into a better or more rational way of life and how it affects the life of individuals. All of these experiences directly influenced my thoughts.

The fact that I was able to complete the two books was a great blessing for me. As you know, *Rethinking Shari'a*, which contains my latest thinking on *fiqh*, was something I had planned to write for a while. One of my goals was not to return until I had completed it.

RETHINKING SHARI'A

ZMH: Let's now talk about this book. It seems to me the seeds were sown in your mind long ago; in a sense it is the product of decades of a personal intellectual search for understanding – this is something that I can identify with. The questions you raise there are not new to your work; you have explored them elsewhere, notably in *The Capacity of Fiqh*. What I found new is your choice of Usuli methodology. First, can you briefly explain what that is? And what was the reason for the choice?

SV: The name Usuli[17] is derived from *usul al-fiqh*, which is the conventional and dominant method used by Muslim jurists for conducting *ijtihad* in deriving *ahkam-e shar'i* from the four valid sources, which in Shi'i *fiqh* are the Qur'an, Hadith, *'aql* (reason) and *ijma'* (consensus). I chose the Usuli approach in order to open a dialogue with the jurists, so as to rebut and challenge their views from within. Since it is the language of the seminaries, the language of the science of *fiqh*, I wanted to base my arguments and claims – which are often challenged or may be controversial – on a common language and methodology. I think that if I had used another methodology or language, I would not have been very successful in communicating effectively, and ultimately bringing my points home. I tried to open a meaningful and constructive conversation with those who agreed with me or opposed me in the hope that we could reach an understanding.

ZMH: There seems to be a paradox here. I mean, if you use the Usuli methodology, aren't you bound to reach the same or similar conclusions as those in the seminaries? In other words, has using this method given you much 'wiggle room' when seeking answers to your question, as you do in *Rethinking Shari'a*?

SV: Of course, as you see in the book, I critically engage with the underlying theoretical doctrines used by the Usuli jurists, and end up questioning their conclusions. But using the same methodology, I argue that we should not extend the domain of Shari'a to the laws that govern our daily life. Usulis cannot prove that Shari'a is applicable to those laws. I find the Usuli method to be the most effective and prudent choice when one seeks to challenge a dominant view from within, i.e. using the same technique but reaching different conclusions. I used it in my earlier books, notably *The Capacity of Fiqh* that you mentioned, in order to reach different conclusions from those of most jurists.

ZMH: Yes, but your arguments are further developed in your new book, and in fact much more radical. You contend that neither the Qur'an nor the Prophet mandated laws governing people's social and political life. This implies that all these laws, rulings that have been instated as *ahkam-e shar'i*

---

17 See Chapter Six; as already mentioned, the term Usuli also denotes those groups in Shi'i seminaries favouring rational analysis (*ijtihad*) in deriving rulings from the valid sources, in contrast to the Akhbari, who favour textual authority, namely Hadith.

throughout Muslim history – ranging from family to penal laws – are not part of Shari'a!

SV: They have never been so; their underlying principles may have been, but not the actual laws themselves. For example, Islam, like other religions, affirms marriage, but the Qur'an did not define the form of marriage and its governing rules, nor the appropriate forms of punishment and retribution as the jurists came to see it. The Prophet did not create a new form or system of marriage; he accepted the customs and ways in which the people at the time practised marriage. He took a similar approach with respect to divorce, punishment, blood-money (*diya*) and inheritance: in all, he approved most of the customs of the time.

I challenge the conventional view that those laws are the best laws, that they are in conformity with the Prophet's Shari'a. I disagree and I don't find them to be his Shari'a at all. The Prophet was an individual living under the rules that governed social relations, the customary laws of society at that time. As a realist, he accepted those laws and approved and respected them, unless they were either considered unjust according to the standards of the time or objected to by society. The core of the Prophet's promotion of Islam was not to inaugurate laws or change them. He did not initiate law-making, it was not his mission.

During the Prophet's ten years in Medina, he had to legislate as part and parcel of the job, as the leader of the community, in order to manage its daily affairs as well as the problems of Muslims in the community. He did make or alter laws at the people's request on a few occasions, all of which I explore in detail in my book; I argue that, if these laws had been part of his Shari'a, they would not have been conditional on the request of the community – i.e., the Prophet would have been required to legislate them routinely, as part of his mission. On the basis of historical evidence, we find that the Prophet intervened and changed these laws only when and if people asked him to. For example, he introduced new laws on women's right to inheritance after women went to him in protest and objected to the existing customary laws regarding the issue.

ZMH: Regardless of how we see it, the Prophet did come to have a great deal of political clout and could therefore influence the laws at the time. The Prophet's time in Medina cannot be seen as inconsequential.

SV: Yes, but its specifics, and the undercurrents of his time in Medina, were very different from how we understand them today. I discuss all this in the book. It depends on how we approach and read the past. Most often, we interpret historical events and their evolution in the light of the present; but if we go deeper and examine the historical evidence to find out what really happened, then we can come to a different understanding. Whether the Prophet sought political power from the outset or not is a matter of interpretation. I believe that he did not. The Prophet preached Islam in Mecca for thirteen years in difficult circumstances, until he was invited by a group in Medina who offered him refuge and protection in return for advice. His political power in Medina was the result of subsequent events; it came by virtue of his leadership, a position he held by popular demand. The Prophet never intervened in laws governing people's life and private affairs unless he was asked – at least, we do not have any historical evidence of it. Were his responses to questions asked by the early Muslims and the problems they confronted, constituted or related to Shari'a? I do not believe so. There is no evidence that they were. Many of his responses to these questions were based on the *'urf* and tradition (Sunna) of the time. We have no reason to consider them part of Shari'a; it is our *fuqaha* who call them Shari'a rulings. We need to rethink all this.

ZMH: What then was the Prophet's Shari'a?

SV: Prophet Mohammad's Shari'a – like that of other prophets – was to invite people to live a just life, one free of crime and with respect for the rights of others. This was what we learn from the Prophet's message in Mecca. The Prophet's real message and Shari'a was what he preached in Mecca. He advised people not to steal, not to lie, to avoid sex outside marriage, and to get along with their neighbours. The Prophet's Shari'a invited individuals to perform good deeds and to avoid various superstitions, polytheism, idolatry. These comprise the main Shari'a of Islam and largely echo the message of other prophets.

Islam, like all religions, warns people against wrongdoing; for example, the Qur'an explicitly says that Allah has permitted trade and has forbidden usury. Here, the Qur'an forbids usury (*riba*) but does not define it.[18] How should we define usury? There has been no consensus on this. The fundamental issue in my opinion is: Who are the people that the Qur'an and Hadith are addressing? What is the Qur'an telling them? This in itself is a big discussion; there are many things for which we do not have answers precise and adequate enough for us to treat them as laws; at least, not concrete ones like, 'Islam's answer to X is Y.'

---

18 The Qur'an, *Baqarah*, 2:275–276.

For example, let us assume that our understanding of the Qur'an and other religions is that that they all favour marriage, that they do not approve of adultery, lying, stealing – things that humans themselves, through their reason, realize are bad and harmful to their lives. All religions expand upon these notions and emphasize that we should choose a path in life that is good and just. That is what Shari'a is. Every religion has its own Shari'a. We see that devotional acts ('ibadat) such as prayer and worship are highly regarded and encouraged in *all* religions, and so is the notion of abstaining from polytheism, idolatry, and superstitions and only worshiping God. Ultimately, I believe that these are what constitute the Shari'a of Islam and other monotheist religions.

ZMH: Of course, such a conception of Shari'a is not shared by the ulema; I mean it does not tally with the consensus that has emerged in Islamic legal tradition.

SV: In my view, any definition we have of Shari'a is an interpretation, on which we have different views. *Fuqaha* may claim that the laws governing people's lives at the time of the Prophet fall in the realm of Shari'a. But I say, they do not. These laws were for the people of that time, the direct address-ees of the Prophet, who enjoined them to live just and decent lives. The laws passed fourteen centuries ago were deemed to be just by the populace, based on their circumstances and their customs, knowledge and experience at the time. But today, if we meet unjust laws, we cannot attribute them to the Prophet's Shari'a, because, in essence and in practice, Shari'a is and always has been intended to fight injustice, so it would be logically incon-sistent and incoherent to approve of an unjust law – it would not be possible.

This shows clearly that we are mistaken if we interpret the Shari'a to include old, archaic laws. My book gives various examples to show that those laws are not, and cannot be, enforceable any longer. People simply do not find them fair and do not and will not accept them. I therefore argue that we need to change our understanding of Shari'a and to limit it to those religious teachings that are valid in all times and all places, and are not in contradiction with evolving human rationality, knowledge and lived experiences.

ZMH: Yes; the term Shari'a appears in the Qur'an, but not in the sense of laws, and was not used in that sense during the time of the Prophet. Why do you think it came to be defined in the course of history as law, and Shari'a and *fiqh* came to be equated?

SV: The first misstep in Islamic history was the title, the idea of caliph, an individual appointed as the Prophet's successor following his death. There is no such a thing as succession to prophecy! Those selected caliphs then came to be in charge of government and politics as well as religious matters. Law and Shari'a were conflated during that very sensitive time, when these successors sought laws to legitimate their rule and to govern their affairs. The laws applied by the Prophet's successors were named and regarded as religious laws and Shari'a. This was the time when governance, religion and politics became intertwined. The jurists who came to join the ranks of government supported such developments and came to identify with Islam and Islamic principles all laws that were passed for proper governance and societal needs.

ZMH: If we take the political context of the time into consideration, it could also be said that their intention was to safeguard the Prophet's teachings, to align day-to-day Muslim life and the laws governing it with what the Qur'an said and with the Prophet's practice.

SV: But the result has been remote from the fundamental teachings of the religion. The problem, as I see it, lies in the theoretical premise of *fiqh* that takes religion to be the same as law-making. This is a definition of Islam that we must rework. The fundamental flaw in the discipline of *fiqh* is that it has become too distant from the moral teachings and basic principles of Islam. For example, one of the basic elements of women's rights is justice, which in today's world, is understood as equality between men and women. Where do we see such a notion of justice for women in the *fuqaha*'s discussion? They insist on keeping unchanged laws that are discriminatory according to the standards of the modern world, on the grounds that they are part of Shari'a. Who can accept this argument in this day and age?

We have around 6,300 verses of the Qur'an; at most, 300 of them relate to legal matters. I ask: What about the other verses? Are they not all part of our religion? There are many verses in the Qur'an that can be reopened in order for us to fight against superstitions, injustice and corruption, providing moral teachings and historical lessons. But today a traditional jurist would approve of legal discrimination against women because he would not be considering today's views and customs. These jurists are not capable of applying Islamic teaching to law. Why? Because justice is an *'urfi* notion, and they do not relate it to today's *'urf* but instead they rely on tradition, on standards from 1,400 years ago. This is wrong and problematic. Instead, justice should be defined by modern standards.

ZMH: Another point that you make in the book is that Usuli jurists engaged in sophisticated rational debates, but they were not prepared to rethink the founding theories and dogmas of *fiqh*. Yet their rational arguments in practice came to justify the Hadith-based conclusions of [their opponents] the Akhbaris. This is an intriguing argument; could you elaborate?

SV: The definitions and conclusions that the Usulis reached in *fiqh* were largely the same as those of the *Akhbaris*. True that the Usulis developed sophisticated logical arguments, in great detail, and went to great lengths to reach their rational conclusions, but they ultimately abandoned them. I discuss this in detail in the last chapter of my book, where I show how the Usulis avoided going where the logic of their own premises and arguments would have led them; they would often resort to consensus (*'ijma*), or would attack anyone who wanted to pursue such arguments to their logical conclusions. Thus they disparaged or discredited the views of those who argued that we do not have a solid basis for regarding all areas of law as coming under the domain of Shari'a; they often resorted to statements like, 'How could we ignore the duties of prayer or fasting? What would remain of Islam!' By not engaging with such views, Usuli jurists failed to do justice to their own methodology and to make a distinctive mark on *fiqh*. In practice, they served to reaffirm and crystalize the *Akhbari* approach and conclusions.

I believe that, as scholars, we should approach issues and analyse them without prejudgement; we must do our best to be unbiased and objective observers, to acknowledge and accept any conclusions that our enquiry leads us to. The problem with the approach taken by the Usulis is that they have failed to keep to the distinction between rulings on devotions (*'ibadat*) and those on the social order (*mu'amalat*). These two sets of rulings are different, and should not be treated as the same. We can retain the former unchanged, but not the latter.[19]

ZMH: I have always wondered why, despite recognizing reason (*'aql*) as a source on a par with the Qur'an and the Sunna, Usuli *fiqh* rulings are more less the same as the other schools of law. But surely there were some who, so to speak, swam against the tide and were prepared to accept the logical

---

19 See Chapter Four, where Abou El Fadl says more or less the same, and my disagreement with Kadivar at the end of Chapter Six over his placing sexual relations in the new category of quasi-rituals.

consequences of the Usuli method? Pluralism and diversity of opinions (*ikhtilaf*) have been inherent to *fiqh* as an enterprise.

SV: Yes, of course there have been alternative voices, but they were muffled. One of those voices, which I discuss at length in my book, is that of Mirza-ye Qomi.[20] He pointed to some extremely important issues at the time (in the eighteenth and nineteenth centuries), and made some controversial statements for which he met an extensive public backlash, for example, when he argued that we are not the addressees of the Qur'an or the Hadith, so we can't take them at face value. In essence, anyone who becomes an expert in Qur'an and Hadith studies would realize this, but everyone tries to find a way to avoid it, seeking arguments that will reach a different conclusion, so as to be able to claim that we are indeed the addressees of the Qur'an and Hadith. Why? Because they feared that abandoning the traditionalist view would essentially mean abandoning the religion of Islam itself. This is all based on an erroneous understanding of religion.

ZMH: Okay, then the question becomes how do we come to know what is or is not part of the Shari'a? In other words, what is a *hukm-e shar'i*?

SV: When we read religious sources, our aim is to understand what God requires from us. The Qur'an is our main source of this understanding, i.e. of *ahkam-e shar'i* – the instructions of the Lawgiver (*shari'*). But our understanding of the Qur'an is not absolute, as I discuss in my book in detail. I do not believe that we can say with certainty what God requires from us today. Because, first, we are not the Qur'an's addressees; secondly, it contains so many ambiguities that we can never be certain of its intention, its real meaning and the implications; and thirdly, some things that the Qur'an says are not related to us. For instance, when the Qur'an says, 'Fight with unbelievers (*mushrikin*),' it is addressing the people of that time who were already at war with the unbelievers. It is not addressing us, for us to act upon it.

This is why, in *Rethinking Shari'a*, I came up with all these introductory arguments, to argue that we should limit Shari'a to the realm of *'ibadat*, not extend it to matters harmful to the daily lives of individuals, unacceptable by our standards of logic and moral conduct. In addition, I do not regard the Hadith as a source of *ahkam-e shar'i*, as they were collected after the Prophet's death, and not according to his wishes but by people voluntarily, which means

---

20 Mirza Abu'l-Qasim Qomi (1738–1816) was a renowned Shi'i jurist, author of an important book on *usul al-fiqh*: *Al-Qawanin al-Muhkama fi'l-Usul* (*The Solid Laws of Usul*). He is also referred to as Muhaqqiq-i Qomi, and Sahib al-Qawanin (Owner/Master of Laws).

that they are not part of the revelatory knowledge. But I value them as historical documents, and believe that they are like other historical sources that will enable us to gain knowledge about Muslims. We can refer to them in certain cases, but for me they are not the source of Shari'a nor of Islam as a faith.

ZMH: If I understand you, you are in effect saying that we do not have such a thing as *hukm-e shar'i* – i.e. religious law – when it comes to the realm of *mu'amalat*, social interactions.

SV: Yes, because if we cannot be certain that the rules governing everyday life are *ahkam-e shar'i*, then imposing them is injustice toward people as well as toward Islam as a religion. It is harmful to people's life. That is what experience has shown us, both in the Islamic Republic of Iran and in groups like ISIS, that claim that they are enforcing Shari'a. We see that the Islamic Republic of Iran cannot enforce many of the laws that it claims to be Shari'a; they are so unjust and out of tune with people's lives that they are not enforceable. People protest against them. Just look around. What we grapple with today are those areas of *fiqh* that concern laws governing *mu'amalat* and not those regarding *'ibadat* (worship), which are not contentious issues for us Muslims today.

Ultimately, I argue that we are making a mistake about the definitions of religion and Shari'a, as well as the role of religion in daily life. The biggest mistake is that we use religion as the source of law-making. This is an obvious and major mistake.

ZMH: Wow, these are such radical views that I don't imagine the *fuqaha* in the seminaries will ever agree with them, at least in our lifetime!

SV: No, because their survival depends on making laws in the name of Islam. They have had the exclusive authority throughout history to legislate in the name of Islam. We can see the consequences: illogicality in the inner workings and governance of Muslim countries. For instance, in the Islamic Republic of Iran, we witness a major contradiction at play, notably the presence of separate institutions that claim to be actively making rules and laws in accordance with the Shari'a. On the one hand, we have an elected parliament charged by the constitution to legislate, but the laws that they pass must be approved by the *fuqaha* of the Guardian Council to ensure that they do not contradict the Shari'a. On the other hand, we have in the seminaries high-ranking jurists (*maraji' al-taqlid*) who on various occasions issue fatwas that are not in conformity with laws passed by parliament and approved by the Guardian Council. This demonstrates that our system of law-making is fundamentally flawed.

Religion should not and does not have anything to do with the making of rules and laws. However, for the past 1,400 years, that is exactly what the *fuqaha* have defined the role of religion to be, and it is quite problematic. Disentangling Islam from law will be a major operation that is not easy to do; it needs time. But we have nonetheless embarked on this trajectory, and I believe it will gain traction once the theoretical and doctrinal reinterpretations gain wider acceptance.

I agreed with her; and I found her arguments clear, coherent and convincing. But, given the ways in which Islam, law and culture have been historically entangled, I could not see her approach being effective as a strategy for addressing issues of gender discrimination. I tried to engage her in a conversation on family law reform, beginning with what I saw as the core problem.

IMPLICATIONS FOR GENDER EQUALITY

ZMH: Can we turn our discussion over to more concrete and practical matters: how to instigate change and reform of family laws in Muslim contexts. One issue is the classical *fiqh* definition of marriage, which treats women as sexual commodities. There are some unsettling passages in classical texts. For example, Muhaqqiq al-Hilli,[21] one of the great jurists whose book is still taught in Shi'i seminaries, writes: 'Marriage etymologically is uniting one thing with another thing . . . it has been said that it is a contract whose object is that of dominion over the vagina (*bad'*), without the right of possession.'[22] Based on your research, where did such a conception of marriage come from? What does the Qur'an tell us about marriage?

SV: These views were based on the *'urf* and practices of people at the time, which came to influence the jurists' interpretations of the Hadith and other sources. Islam – like other religions – has simply embraced marriage and frowned upon sex outside marriage (*zina*), but has not defined either, because that is the job of *'urf* , i.e. people's collective knowledge, to define marriage, *zina*, and the like. The concept of marriage is fluid and may change over time, as demonstrated in the various forms of marriage that existed in the past. For example, in [Shi'i] *fiqh*, we have temporary and permanent

---

21 A thirteenth-century jurist, author of the great jurisprudential book *Sharayi' al-Islam*.
22 Hilli, 1985, p. 428.

marriage, neither of which was invented by Islam; they were the practice of the time, they existed because custom recognized and accepted them.

There may be other forms of partnership that we might consider to be marriage. As for your second question, neither the Qur'an nor the Prophet took it upon themselves to define marriage, or any other social institution; rather they delegated them to the authority of 'urf and human experience. People themselves, through their collective knowledge and experience in the course of time, have developed ways of organizing themselves. We should not expect Islam and the Prophet to dictate or define everything for us. Some rules of right or wrong are matters of morality, which are already intuitively known or accepted by most individuals. People and nations are subject to change over time. For example, if *fiqh* has provided us with a definition of theft, it does not mean that we should define theft in the same way; we may define it differently today, in the light of our own collective knowledge and experience.

However, I would like to make a point about marriage. We can infer from the Qur'an and Hadith that sexual relationships outside marriage were disapproved. Nevertheless, it was left open to people's discretion to define marriage according to custom. Ultimately, marriage is a matter of mutual consent of two adults who agree to live together, without compulsion, force or deception. That is the proper definition of marriage, no matter what forms it takes.

ZMH: You are right; but to be honest, it is not enough to say, as you do, that neither the Qur'an nor the Prophet have given us a definition of marriage. Why? Because we have to deal with the question of legitimacy; look, *fiqh* rulings are still the source of family laws and gender norms in Muslim contexts, and they are defended in the name of Islam, and justified through its textual sources. I believe that to challenge these patriarchal rulings we also need to recover and reclaim the ethics of equality and gender justice in the Qur'an. This is what Muslim feminists are doing, and I see it as a viable path toward gender equality and reform in our contexts. So let me reformulate my question and expand it. Based on your research, do you think that the Qur'an provides us with such ethics?

SV: In my view, yes. But first, there is something that I'd like to say. For me, Islam is not an inherited religion; I am not Muslim because my parents are Muslims. What I am saying is based on my research – I have done my best to approach the textual and historical sources without bias, as I do not think Islam needs to be defended! I truly believe that Islam does not endorse any form of discrimination against anyone. Its method for eliminating discrimination, for transforming people and society, is gradual. The Qur'an time and again tells men to consort with their wives in accordance with what is accepted as just and good (*bilma'ruf*). Or, take the Prophet's own conduct with women, or the laws that were reformed in the interests of women. These and many other verses indicate the Qur'an's ethical emphasis, warning people against unethical action, because religion is bound by ethics and justice. The standards of ethics and justice are both time- and context-bound.

The fact is that the Qur'an spoke to people in the light of their *'urf*, taking into consideration the level of ethics and knowledge, but not in a manner or language that would later allow someone to say, 'Women cannot enjoy equality because of what this or that verse in the Qur'an says.' We do not have anything in the Qur'an that limits women's quest for equal rights, there is no barrier. Men and women are equally accountable for their actions in this life and the afterlife; there is ontological, cosmological, eschatological equality between men and women.

The Prophet of Islam tried hard to improve women's rights and status. Fourteen centuries ago, women were given property rights; the Qur'an (4:32) says 'For men a share of what they have earned, and for women a share of what they have earned.' The Qur'an recognizes women's right to choose their spouses, and removes their father's right to do so; it gives them the right to own the customary marriage payment (*mahr*), which previously went to the father or guardian. Women did not have the right to inheritance, and they went to the Prophet and said, 'We too want to inherit,' and the Qur'an provided them with that right. Men objected, but the Prophet insisted, and it was established. If the revelations in Medina had continued (the Prophet's time in Medina was only ten years, for most of which he was preoccupied with battles), and if women had reached the stage [of consciousness] to ask the Prophet for equal rights with men, I believe they would have obtained them.

Equality in rights for women today is a just demand, and Islam cannot be against it. I have repeatedly said that those who say otherwise are propagating a religion that is good only for them; it will not be accepted by just people. I myself will never accept such a religion. If Islam has explicitly condoned discrimination against me, a woman, I will reject such an Islam. What justice requires in given conditions of time and place is not in contradiction with Islam.

ZMH: My next question is, how can we Muslim women attempt to challenge discriminatory laws from within, in contexts where religion and law
are historically and culturally so closely entangled?

SV: I believe that we must rethink the theoretical foundations of *fiqh*. As I
show in my two books, *The Capacity of Fiqh* and *Rethinking Shari'a*, these
foundations confront us with serious theoretical problems that must be
critically examined and rethought from within. We can return to them only
after a thoughtful and comprehensive study of the foundations of *usul
al-fiqh*. This is exactly why I choose Usuli methodology for my research, in
order to analyse and criticize from within, with the aim of opening the way
for reform.

There I show how the jurists over the centuries created the idea that the
laws regulating our everyday life should be based on Islam. One of the
doctrinal foundations of *fiqh* is that Islam defines *everything* and has a
ruling (*hukm*) for everything. I disagree with this view. I believe that the
religion of Islam did not have a mission to make laws governing our daily
life. What the *fuqaha* claim to be Shari'a laws were elements of *'urfi* law at
the time of revelation. There is no evidence that these laws were intended
for all people in all places and at all times. We have no reason to call them
Shari'a and to enforce them now. The laws governing our daily life are based
on custom; custom defines and determines the source of law and legislation. This is not to deny that the Qur'an, religious dogma and teaching
inevitably come to shape or affect our understanding of custom. For example, people may base their disapproval of relationships outside of marriage
upon their religious beliefs, and this will be reflected in their customs and
norms; then in modern times our representatives in parliament may legislate against such relationships; that is where religious doctrine, values and
customs come into play.

I repeat my argument about Shari'a, and the understanding that religion
should not be referred to as a source for our laws. I believe that women can
engage in their fight against inequality and discrimination while arguing
that these forms of injustice do not stem from religion. When faced with
discriminatory views and challenges, we simply have to argue and convince
our opponents that religion does not approve of discrimination and
inequality. Clearly, our opponents cannot deny that, or they would lose face
in the court of public opinion. Today, it has become increasingly costly for
jurists to remain steadfast in their views on the virtues of discrimination
between the sexes. We are equipped with rational, logical, Shari'a-based

and Qur'anic rationalizations and evidence to defend and corroborate our views on equality and the fight against discrimination, and we should not only use them, but we must insist on them. This is what I tried to do in my first book, *Women, Jurisprudence, Islam*. I sought, first, to examine and refute the arguments made by jurists that such discrimination is somehow Shari'a-based; and second, to provide counter-arguments in defence of equality. I believe we have sufficient evidence for both elements of the argument, be it Shari'a-based justifications or those based on reason and logic.

ZMH: Am I right to say that your project for reforming family laws is to take them out of the realm of *fiqh?*

SV: Yes, this is my project, and I have repeatedly said in my books that *fiqh's* era of law-making is over, and the *fuqaha* must loosen their grip over the rules guiding day-to-day life and leave that to the discretion of the lawmakers and the people. Muslims are going through a difficult time; women and religious minorities living in Muslim countries are not treated as full humans. We must untangle the knot by which the *fuqaha* tied Islam to law so that Muslims can live in peace and prosper, so that women can achieve their rights. This is the core problem: to bring law-making into the hands of the people, to be done in a democratic way. And all my effort is directed to this end.

We Muslim women have a long path to travel to achieve reform in the sense of changing pre-existing beliefs about religion.

AN UPDATE

Since her return to Iran, I have been in regular touch with Vasmaghi concerning my editing of the English transcript of our conversation. I have followed her activities with both admiration and anxiety.

On her release from Evin prison on 4 November 2017, Vasmaghi appealed against the five-year sentence that Tehran Revolutionary Court had issued in 2015 while she was in Sweden. The appeal hearing was held on 16 May 2018 and as a result her sentence was suspended.[23] In September 2019, when she attempted to travel to Europe for a seminar, she was banned from leaving the country. But she was not silenced; in November 2019, following the violent crackdown on demonstrators who had protested the sudden and dramatic

---

23 https://www.zeitoons.com/52164

increase in oil prices, Vasmaghi, along with seventy-six other high-profile individuals, signed a public petition, "Respect People's Demands". In June 2020 the legal divisions of the Revolutionary Guard's Intelligence Organization and the Intelligence Ministry filed a complaint against Vasmaghi, accusing her of 'activities against the state' in connection with the petition. She refused to attend the closed Revolutionary Court hearing on the grounds of the court's lack of jurisdiction and improper procedures like closing the hearing to the public. Instead, she made her defence statement public and explained her reasons for rejecting the unfounded allegations and not appearing in court. In August, the Revolutionary Court sentenced her to one year in prison, which was confirmed by the Court of Appeals, in addition to the previous five-year suspended sentence.[24]

Despite all this harassment, Vasmaghi has continued her public activities; her essays and opinion pieces have regularly appeared in print and online media, both in Iran and abroad.[25] She has also been a regular commentator on current affairs on BBC Persian, Voice of America and other radio and TV channels outside Iran. She is also active on social media; 'Dr Vasmaghi's Unofficial Channel' was launched on Telegram, featuring as its first post a disclaimer: 'This is not Dr Vasmaghi's official channel and she is not responsible for its contents.' This was followed by a biography and list of her books, excerpts from her books and articles, as well as audio and video files of her online participation in seminars both inside and outside Iran. Among them are in-depth discussions of *Rethinking Shari'a* at the Islamic Association of Engineers, one of the professional bodies that played a role in shaping the Islamic ideology of the 1979 Revolution.[26] Nineteen of these discussions were held between 7 February 2019 and 27 February 2020, each session lasting for four hours; in each

---

24 "Iranian poet and academic Sedigeh Vasmaghi faces six years in prison", *Pen International*, https://pen-international.org/news/iran-iranian-poet-and-academic-sedigeh-vasmaghi-faces-six-years-in-prison; see also https://icorn.org/sites/default/files/attachements/sedigeh_defence_statment_english.pdf; for her defence statement, see https://ifex.org/iranian-lawyer-poet-and-activist-sedigeh-vasmaghi-on-trial-for-threatening-national-security/

25 For instance, two conversations with Yasir Arab, on Aparat online TV in Iran in August 2019, one on the "Critique of the *fuqaha*," the other on "The end of compulsory hijab," in the *Kherad-e jensi* (Sexual Wisdom) series; both available on Youtube: https://www.aparat.com/v/Y0MCG; https://youtu.be/OyKRJ5VYkqI

26 Founded in 1957, by the early 1990s the Association had become a platform for religious reformism and the emerging critique of the Islamic state. See Mir-Hosseini & Tapper, 2006, pp. 63–65.

one, Vasmaghi first presented a section of the book, then there were questions and answers and discussion.[27]

In February 2019 there appeared on her 'Unofficial' channel three recordings of discussions of *The Capacity of Fiqh*, in which she responds to questions she has received – very much in the manner of ulema dealing with online enquiries. The questions, submitted in a written form, ranged from theological issues, such as belief in resurrection and Qur'an as the word of God; to *fiqhi* rulings relating to *'ibadat*, such as saying prayers in Persian, fasting during menstruation; to social and political issues, such as hijab, banning women's voices, the age of marriage, and the permissibility of cohabitation. To each, Vasmaghi begins with the phrase 'a friend asks . . .' and injects into each response phrases such as 'this is my perspective' and 'this is what I came to understand through the study of sources.' In her answers she refers to ethical issues, Qur'anic teachings and human rights. Interestingly, for 'human rights' she uses the term *hoquq-e ensani* instead of the conventional *hoquq-e bashar* – for a Persian speaker the latter is associated with international human rights law, the former with the philosophy behind it.

I have been so impressed with Vasmaghi's courage and conviction, and what she has achieved against all odds since her return to Iran. In July 2020, we had a follow-up conversation – this time over an excellent connection.

ZMH: You have been very active since your return; I follow your Telegram channel and have listened to many of your lectures online. First I want to salute you for your courage for making your views public in the present political climate in Iran, where voicing dissent against the domination of *fiqh* is costly. Can I ask you how you assess the impact of your *Rethinking Shari'a* in discussion forums?

SV: As a researcher I must remain true to my findings, the truths that I discover, and share them honestly with others. I need to do this even if it works against me; many times, in the course of the lectures I was giving based on my research for *Rethinking Shari'a*, friends came to me and said that it would better not to talk about certain sections of the book relating to the Qur'an, or to say them in a modified and discreet manner. I said explicitly 'I will not dissimulate (*taqiyeh*) when it comes to my research; whatever I find, I say it honestly and explicitly, even if it may put me in danger.' I expect the same from others. Those who disagree can provide

---

27 https://t.me/DrVasmaghi

counter-arguments, if they have any. If they don't, they can't expect me to keep silent. I don't accept this. I have spoken with the language of reason and I hope others will respond with the same language.

ZMH: I also notice that reformist thinkers have not engaged with your book.

SV: Yes, this has been the case. Some of them came to my talks; you know that for over a year there were sessions at the Society of Engineering where I presented the book, followed by discussion. I received praise, some spoke in support, some of them from the Qom seminary expressed a wish for this kind of scholarship to reach Qom and be debated there. I know that [the ulema] read my work, but they aren't willing to support me openly. One reason is that certain taboos will be broken; and the other is that this time it is a woman who has entered the arena to express these ideas. It's awkward for the clerical establishment to have a woman as an interlocutor; in our society, many men, especially the clerics, think that [knowledge of religion] is their exclusive realm; they are not prepared to value or accept what a woman says. Patriarchy and male arrogance exist in our society. I always think that had a man expressed my views, they would been received quite differently. Of course, that man would have faced a greater risk, but the impact of these views would have been much greater. But now that they are expressed by a woman, because of their male arrogance, men are not prepared to come out in affirmation and help to spread these kinds of debates in society.

ZMH: As far as I know, you are the only woman in the country with train-ing in the Islamic sciences and the knowledge and courage to engage so critically with doctrines and dogmas in *fiqh*. There may be other female scholars, but none have been as direct and outspoken as you. This, in my view, is what makes your voice and work so significant. Reading your work and listening to your talks, knowing the enormity of the challenges you have faced in your personal and public life, I have often wondered . . . I don't know how to put it . . . what is it that drives you to do what you do against all odds? I feel that one can't do this kind of work without deep conviction, without faith (*iman*).

SV: You are right; I really have *iman* in what I am doing, and I think I have chosen the right path, that is to say, I feel this is the purpose of my life, my responsibility. For this reason, I accept all these hardships. I have difficulty reading, which makes doing research complicated. I really believe in what I am doing, and think that the path that I have chosen is worth devoting all my life to. That is why I came back from Europe to Iran; I was prepared to appear in court, to go to prison, but to be here in the field, to be in a place that needs my work, where my audience is, where people are suffering because of the rule of *fiqh* (*hakimat-e fiqh*) . . . I felt that I needed to come back home to my work; that I couldn't do this from afar.

In the prefaces of all her books, Vasmaghi has acknowledged the support of her husband. In *Rethinking Shari'a*, she devotes a paragraph to express her appreciation of his companionship while working on the book, how at times the 'precise points' that he raised led her to do further thinking and research. I had seen them together when they were in Europe, and admired their relationship, his loving and caring ways of helping her to navigate through public meetings. I asked her how she manages to do the research and writing given her eye condition.

ZMH: I know your husband is always by your side; you have also acknowledged him in all your books; I have seen you together, you are indeed a team!

SV: Mohammad is my biggest ally, the one who constantly reads to me, and helps me in my research and writing down what I say. For instance, we were in Sweden when I was completed *Rethinking Shari'a*, though I had begun the writing before leaving Iran; I still needed to do more research, and Mohammad did all this for me; I dictated and he wrote, and that's how the book was written. Here [in Tehran] I also have friends who help. Now that I am working on a new project, there is one person who reads to me three days a week, and another for three other days; and Mohammad reads to me every night. He also takes notes for me and we go through them together. I could not do what I do without his help; he does it because he shares my goals.

As this goes to press, Sedigheh Vasmaghi is awaiting a court appearance, and cannot leave the country again; but she is working on another book. Her clear vision and her articulate and informed critique of the domination of *fiqh* over every aspect of life, in particular law-making, resonate with many Iranians. She has carved out a proper place in Iranian reformist thought that previously lacked a woman's voice and a strong advocate for gender equality. Her being in Iran also matters: she can now present her work and ideas in a variety of fora, and interact with different audiences. Talks given by religious scholars and intellectuals have played an important role in shaping the new religious discourses. Women have participated largely as spectators, but now Vasmaghi is the main speaker with the knowledge and necessary credentials to challenge archaic patriarchal *fiqh* rulings. She is respected equally by religious and secular Iranians.

Conclusion: Looking Back
to Look Forward

Justice is at once a prerequisite for and a requirement of religious rules. Justice in turn, aims to fulfill needs, attain rights, and eliminate discrimination and inequality.

Abdulkarim Soroush

I t was the injustices arising from *fiqh* rulings, and the absence of women's voices and experiences in today's Muslim legal systems, that brought me and other women together to launch Musawah, a global movement for equality and justice in the Muslim family. In the *Framework for Action* we set out our vision:

> We hold the principles of Islam to be a source of justice, equality, fairness and dignity for all human beings . . .We, as Muslims and citizens of modern nations, declare that equality and justice in the family are both necessary and possible. The time for realising these values in our laws and practices is now.
>
> Musawah declares that equality in the family is necessary because many aspects of our current Muslim family laws and practices are unjust and do not respond to the lives and experiences of Muslim families and individuals. Musawah declares that equality in the family is possible through a holistic approach that brings together Islamic teachings, universal human rights principles, fundamental rights and constitutional guarantees, and the lived realities of women and men today.[1]

---

1 https://www.musawah.org/resources/musawah-framework-for-action/

But then – and even now, though much less – many perceived our project to reconcile Islam and feminism as futile. At the launch of Musawah in February 2009, the divide between Islam and feminism was still clearly present among the 250-odd participants. There were heated exchanges – which reflected tensions in the planning committee.[2] What was encouraging, however, was the keenness of many younger participants who found the feminist engagement with religion empowering and liberating. One young woman exclaimed: 'I feel like someone opened a window into my mind and let in the fresh air. It feels so good!' A journalist observed: 'How lucky that young woman is, I thought. Just over twenty years ago, I felt as though I had to smash the window into my mind open myself, fists bleeding and bruised, to catch some of that fresh air.'[3]

In June the same year, we in Musawah gave our first short course, designed to help to build participants' knowledge and courage to criticize discriminatory laws, policies and practices justified in the name of Islam, and to speak out about their impact on women's rights and fundamental liberties. It was so reassuring to see their enthusiasm and how they were discovering the potential of 'Islamic feminism'. Many of them wrote to Musawah; for example:

The course was more than a breath of fresh air to the mind and the heart, it felt more like a journey bringing you finally back home.

I managed to challenge 25 conservative mullahs who were saying that women are created inferior to men and there is no way out . . . And you know what, I managed to shut them up. At the end, people who were opposing them but were not courageous enough to say anything 'against Islam' (because the ulema themselves are walking talking Islam) were very pleased.

It was an exciting time for me too. Although I had been unable to return to Iran since 2006, the rise of the Green Movement in June 2009 gave me more hope. Thirty years into an 'Islamic Republic' committed to imposing laws based on pre-modern, patriarchal interpretations of Shari'a, women and young people took to the streets to protest the widely accepted corruption of the system and asked, 'Where is my vote?'

---

2 Mir-Hosseini, 2009b.
3 Mir-Hosseini, 2009b; Mona Eltahawy in *The Jerusalem Report* 25, 30 March 2009.

Inspired by the reception of Musawah's launch on the one hand and by the Green Movement on the other, and reflecting on how far things had moved for me in the decade since the publication of *Islam and Gender*, I embarked on a new project that has resulted, a decade later, in this book: a further account of my journey to knowledge, by way of conversations with a number of prominent Muslim reformist thinkers, from varied contexts, who have both influenced my journey and been travelling in the same direction as me – toward the construction of egalitarian gender rights from within an Islamic framework.

The preceding chapters have revealed similarities and differences in the ways we came to experience and learn about our faith and religious tradition, as well as our evolving perspectives and approaches in relating to Islam's textual sources. We have all faced the challenge of negotiating the divergence between modern notions of justice that include gender equality, and the assumptions that underpin established patriarchal understandings of Shari'a as articulated in classical *fiqh* rulings. In different ways, we have all brought Islamic legal tradition into conversation with human rights and feminist frameworks, and sought to demonstrate that approaches from both perspectives, far from mutually opposed, can be mutually reinforcing. We all deplore the injustices that arise from patriarchal customs and laws based on classical *fiqh*, and argue for defensible and coherent alternatives within a framework that recognizes the equality and justice that are inherent to Islam.

There are of course some disagreements and misunderstandings in our positions on the main issues that this book addresses: Shari'a, gender equality and justice. In narrating these conversations, I neither intended to compare the merits or shortcomings of each approach, nor did I want to synthesize a single 'reform methodology'. What works in one context might not work in another context or time. We all concurred on two premises as necessary, though not sufficient, for the construction of gender egalitarian laws from within the Islamic tradition. The first premise is the recognition that the main issues are socially constructed; understandings of gender equality and justice are shaped and change in interaction with ideological, political, socio-economic forces, and people's experiences and expectations. The same goes for understandings of Shari'a, the interpretations of Islam's sacred texts and the legal rulings derived from them.

The second premise is that the textual sources of Islam are not inherently patriarchal, nor do they set out an exhaustive set of eternal laws. The Qur'an upholds justice and exhorts Muslims to stand for justice; but it does not define justice, rather it indicates the path to follow toward justice, the meaning of which is always time- and context-bound. It gives us ethical guidance and principles for the creation of just laws.

The journeys that we have travelled were largely shaped and mediated by our varied experiences of the rise of political Islam in the second part of the last century. The instrumental use of Shari'a as the source of political legitimacy has not only exposed the intimate links between theology and politics, but put the issue of gender justice in the Shari'a at the centre of contestation. On the one side, Islamist movements of various hues have evoked pre-modern and patriarchal understandings of the Shari'a to deprive women of the personal, civil and political rights they had gained around the world. On the other side, new forms of reformist scholarship and activism, including Musawah and my interlocutors, have challenged these understandings from within the Islamic tradition.

The question of gender equality in Muslim contexts has become intensely political, and in all likelihood can only be resolved through political means. Enmeshed in an intricate dialectic between religion, politics and practice, the struggle for gender equality has been part of a larger struggle for social justice, and an essential component of this struggle is the democratization of the production of religious knowledge. It is precisely for this reason that Muslim reformist and feminist scholars – such as those who speak in this book, along with activists such as those in Musawah – have something constructive to offer.

First, by transcending polarizations between 'secular' and 'religious' feminism, and between 'Islam' and 'human rights', they reveal the real site of ideological and political contestation, which is between patriarchal and authoritarian forces on the one side, and egalitarian and democratic ones on the other, whether they come in a religious or a secular guise. Secondly, by providing egalitarian interpretations of Islam's textual sources, the reformist and feminist scholars contest patriarchal and unjust laws from within religious tradition. This has the potential to break the monopoly of religious knowledge by specialists (the ulema) and its manipulation by state authorities, which constitute a major obstacle for Muslim women in their quest for equality and dignity.

Realizing this potential entails two linked processes: recovering and reclaiming the ethical and egalitarian ethos in Islam's sacred texts, and exposing the relationship between the production of religious knowledge and the practices of power. It is only in this way that we can begin to transform the deep structures that have formed our religious, cultural and political realities.

* * * * *

In the course of research for this book, I came across Cantwell Smith's 1981 collection of essays, *On Understanding Islam*.[4] In one of the essays, "Islamic Law: Shari'a and *Shar*'", originally published in 1965, he provides evidence that, for early Muslim scholars, Shari'a was primarily a 'moral' rather than a legal concept; it involved neither obedience to nor transgression of a law, but obedience to God. He showed that the term was hardly used by early Muslim theologians, while another term, *shar*', with the sense of 'moral imperative', had greater currency.

The essay ends with two hypotheses that both challenge common understandings of Shari'a and invite us to explore it further. First, for early Muslim scholars, 'law does not determine right and wrong. Only God can, and only God does, do that.' Secondly,

> the dictum that the central fact of Islam as a religion is the idea of law should be modified in the direction of saying that the central Islamic fact religiously has been the idea of moral responsibility. The law is the result of that responsibility, not its cause; the sociological and mundane product, not its cosmic basis.[5]

Smith still speaks to me; his hypotheses takes me back to my fieldwork in the early 1980s in family courts in Tehran, with which this book began, and where the judges claimed that the law was based on Shari'a. Perhaps the women I saw asking, 'Is this justice? Is this Islam?', had a better understanding of the Shari'a than the clerical judges and the system they represented.

---

4 Smith, 1981. The book contains previously published and unpublished essays, and his reflections on them.
5 Smith, 1981, pp. 108–109.

Bibliography

'Abd Al 'Ati, Hammuda, 1997. *The Family Structure in Islam*. Indianapolis: American Trust Publications.

Abou El Fadl, Khaled, 1997. *The Authoritative and the Authoritarian in Islamic Discourses: A Contemporary Case Study*, 2nd edition revised and expanded, Austin, TX: Dar Taiba.

Abou El Fadl, Khaled, 2001a. *And God Knows the Soldiers: The Authoritative and the Authoritarian in Islamic Discourses*, Lanham, MD: University Press of America.

Abou El Fadl, Khaled, 2001b. *Speaking in God's Name: Islamic Law, Authority and Women*, Oxford: Oneworld.

Abou El Fadl, Khaled, 2004. *Islam and the Challenge of Democracy*, Princeton University Press.

Abou El Fadl, Khaled, 2005. "Dogs in the Islamic Tradition and Nature," *Encyclopaedia of Nature and Religion*, New York: Continuum International. https://www.searchforbeauty. org/explore/dogs-in-islam/

Abou El Fadl, Khaled, 2006. *The Search for Beauty in Islam: A Conference of the Books*, Lanham, MD: Rowman & Littlefield.

Abou El Fadl, Khaled, 2007. *The Great Theft: Wrestling Islam from the Extremists*, New York: HarperSanFrancisco.

Abou El Fadl, Khaled, 2014. *Reasoning with God: Reclaiming Shari'ah in the Modern Age*, Lanham, MD: Rowman & Littlefield.

Abou-Bakr, Omaima (ed.), 2013. *Feminist and Islamic Perspectives: New Horizons of Knowledge and Reform*, Cairo, Egypt: Women and Memory Forum with the Danish-Egyptian Dialogue Institute and the Danish Center for Research on Women and Gender.

Abou-Bakr, Omaima, 2015. "Imperative Legacy of *Qiwamah* as an Exegetical Construct," in Ziba Mir-Hosseini, Mulki Al-Sharmani & Jana Rumminger (eds), *Men in Charge? Rethinking Male Authority in Muslim Legal Tradition*, London: Oneworld, pp. 44–65.

Abu Zayd, Nasr Hamid, 2006. *Reformation of Islamic Thought: A Critical Historical Analysis*, Amsterdam University Press.

Abu Zayd, Nasr Hamid, 2011. "Toward Understanding the Qur'an's Worldview: An Autobiographical Reflection," in Gabriel Said Reynolds (ed.), *New Perspectives on the Qur'an: The Qur'an in its Historical Context*, London: Routledge, pp. 47–87.

Abu Zayd, Nasr Hamid, 2013. "The Status of Women between the Qur'an and *Fiqh*," in Ziba Mir-Hosseini, Kari Vogt, Lena Larsen and Christian Moe (eds), *Gender Equality in Muslim Family Law: Justice and Ethics in the Islamic Legal Tradition*, London: I.B. Tauris, pp. 153–68.

Abu-Odeh, Lama, 2004. "Modernizing Islamic Law: The Case of Egypt," *Vanderbilt Journal of Transnational Law* 37 (4), pp. 1043–146.

AFTURD (Association des Femmes Tunisiennes pour la Recherche et le Développement), 2006. *Egalité dans l'Héritage: Pour Une Citoyenneté Pleine et Entière*, Tunis: AFTURD.

Ahmed, Leila, 1992. *Women and Gender in Islam: Historical Roots of a Modern Debate*, New Haven: Yale University Press.

Al-Hibri, Azizah, 1982. "A Study of Islamic Herstory: Or How Did We Get Into This Mess," *Islam and Women*, special issue of *Women's Studies International Forum* 5 (2), pp. 207–19.

Al-Hibri, Azizah, 2003. "An Islamic Perspective on Domestic Violence," *Fordham International Law Journal* 27 (1), pp. 195–224.

Ali, Kecia, 2003. "Progressive Muslims and Islamic Jurisprudence: The Necessity for Critical Engagement with Marriage and Divorce Law," in Omid Safi (ed.), *Progressive Muslims: On Justice, Gender, and Pluralism*, Oxford: Oneworld, pp. 163–89.

Ali, Kecia, 2007. "Religious Practices: Obedience and Disobedience in Islamic Discourses," in Suad Joseph (ed.), *Encyclopedia of Women in Islamic Cultures* vol. 5, Leiden: Brill, pp. 309–13.

Ali, Kecia, 2010. *Marriage and Slavery in Early Islam*. Cambridge, MA: Harvard University Press.

Ali, Kecia, Juliana Hammer, and Laury Silvers, 2012. *A Jihad for Justice: Honoring the Work and Life of Amina Wadud*, https://www.bu.edu/religion/files/2010/03/A-Jihad-for-Justice-for-Amina-Wadud-2012-1.pdf

Ali, Kecia, n.d. "Muslim Sexual Ethics: Understanding a Difficult Verse, Qur'an 4:34," http://www.brandeis.edu/projects/fse/muslim/diff-verse.html, accessed 1 Jan 2014.

Alipour, Farahmand, 2013. "A Woman Rethinking Islamic Jurisprudence," *Majalla*, 5 December; https://eng.majalla.com/2013/12/article55246939/a-woman-rethinking-islamic-jurisprudence

Al-Qaradawi, Yusuf, 1967. *Al-halal wa al-haram fi al-Islam (Halal and Haram in Islam)*, Beirut, Damascus: Al-Maktabah al-Islami; trans. Kamal El-Helbawy, M. Moinuddin Siddiqui, Syed Shukry as *The Lawful and the Prohibited in Islam*, Indianapolis: American Trust Publications, 1980.

Al-Sharqawi, Nadia, and Boucheri Al-Ghazali, 2014. *Mubadrat ta'miq va tasil al-marifa bimafhumi alqiwamah va alwilayah (Initiative to deepen and interconnect knowledge on the concepts of qiwamah and wilayah)*, Rabat: Rabita Mohammedia.

Amirpur, Katajun, 2015. *New Thinking in Islam: Jihad for Freedom, Democracy and Women's Rights*, London: Gingko Library.

Anderson, James Norman, 1976. *Law Reforms in the Muslim World*, London: Athlone.

An-Na'im, Abdullahi Ahmed, 1987. "Translator's Introduction," in Mahmoud Mohamed Taha, *The Second Message of Islam*, Syracuse University Press, pp. 1–30.

An-Na'im, Abdullahi Ahmed, 1990. *Toward an Islamic Reformation: Civil Liberties, Human Rights, and International Law*, Cairo University Press.

An-Na'im, Abdullahi Ahmed (ed.), 1992. *Human Rights in Cross-Cultural Perspectives: A Quest for Consensus*, Pennsylvania University Press.

An-Na'im, Abdullahi Ahmed, 1995. "The Dichotomy between Religious and Secular Discourse in Islamic Societies," in Mahnaz Afkhami (ed.), *Faith and Freedom: Women's Human Rights in the Muslim World*, London, I.B. Tauris, pp. 51–60.

An-Na'im, Abdullahi Ahmed, 1998–99. "Shari'a and Positive Legislation: Is an Islamic State Possible or Viable?" *Yearbook of Islamic and Middle Eastern Law* 5, pp. 29–41.

An-Na'im, Abdullahi Ahmed, 2008. *Islam and the Secular State. Negotiating the Future of Shari'a*, Harvard University Press.

An-Na'im, Abdullahi Ahmed, 2015. "Islamic Politics and the Neutral State: A Friendly Amendment to Rawls?" in Tom Bailey and Valentina Gentile (eds), *Rawls and Religion*, New York: Columbia University Press, pp. 242–65.

An-Na'im, Abdullahi Ahmed, 2021. *Decolonizing Human Rights*, Cambridge University Press.

Anwar, Zainah and Rashidah Abdullah (eds), 2000. *Islam, Reproductive Health and Women's Rights*, Kuala Lumpur: Sisters in Islam.

Badran, Margot, 2002. "Islamic Feminism: what's in a name?" *Al-Ahram Weekly Online*, 17–23 January, https://web.archive.org/web/20150320074746/http://weekly.ahram.org.eg/2002/569/cu1.htm

Barlas, Asma, 2002. *Believing Women in Islam: Unreading Patriarchal Interpretations of the Qur'an*, Austin: Texas University Press.

Bauer, Karen, 2015. *Gender Hierarchy in the Qur'an: Medieval Interpretations, Modern Responses*, Cambridge University Press.

Benchekroun, Siham (ed.), 2017. *Women's Inheritance: A Multidisciplinary Perspective on Inheritance in Morocco*, Rabat: Emoreintes Éditions & Université international de Rabat.

Bhojani, Ali-Reza, 2017. *Moral Rationalism and Shari'a: Independent Rationality in Modern Shi'i Usul al-Fiqh*, London: Routledge.

Boulby, Marion, 1988. "The Islamic Challenge: Tunisia Since Independence," *Third World Quarterly*, 10 (2), pp. 590–614.

Brown, Jonathan A.C., 2009. "Hadith," in *Islamic Studies*, Oxford Bibliographies https://www.oxfordbibliographies.com/view/document/obo-9780195390155/obo-9780195390155-0030.xml#obo-9780195390155-0030-bibItem-0003

Charrad, Mounira, 2001. *States and Women's Rights: The Making of Postcolonial Tunisia, Algeria and Morocco*, Berkeley: University of California Press.

Chiba, Masaji (ed.), 1986. *Asian Indigenous Law in Interaction with Received Law*, London & New York: Kegan Paul International.

Duderija, Adis, 2011. *Constructing a Religiously Ideal 'Believer' and 'Woman' in Islam: Neo-traditional Salafi and Progressive Muslims' Methods of Interpretation*, Basingstoke: Palgrave Macmillan.

Duderija, Adis, 2015. "Toward a Scriptural Hermeneutics of Islamic Feminism," *Journal of Feminist Studies in Religion*, 31 (2), pp. 45–64.

Duderija, Adis, 2017. *The Imperatives of Progressive Muslims*, London: Routledge.

el-Husseini, Rola, 2008. "Women, Work and Political Participation in Lebanese Shia Contemporary Thought: The Writings of Ayatollahs Fadlallah and Shams al-Din," *Comparative Studies of Asia and the Middle East*, 28 (2), pp. 273–82.

El-Zein, Amira, 2017. *Islam, Arabs, and the Intelligent World of the Jinn*, New York: Syracuse University Press.

Elewa, Ahmed and Laury Silvers, 2010–11. "'I am One of the People:' A Survey and Analysis of Legal Arguments on Women-Led Prayer in Islam," *Journal of Law and Religion*, 26 (1), pp. 141–71.

Emon, Anver, 2018. "Ijtihad," in Anver Emon and Rumee Ahmed (eds), *The Oxford Handbook of Islamic Law*, Oxford: Oxford University Press, pp. 182–206.

Erwin, Courtney, 2015. "Inheritance Law Reform in Morocco: At the Intersection of Human Rights and Religious Identity," https://ilg2.org/2015/10/29/inheritance-law-reform-in-morocco-at-the-intersection-of-human-rights-and-religious-identity/

Eshkevari, Hassan Yousefi, 2013. "Rethinking Men's Authority over Women: *Qiwama, Wilaya* and their Underlying Assumptions," in Ziba Mir-Hosseini, Kari Vogt, Lena Larsen and Christian Moe (eds), *Gender Equality in Muslim Family Law: Justice and Ethics in the Islamic Legal Tradition*, London: I.B. Tauris, pp. 191–212.

Fazal, Imran (ed.), [2011]. *Speaking in God's Name: Re-Examining Gender in Islam* https://www.academia.edu/44993169/SPEAKING_IN_GOD_S_NAME_RE_EXAMINING_GENDER_IN_ISLAM

Ferrari, Silvio, 2006. "Adapting Divine Law to Change: The Experience of the Roman Catholic Church (with some references to Jewish and Islamic Law)," *Cardozo Law Review*, 28 (1), pp. 53–65.

Filali, Kenza, 2018. "Asma Lamrabet explique les raisons de sa démission de la Rabita Mohammadia," *Le Desk*, 26 March, https://ledesk.ma/2018/03/26/asma-lamrabet-explique-les-raisons-de-sa-demission-de-la-rabita-mohammadia/.

Foblets, Marie-Claire, 2010. "Foreword and Acknowledgements: Islam and the Requirements of Liberal Democratic Principles," in Marie Claire Foblets and Jean-Yves Carlier (eds), *Islam & Europe: Crises are Challenges*, Leuven University Press, pp. 7–12.

Foer, Franklin, 2002. "Moral Hazard: The Life of a Liberal Muslim," *The New Republic* November 18; https://newrepublic.com/article/136609/moral-hazard

Ghazali, Mohammad, 1989. *Al-Sunna al-nabawiyya bayna ahl al-fiqh wa ahl al-hadith (The Prophetic Sunna: Between the Jurists and Traditionalists)*, Cairo: Dar al-Shuruq.

Gilligan, Carol, 2011. *Joining the Resistance*, Cambridge: Polity Press.

Gray, Doris, 2013. *Beyond Islamism and Feminism: Gender and Equality in North Africa*, London, I.B. Tauris.

Grenshaw, Kimberlé, 1989. "Demarginalizing the Intersection of Race and Sex: A Black Feminist Critique of Antidiscrimination Doctrine, Feminist Theory and Antiracist Politics," *University of Chicago Legal Forum*, 1989 (1), Article 8; http://chicagounbound.uchicago.edu/uclf/vol1989/iss1/8

Hammer, Juliane, 2012. *American Muslim Women, Religious Authority, and Activism: More than a Prayer*, Austin: University of Texas Press.

Harding, Sandra (ed.), 2004. *The Feminist Standpoint Theory Reader: Intellectual and Political Controversies*, London: Routledge.

Hassan, Riffat, 1987. "Equal before Allah? Women-Man Equality in the Islamic Tradition," *Harvard Divinity Bulletin* 17 (2); accessible at http://new.wluml.org/node/253.

Hassan, Riffat, 1999. "Feminism in Islam," in Arvind Sharma and Kate Young (eds), *Feminism and World Religions*, New York: SUNY Press, pp. 248–78.

Hermansen, Marcia, 2013. "New Voices of Women Theologians," in Ednan Aslan, Elif Medeni and Marcia Hermansen (eds), *Muslima Theology: Voices of Muslim Women Theologians*, Frankfurt-am-Main: Peter Lang, pp. 11–34.

Hidayatullah, Aysha, 2014. *Feminist Edges of the Qur'an*, Oxford: Oxford University Press.

Hilli, Muhaqqiq, 1985. *Sharayi' al-Islam*, Vol. II, trans. A.A. Yazdi, compiled by Muhammad Taqi Danish-Pazhuh, Tehran University Press.

Hull, Akasha Gloria, Patricia Bell-Scott, and Barbara Smith, 1982. *All the Women Are White, All the Blacks Are Men, But Some of Us Are Brave*, New York: The Feminist Press.

Husni, Ronak, and Daniel Newman (eds), 2007. *Muslim Women in Law and Society: Annotated Translation of al-Tahir al-Haddad's* Imra'tuna fi'l-shari'a wa'l-mujtama', *with an Introduction*, London: Routledge.

Ibn Qayyim al-Jawziyya, 1956. *I'lam ul Muwaqqi'in 'an Rabb al 'Alamin*, 3, Beirut: Dar al-Fikr al-'Arabi.

Ibn Rushd, 1996. *The Distinguished Jurist's Primer*, vol. II (*Bidayat al-Mujtahid wa Nihayat al-Muqtasid*), trans. Imran Ahsan Khan Nyazee, Reading: Garnet.

Iqbal, Muhammad, 1934. *The Reconstruction of Religious Thought in Islam*, Oxford University Press.

Islahi, Amin, 1979. *Taddabur-i Qur'an: muqaddimah va tafasir-i Mawlana Amin Ahsan Islahi (Pondering on the Qur'an: Introduction and Exegeses of Mawlana Amin Ahsan Islahi)*, Delhi: World Islamic Publications.

Kadivar, Mohsen, 1994. *Nazariyeh-ha-ye Dowlat dar Feqh-e Shi'i (Theories of the State in Shi'i Jurisprudence)*, Tehran: Ney.

Kadivar, Mohsen, 1999a. *Hokumat-e Vela'i (Theocratic State)*, Tehran: Ney.

Kadivar, Mohsen, 1999b. "*Din, modara va khoshunat*" (Religion, Tolerance and Violence), *Kian*, 45 (Bahman/Esfand 1377); available at https://kadivar.com/689/

Kadivar, Mohsen, 2008. *Haqq ol-Nass: Islam va Hoquq-e Bashar (The Rights of Humankind; Islam and Human Rights)*, Tehran: Kavir.

Kadivar, Mohsen, 2011a. "From Traditional Islam to Islam as an End Itself," *Die Welt des Islams*, 51, pp. 459–84.

Kadivar, Mohsen, 2011b. "Muslim Marriage with People of the Book," 21 Bahman 1391; http://kadivar.com/?p=10352

Kadivar, Mohsen, 2013. "Revisiting Women's Rights in Islam: 'Egalitarian Justice' in Lieu of 'Deserts-based Justice,'" in Ziba Mir-Hosseini, Kari Vogt, Lena Larsen and Christian Moe (eds), *Gender Equality in Muslim Family Law: Justice and Ethics in the Islamic Legal Tradition*, London: I.B. Tauris, pp. 213–34.

Kadivar, Mohsen, 2015a. *Dar Mahzar-e Faqih-e Azad; Ostad Hossein Ali Montazeri Najafabadi (In the Presence of a Noble Theologian: My Mentor Ayatollah Montazeri (1922–2009))*, 3rd edition; https://kadivar.com/14618/

Kadivar, Mohsen, 2015b. "Ijtihad in Usul al-Fiqh: Reforming Islamic Thought through Structural Ijtihad," *Iran Nameh*, 30 (3), pp. xx–xxvii.

Kadivar, Mohsen, 2017. "*Intizar az Din va Nou-andishi-ye Dini*" (Expectation of Religion and Reformist Thinking); Part 1 https://kadivar.com/16093/; Part 2 https://kadivar.com/16139/; Part 3 https://kadivar.com/16168/

Kadivar, Mohsen, 2020. "*Nesbat-e Din va Siyasat*" (The Relationship of Religion and Politics); https://kadivar.com/18422/

Kadivar, Mohsen, 2021a. *Human Rights and Reformist Islam*, Edinburgh University Press.

Kadivar, Mohsen, 2021b. *Blasphemy and Apostasy in Islam*, Edinburgh University Press.

Kamali, Mohammad Hashim, 1998. "Punishment in Islamic Law: A Critique of the Hudud Bill of Kelantan, Malaysia," *Arab Law Quarterly*, 13 (3), pp. 203–34.

Kapur, Ratna, 2012. "Unveiling Equality: Disciplining the 'Other' Woman Through the Human Rights Discourse," in Anver M. Emon, Mark S. Ellis and Benjamin Glahn (eds), *Islamic Law and International Human Rights Law*, Oxford University Press, pp. 265–90.

Kasraoui, Safaa, 2018a. "Islamic Feminist Asma Lamrabet Opens Up About her Resignation," *Morocco World News*, 26 March, https://www.moroccoworldnews.com/2018/03/243173/islamic-feminist-asma-lamrabet-opens-resignation/

Kasraoui, Safaa, 2018b. "Inheritance Debate and the Call for Gender Equality Persists in Morocco," *Morocco World News*, 8 April, https://www.moroccoworldnews.com/2018/04/244028/inheritance-debate-call-gender-equality-persist-morocco/

Keddie, Nikki, 2007. *Women in the Middle East: Past and Present*, Princeton University Press.

Kelly, Patricia, 1996. "Finding Common Ground: Islamic Values and Gender Equity in Tunisia's Reformed Personal Status Code," in *Shifting Boundaries in Marriage and Divorce in Muslim Communities*, Special Dossier, Women Living Under Muslim Laws, 1, pp. 74–105.

Kermani, Navid, 2004. "From Revelation to Interpretation: Nasr Hamid Abu Zayd and the Literary Study of the Qur'an," in Suha Taji-Farouki (ed.), *Modern Muslim Intellectuals and the Qur'an*, Oxford University Press, pp. 169–92.

Khan, Shayan Afzal, 2007. *Unveiling the Ideal: A New Look at Early Muslim Women*, Kuala Lumpur: Sisters in Islam.

Kurzman, Charles (ed.), 1998. *Liberal Islam: A Sourcebook*, Oxford University Press.

Kurzman, Charles (ed.), 2002. *Modernist Islam 1840–1940: A Sourcebook*, Oxford University Press.

Lamrabet, Asma, 2002. *Musulmane tout simplement (Simply Muslim)*, Paris: Tawhid; http://www.asma-lamrabet.com/publications/musulmane-tout-simplement-editions-tawhid-2002/

Lamrabet, Asma, 2003. *Aïcha, épouse du Prophète ou l'islam au féminin (Aisha: The Prophet's Wife or Feminine Islam)*, Paris: Tawhid.

Lamrabet, Asma, 2007. *Le Coran et les femmes: Une lecture de libération*, Paris: Tawhid.

Lamrabet, Asma, 2012. *Femmes et hommes dans le Coran: Quelle égalité?*, Paris: Albouraq.

Lamrabet, Asma, 2016. *Women in the Qur'an. An Emancipatory Reading*, trans. of *Le Coran et les Femmes* by Myriam François-Cerrah, England: Square View.

Lamrabet, Asma, 2016b. "Fatima Mernissi as I know her", http://arabic.musawah.org/sites/default/files/FatimaAsIKnewHerASMALAMRABET.pdf

Lamrabet, Asma, 2018. *Women and Men in the Qur'an*, trans. of *Femmes et hommes dans le Coran* by Muneera Salem-Murdock, Basingstoke: Palgrave Macmillan.

Lamrabet, Asma, 2019. "Le 'voile' dit-Islamique: Une relecture des concepts," (*The so-called Islamic 'veil': A reinterpretation of concepts*), http://www.asma-lamrabet.com/articles/le-voile-dit-islamique-une-relecture-des-concepts/

Lau, Martin, 2007. "Twenty-Five Years of Hudood Ordinances," *Washington & Lee Law Review*, 64, pp. 1291–14.

Lindholm, Tore and Kari Vogt (eds), 1993. *Islamic Law Reform and Human Rights: Challenges and Rejoinders*, Oslo: Nordic Human Rights Publications.

Lindsey, Ursula, 2018. "Can Muslim Feminism Find a Third Way?" *New York Times*, 11 April.

MacIntyre, Alasdair, 1988. *Whose Justice? Which Rationality?* Indiana: University of Notre Dame Press.

Mahmood, Tahir, 1972. *Family Law Reforms in the Muslim World*, Bombay: N M Tripathi.

Mahmoud, Mohamed, 2006. "To Beat or Not to Beat: On Exegetical Dilemmas over Qur'an 4:34," *Journal of the American Oriental Society* 126 (4), pp. 537–50.

Mas'ud, Muhammad Khalid, 2003. *Iqbal's Reconstruction of Ijtihad*, 2nd edn, Lahore: Iqbal Academy.

Masud, Muhammad Khalid, Kari Vogt, Lena Larson and Christian Moe (eds), 2021. *Freedom of Expression in Islam. Challenging Apostasy and Blasphemy Laws*, London: I.B. Tauris.

Matsunaga, Yasuyiki, 2008. "Mohsen Kadivar, an Advocate of Post-revivalist Islam in Iran," *Br. J. Middle East Studies* 34 (3), pp. 317–29.

Mavani, Hamid, 2020. "Structural Ijtihad: A Radical Paradigm Shift in Twelver Shi'i Legal Theory," in David R. Vishanoff (ed.), *Islamic Law and Ethics*, Herndon VA: International Institute of Islamic Thought, pp. 52–74.

Mende, Claudia, 2018. "Feminist Asma Lamrabet under Pressure," *Al-Qantara*, 23 April, https://en.qantara.de/content/islamic-inheritance-law-in-morocco-and-tunisia-feminist-asma-lamrabet-under-pressure

Mernissi, Fatima, 1987. *Le Harem politique: Le prophète et les femmes*, Paris: Editions Albin Michel.

Mernissi, Fatima, 1991. *Women and Islam: An Historical and Theological Enquiry*, trans. of *Le harem politique* by Mary Jo Lakeland, Oxford: Blackwell; also issued as *The Veil and Male Elite: A Feminist Interpretation of Women's Rights in Islam*, Reading, MA: Addison-Wesley.

Mir-Hosseini, Ziba, 1996. "Stretching the Limits: a Feminist Reading of the Shari'a in Post-Khomeini Iran," in Mai Yamani (ed.), *Islam and Feminism: Legal and Literary Perspectives*, London: Ithaca Press, pp. 285–319.

Mir-Hosseini, Ziba, 1999. *Islam and Gender: The Religious Debate in Contemporary Iran*, Newhaven: Princeton University Press.

Mir-Hosseini, Ziba, 2002. "Negotiating the Politics of Gender in Iran: An Ethnography of a Documentary," in Richard Tapper (ed.), *The New Iranian Cinema*, London: I.B. Tauris, pp. 167–99.

Mir-Hosseini, Ziba, 2003. "The Construction of Gender in Islamic Legal Thought: Strategies for Reform," *Hawwa: Journal of Women in the Middle East and the Islamic World*, 1 (1), pp. 1–28.

Mir-Hosseini, Ziba, 2004. "Islamic Law and Feminism: The Story of a Relationship," *Yearbook of Islamic and Middle Eastern Law*, 9, pp. 32–42.

Mir-Hosseini, Ziba, 2006. "Muslim Women's Quest for Equality: Between Islamic Law and Feminism," *Critical Inquiry*, 32 (1), pp. 629–45.

Mir-Hosseini, Ziba, 2007. "Islam and Gender Justice," in Vincent Cornell and Omid Safi (eds), *Voices of Islam 5, Voices of Diversity and Change*, Westport: Greenwood, pp. 85–113.

Mir-Hosseini, Ziba, 2009. "Toward Gender Equality: Muslim Family Laws and the *Shari'ah*," in Zainah Anwar (ed.), *Wanted: Equality and Justice in the Muslim Family*, Kuala Lumpur: Musawah, An Initiative of Sisters in Islam, pp. 23–63. Available at http://www.musawah. org/wanted-equality-and-justice-muslim-family-english.

Mir-Hosseini, Ziba, 2010a. "Being From There: Dilemmas of a Native Anthropologist," in Shahnaz Nadjmabadi (ed.), *Conceptualizing Iranian Anthropology*, Oxford: Berghahn, pp. 180–191.

Mir-Hosseini, Ziba, 2010b. "Secularization of Shari'a in Iran," in Marie-Claire Foblets and Jean-Yves Carlier (eds), *Islam & Europe: Crises are Challenges*, Leuven University Press, pp. 109–15.

Mir-Hosseini, Ziba, 2010c. "Understanding Islamic Feminism: Interview with Ziba Mir-Hosseini," by Yoginder Sikand, *Monthly Review Online*, 9 Feb. https://mronline. org/2010/02/09/understanding-islamic-feminism-interview-with-ziba-mir-hosseini/

Mir-Hosseini, Ziba, 2011. "Beyond 'Islam' vs 'Feminism,'" *IDS Bulletin* 42 (1), pp. 67–77; https://ziba.bnbhosting.de/wp-content/uploads/2021/11/mir-hosseini-article-beyond-islam-vs-feminism-2011.pdf

Mir-Hosseini, Ziba, 2012a. "Sexuality and Inequality: The Marriage Contract and Muslim Legal Tradition," in Anissa Helie and Homa Hoodfar (eds), *Sexuality in Muslim Contexts: Restrictions and Resistance*, London: Zed Press, pp. 124–48.

Mir-Hosseini, Ziba, 2012b. "The Politics of Divorce Laws in Iran: Ideology versus Practice," in Rubya Mehdi, Werner Menski, and Jørgen Nielsen (eds), *Interpreting Divorce Laws in Islam*, Copenhagen: DJØF Publishing, pp. 65–83.

Mir-Hosseini, Ziba, 2013a, "Out of This Dead-end," *Critical Muslim* 8, Special Issue *Men in Islam*, pp. 47–59.

Mir-Hosseini, Ziba, 2013b. "Justice, Equality and Muslim Family Laws: New Ideas, New Prospects," in Ziba Mir-Hosseini, Kari Vogt, Lena Larsen, and Christian Moe (eds.), *Gender and Equality in Muslim Family Law: Justice and Ethics in the Islamic Legal Tradition*, London, I.B. Tauris, pp. 7–34.

Mir-Hosseini, Ziba, 2015. "Muslim Legal Tradition and the Challenge of Equality," in Ziba Mir-Hosseini, Mulki Al-Sharmani & Jana Rumminger (eds), *Men in Charge? Rethinking Male Authority in Muslim Legal Tradition*, London: Oneworld, pp. 13–43.

Mir-Hosseini, Ziba, 2016. "Honouring Fatima Mernissi," in "Honouring a Fierce Feminist Foremother," Special Issue of *Musawah Vision*, 20; http://arabic.musawah. org/sites/default/files/MusawahVision20EN.pdf

Mir-Hosseini, Ziba, 2017. "Islam, Gender and Democracy in Iran," in Jocelyn Cesari and Jose Casanova (eds), *Islam, Gender and Democracy*, Oxford University Press, pp. 211–36.

Mir-Hosseini, Ziba, 2019. "Commentary on the Research: Why Islamic Feminism, and Why Now?" in Fethi B Jomaa Ahmed (ed.), *Issues of Gender Rights and Duties: Islamic Feminism Versus Principles of Islamic Legislation* (Islam & Applied Ethics, Book 12), Doha: Research Center for Islamic Legislation and Ethics, Hamid Bin Khalifa University Press, pp. 83–115; https://www.cilecenter.org/publications/publications/1214-issues-gender-rights-and-duties-islamic-feminism-versus-principles

Mir-Hosseini, Ziba, and Richard Tapper, 2006. *Islam and Democracy in Iran: Eshkevari and the Quest for Reform*, London: I.B. Tauris.

Mir-Hosseini, Ziba, and Vanja Hamzic, 2010. *Control and Sexuality: The Revival of Zina Laws in Muslim Contexts*, London: Women Living Under Muslim Laws.

Mir-Hosseini, Ziba, Mulki Al-Sharmani and Jana Rumminger (eds), 2015. *Men in Charge? Rethinking Male Authority in Muslim Legal Tradition*, London: Oneworld.

Moosa, Ibrahim, 2000. "Introduction," in Fazlur Rahman, *Revival and Reform in Islam*, Oxford: Oneworld.

Murata, Sachiko, 1992. *The Tao of Islam: A Source Book on Gender Relationships in Islamic Thought*, Albany NY: SUNY Press.

Musawah, 2016. "Honouring a Fierce Feminist Foremother," Special Issue of *Musawah Vision*, 20, http://arabic.musawah.org/sites/default/files/MusawahVision20EN.pdf

Nasr, Seyyed Hossein (ed.), 2015. *The Study Qur'an: A New Translation and Commentary*, New York: Harper One.

Osanloo, Arzoo, 2014. "From Status to Rights: The Shifting Dimensions of Women's Affairs and Family Law in Iran," in Mulki Al-Sharmani (ed.), *Feminist Activism, Women's Rights and Legal Reform*, London: ZED Books, pp. 125–50.

Rahman, Fazlur, 1965. "The Concept of *Hadd* in Islamic Law," *Islamic Studies* 4, pp. 237–52.

Rahman, Fazlur, 1980a. *Major Themes of the Qur'an*, Chicago University Press.

Rahman, Fazlur, 1980b. "A Survey of Modernization of Muslim Family Law." *International Journal of Middle Eastern Studies* 11 (4), pp. 451–65.

Rahman, Fazlur, 1982a. *Islam and Modernity: Transformation of an Intellectual Tradition*, University of Chicago Press.

Rahman, Fazlur, 1982b. "Status of Women in Islam: A Modernist Interpretation," in Hanna Papanek & Gail Minault (eds), *Separate Worlds: Studies of Purdah in South Asia*, Delhi: Chanakya Publications, pp. 285–310; revised version in Guity Nashat (ed.). *Women and Revolution in Iran*, Boulder COL, Westview Press, 1983, pp. 37–54.

Rahman, Fazlur, 1986. "Islam and political action: politics in the service of religion," in Nigel Biggar, Jamie Scot and William Schweiker (eds), *Cities of Gods: Faith, Politics and Pluralism in Judaism, Christianity and Islam*, Westport CT: Greenwood Press.

Rahman, Fazlur, 2000. *Revival and Reform in Islam*, with an Introduction by Ebrahim Moosa, Oxford: Oneworld.

Ramadan, Tariq, 2005. "An International call for Moratorium on corporal punishment, stoning and the death penalty in the Islamic World," https://tariqramadan.com/an-international-call-for-moratorium-on-corporal-punishment-stoning-and-the-death-penalty-in-the-islamic-world

Ramazanoglu, Caroline, with Janet Holland, 2002. *Feminist Methodology: Challenges and Choice*, London: Sage.

Rampoldi, Milena, 2016. "Iran's Sedigheh Vasmaghi says Islam is Never Opposed to Equal Rights for Women," *Pressenza*, 6 February; https://www.pressenza.com/2016/02/irans-sedigheh-vasmaghi-says-islam-is-never-opposed-to-equal-rights-for-women/

Rapoport, Yossef, 2005. *Marriage, Money and Divorce in Medieval Islamic Society*, Cambridge University Press.

Reda, Nevin & Yasmin Amin (eds), 2020. *Islamic Interpretive Tradition and Gender Justice: Processes of Canonization, Subversion, and Change*, Montreal/Chicago: McGill-Queen's University Press.

Ridgeon, Lloyd, 2021. *Hijab – Three Modern Iranian Seminarian Perspectives*, London: Gingko Library.

Roodi, Zahra, 1999. *Baha-ye Azadi: Defa'iyat-e Mohsen Kadivar dar Dadgah-e Vizheh-ye Rouhaniyat* (*The Price of Freedom: Mohsen Kadivar's Defence at the Special Clergy Court*), Tehran: Ney, 1378.

Sadri, Ahmed, 2001. "Sacred Defense of Secularism: The Political Theology of Soroush, Shabestari and Kadivar," *International Journal of Politics, Culture and Society*, 15 (2), pp. 257–70.

Saeed, Abdullah, 2004. "Fazlur Rahman: a Framework for Interpreting the Ethico-Legal Content of the Qur'an," in Suha Taji-Farouki (ed.), *Modern Muslim Intellectuals and the Qur'an*, Oxford University Press, pp. 37–66.

Safari, Ellie, 2007. *The Noble Struggle of Amina Wadud*, https://www.wmm.com/catalog/film/the-noble-struggle-of-amina-wadud/.

Salem, Norma, 1984. "Islam and the Status of Women in Tunisia," in Freda Hussain (ed.), *Muslim Women*, London: Croom Helm, pp. 141–68.

Salime, Zakia, 2011. *Between Feminism and Islam: Human Rights and Sharia Law in Morocco*, University of Minnesota Press.

Seedat, Fatima, 2013a. "When Islam and Feminism Converge," *The Muslim World*, 103 (3), pp. 404–20.

Seedat, Fatima, 2013b. "Islam, Feminism, and Islamic Feminism: Between Inadequacy and Inevitability," *Journal of Feminist Studies in Religion*, 29 (2), pp. 25–45.

Shaikh, Sa'diyya, 2007. "A Tafsir of Praxis: Gender, Marital Violence and Resistance in a South African Community," in Dan Maguire and Sa'diyya Shaikh (eds), *Violence Against Women in Contemporary World Religions: Roots and Cures*, Ohio: The Pilgrim Press, pp. 66–89. https://www.academia.edu/253003

Shamloo, Ahmad, 1979. "*Dar in Bombast*" (In This Dead End), *Bamdad*, 20 Mordad 1358. For English translations, see Franklin Lewis, https://www.academia.edu/37959405/_In_This_Dead_End_poem_by_Ahmad_Shamlu_translated_Franklin_Lewis; and https://www.youtube.com/watch?v=LDiOcUSZgyg

Shams al-Din, Muhammad Mahdi, 2009. *Hudud-e Mosharekat-e Siyasi-ye Zanan* (*Boundaries of Women's Political Participation*), Tehran: Be'sat, 1388.

Siavoshi, Sussan, 2017. *Montazeri: The Life and Thought of Iran's Revolutionary Ayatollah*, Cambridge University Press.

Sirri, Lana, 2021. *Islamic Feminism: Discourses on Gender and Sexuality in Contemporary Islam*, London & New York: Routledge.

Sisters in Islam, 2002. *Polygamy is not a Right for Men*, https://sistersinislam.org/web/assets/uploads/2019/10/Islam-and-polygamy.pdf

Smith, William Cantwell, 1981. *On Understanding Islam, Selected Essays*, The Hague: Mouton.

Sonbol, Amira El Azhary (ed.), 1996. *Women, Family and Divorce Laws in Islamic History*, Syracuse University Press.

Sonbol, Amira El Azhary, 1998. "Ta'a and Modern Legal Reform: A Reading," *Islam and Christian-Muslim Relations*, 9 (3), pp. 285–94.

Sonn, Tamara, 1991. "Fazlur Rahman's Islamic Methodology," *The Muslim World*, 81 (3–4), pp. 212–30.

Sonn, Tamara, 1998. "Fazlur Rahman and Islamic Feminism," in Earle H. Waugh and Frederic M. Denny (eds), *The Shaping of An American Islamic Discourse: A Memorial to Fazlur Rahman*, Atlanta: Scholars Press, pp. 123–45.

Stowasser, Barbara, 1993. "Women's Issues in Modern Islamic Thought," in Judith E. Tucker (ed.), *Arab Women: Old Boundaries, New Frontiers*, Bloomington: Indiana University Press, pp. 3–28.

Taha, Mahmoud Mohamed, 1987. *The Second Message of Islam*, trans. Abdullahi Ahmed An-Na'im, Syracuse University Press.

Tripp, Aili Mari, 2019. *Seeking Legitimacy: Why Arab Autocracies Adopt Women's Rights*, Cambridge University Press.

Tucker, Judith. 2000. *In the House of Law: Gender and Islamic Law in Ottoman Syria and Palestine*, Berkeley: University of California Press.

Vasmaghi, Sedigheh, 2009a. *Beza'at-e Feqh va Gostareh-e Nofuz-e Foqaha (The Capacity of Fiqh and the Extent of the Influence of the Fuqaha)*, privately published.

Vasmaghi, Sedigheh, 2009b. *Zan, Fiqh, Islam*, 2nd edn, Tehran: Samadieh.

Vasmaghi, Sedigheh, 2014a. *Women, Jurisprudence, Islam*, trans. of *Zan, Fiqh, Islam* by Ashna and Philip G Kreyenbroek, Wiesbaden: Harrassowitz.

Vasmaghi, Sedigheh, 2014b. *Hatman Rahi Hast (Surely, There is a Way)*, Paris: Kharavan.

Vasmaghi, Sedigheh, 2017. *Bazkhani-ye Shari'at (Rethinking Shari'a)*, Tehran: Qalam.

Vasmaghi, Sedigheh, 2018. *Al Mar'ih, Al Fiqh, Al Islam* (Arabic trans. of *Zan, Fiqh, Islam*), Beirut: Dar al Kitab al Lubnani; Cairo: Dar al Kitab Al Masri.

Vogt, Kari, Lena Larsen and Christian Moe (eds), 2008. *New Directions in Islamic Thought: Exploring Reform and Muslim Tradition*, London: I.B. Tauris.

Wadud, Amina, 1999. *Qur'an and Woman: Rereading the Sacred Text from a Woman's Perspective*, Oxford University Press (first published in 1992 in Kuala Lumpur by Penerbit Fajar Bakati Sdn. Bhd.).

Wadud, Amina, 2006. *Inside the Gender Jihad: Women's Reform in Islam*, Oxford: Oneworld.

Wadud, Amina, 2009. "Islam Beyond Patriarchy Through Gender Inclusive Analysis," in Zainah Anwar (ed.), *Wanted: Equality and Justice in the Muslim Family*, Kuala Lumpur: Musawah, an Initiative of Sisters in Islam, pp. 95–112.

Wadud, Amina, 2016. "We were Sisters in Soul," in "Honouring a Fierce Feminist Foremother," Special Issue of *Musawah Vision*, 20; http://arabic.musawah.org/sites/default/files/MusawahVision20EN.pdf

Waki' ibn Hayyan, Muhammad b. Khalaf, *Akhbar al-Qudah (Judges' News)*, Egypt: Matba'at al-Sa'adah, 1947.

Waugh, Earle H., and Frederic M. Denny (eds), 1998. *The Shaping of An American Islamic Discourse: A Memorial to Fazlur Rahman*, Atlanta: Scholars Press.

Welchman, Lynn, 2011. "A Husband's Authority: Emerging Formulations in Muslim Family Laws," *International Journal of Law, Policy and the Family*, 25 (1), pp. 1–23.

Zomorrod, Farida, 2019. "Issues of Gender Rights and Duties: Islamic Feminism Versus Principles of Islamic Legislation," in Fethi B. Jomaa Ahmed (ed.), *Issues of Gender Rights and Duties: Islamic Feminism Versus Principles of Islamic Legislation* (Islam & Applied Ethics, Book 12), Doha: Research Center for Islamic Legislation and Ethics, Hamid Bin Khalifa University Press, pp. 17–82; https://www.cilecenter.org/publications/publications/1214-issues-gender-rights-and-duties-islamic-feminism-versus-principles

Index